The Echo of Battle

The Echo of Battle

THE ARMY'S WAY OF WAR

Brian McAllister Linn

HARVARD UNIVERSITY PRESS

Cambridge, Massachusetts
London, England

First Harvard University Press paperback edition, 2009

Library of Congress Cataloging-in-Publication Data
Linn, Brian McAllister.
The echo of battle : the army's way of war / Brian McAllister Linn.
    p.   cm.
  Includes bibliographical references and index.
  ISBN 978-0-674-02651-3 (cloth : alk. paper)
  ISBN 978-0-674-03479-2 (pbk.)
  1. United States. Army—History—20th century.   2. Military art and
science—United States—History—20th century.   3. United States—Military
policy.   I. Title.
UA25 .L63   2007
355.033573—dc22   2007282197

CONTENTS

The Echo of Battle

PROLOGUE

No topic today unites and divides Americans more than war. But what does it mean? Even the people charged with its prosecution disagree. Former Secretary of Defense Donald Rumsfeld's declaration shortly after the terrorist attacks on 11 September 2001 that "even the vocabulary of this war will be different" exemplifies the present difficulty in conceptualizing warfare.[1] The strong, and often vitriolic, clashes among senior officers in the Gulf War and the Balkan conflicts stemmed, to large degree, from their differing concepts of war. Today, as our armed forces fight a "Global War on Terror" (called—ironically, in some quarters—GWOT, "Gee, what?" or—more ominously—the "Long War"), the commanders of the armed forces seem no more able than their civilian leaders to define the enemy, the objective, or the meaning of victory. Perhaps not surprisingly, GWOT's two most significant campaigns, Afghanistan and Iraq, have been characterized by bitter disagreement within the military over war planning and execution, much of it stemming from irreconcilable definitions of war.

Even before GWOT, the defense community was in the midst of a vibrant debate over whether the nature of war itself had changed. Advocates offered the prospect of a glittering future through a "Revolution in Military Affairs," "Military Transformation," and a "New American Way of War." But their voices were only some, if perhaps the most strident, in a much larger discussion. Others defended the relevance of military philosophers such as Henri Jomini and Carl von Clausewitz, while still others advocated what General Wesley K. Clark termed "modern war—limited, carefully constrained in geography, scope, weaponry, and effects."[2] The debate, like the defense community, overflowed with buzzwords—asymmetric conflict, fourth-generation warfare, shock and awe, full spectrum dominance—many of which quickly became passé. And with some significant exceptions, much of this debate confined itself to hypothetical threats, to the relative merits of weapons systems, and to new tactical organizations.

This failure of military intellectuals to agree on a concept of war might seem surprising, given that virtually everyone in the armed forces claims to be a "warfighter" and every few years at least one of the services proclaims its intention to make each member a "warrior."[3] The bleak warren of the Pentagon is crowded with military staffers working fourteen-hour days to analyze the lessons of past wars, plan for current wars, and envision the next war. The army, navy, and air force each have war colleges, the marines have the School of Advanced Warfighting, and each service sponsors professional journals to discuss war and its ramifications. If there is one thing that the nation's officers should agree on, it is war.

Yet much anecdotal evidence suggests otherwise. Until very recently, a common joke at all the war colleges was that the one subject *not* studied was war. In 2005 a Department of Defense agency offered $5,000 for the best essay on the "new principles of war," thus paradoxically implying both that war was subject to scientific laws (principles) and that these laws were transitory and situational (new). Such confusion is by no means uncommon. The Pentagon routinely issues directives purporting to give a concept of war that are little more than gibberish. For example: "Joint Adaptive Expeditionary Warfare requires capabilities organized cross-enterprise, adapting dynamically to uncertainty and turbulence in a multi-dimensional, nonlinear, competitive environment."[4] All of this suggests that military leaders are no longer certain of what the term "war" means and thus can no longer explain it to their civilian superiors, the public, or even to themselves.

The premise that historical analysis can clarify contemporary military issues—or, in military parlance, that history provides applicable "lessons learned" for the present and future—is one of the cardinal tenets of American military thought. But the search for a usable past has tended to follow three distinct lines of inquiry. Some have studied prominent military officers, in the process encountering the problem of separating the individual's own views on war from a broader service consensus. Others have studied military reform movements, seeking to establish a collective professional ethos that promoted transformation.[5] Most have tried to distill lessons from the actual conduct of warfare. But studying military practice on the battlefield provides only a partial perspective. Despite thousands of books on combat and campaigns, what most people term the "American way of war" is really a more limited effort to explain the "American way of battle."[6]

Appreciating a national way of war requires going beyond the narrative of operations, beyond debates on the merits of attrition or annihilation, firepower or mobility, military genius or collective professional ability. It requires the essential recognition that the way a military force conducts war very much depends on how it prepares for war. Preparation occurs in peacetime, often over several decades, and is greatly influenced by the service's perception of its own martial traditions, its interpretations of lessons learned from recent conflicts, its understanding of current threats and opportunities, and its vision of future wars.

General John R. Galvin recognized this crucial relationship between prewar concepts and wartime conduct. "When we think about the possibilities of conflict we tend to invent for ourselves a comfortable vision of war . . . a combat environment that is consistent and predictable . . . one that fits our plans, our assumptions, our hopes, and our preconceived ideas. We arrange in our minds a war we can comprehend on our own terms, usually with an enemy who looks like us and acts like us. This comfortable conceptualization becomes the accepted way of seeing things . . . until it comes under serious challenge as a result of some major event—usually a military disaster."[7] As Galvin himself acknowledged, only a few officers create and disseminate their service's vision of war; the vast majority simply accept it without question. Seen in this context, the army's way of war owes as much or more to intellectuals such as Joseph Totten and Donn Starry as it does to practitioners such as Ulysses S. Grant or Douglas MacArthur.

Army officers and military historians, past and present, assume that the service shares a common definition of war. Indeed, this assumption is central to the regular army's institutional self-identity. Since its inception, it has maintained that "modern warfare," a term whose specific meaning has changed radically, is too complex to be trusted to gifted amateurs, who may or may not appear when the nation is in crisis. Only professional officers who have devoted a lifetime to understanding warfare are qualified to wage it. Internal debates may rage over the means of waging war, but the army's basic concept of war itself has not changed. Or has it?

Far from displaying the rigid organizational unanimity often ascribed to the "military mind," the army has been engaged in prolonged and often acrimonious debate over the nature of both war and national defense. In the process, the army has developed three distinct intellectual traditions that together make up the "army way of war." The three traditions are not mutually exclusive. Most officers adopt concepts derived from all three, though if pressed they will usually champion one. These traditions are not sequential. At many times two of them have overlapped and the third has almost disappeared. Nor are they always in opposition. At times their proponents have reached consensus on policies, weaponry, or the nature of current and future conflict. But instances of brief agreement on the army's way of war should not obscure the reality that these three traditions think about warfare in fundamentally different ways.

The first of these martial philosophies is espoused by a group that I will call the Guardians, and it was the dominant military paradigm for much of the nineteenth century. Its military intellectuals postulated that war was both an art and a science, the former consisting largely of the application of the latter. As a science, war was subject to laws and principles which, if applied, provided the means to anticipate or even predict the consequences of specific actions or policies. Only an officer who had mastered the science of war could be trusted to practice it as an art.

After the experience of the Revolution and the War of 1812, the Guardians envisioned the primary threat to the nation as a sudden naval raid on Atlantic coastal cities. A devastating blow to these urban areas might not only cripple the U.S. war effort but might also provide the springboard for continental invasion. Guardians saw a solution to this threat in harbor fortifications, the newest weaponry, and a small, elite corps of military specialists supported, if necessary, by masses of patriotic citizen-soldiers. Once these defenses were in place, the nation would have absolute and relatively cheap security, able to deter any current or future adversary.

The legacy of this military tradition continued long after the disappearance of the threat on which it was based. Indeed, in some respects much of today's dialogue about homeland security and a ballistic missile shield harks back to the Guardians' nineteenth-century vision. Their legacy can be seen as well in some officers' view of war as an engineering project in which the application of scientific principles by skilled technicians all but guarantees success. This perspective was manifest in the Powell Doctrine, named after the chairman of the Joint Chiefs of Staff Colin Powell, which imposed strict preconditions on the deployment of military forces. It is also apparent in *Army Vision 2010,* a "conceptual template" asserting that, irrespective of what the enemy does, the army will "win decisively" through "dominant maneuver," "precision engagement," and "full dimensional protection."[8]

A strong contrast to the vision of the Guardians was that of the Heroes. Their tradition emphasized the human element, and defined warfare by personal intangibles such as military genius, experience, courage, morale, and discipline. Heroes reduced war to its simplest terms—as armed violence directed toward the achievement of an end. This approach encouraged adaptability and innovation; it fostered an ability to separate the essential from the trivial, and it allowed Heroes to make a relatively easy transition from one form of warfare to another. George S. Patton, for example, could within two decades champion armored industrial warfare, then the horse cavalry, and then armored warfare once again, without ever compromising his essential belief that "war is an art and as such is not susceptible of explanation by fixed formula."[9]

Heroes characteristically dismiss those who seek to impose predictability and order on a phenomenon they view as chaotic, violent, and emotional. Like Patton, they believe that "wars are fought with men, not weapons. It is the spirit of the [man] who fights, and of the [man] who leads which gains the victory."[10] At its best, the Heroic concept of war provides both an intellectual and practical framework contributing not only to battlefield victory but also to success in a wide variety of military operations. But the Heroic tradition lends itself to emotional posturing, to elitism or selfishness, to General Tommy Franks' grandiose proclamation, "I'm a warfighter, not a manager."[11] And it can produce muddy-boots fundamentalism, the anti-intellectual reductionism manifested in slogans such as "War means fighting and fighting means killing," or "The Army's job is to kill people and break things."

A group that I call the Managers is often opposed to both the Guardians and the Heroes. In their view, the Civil War and the German wars of unification in the nineteenth century transformed the nature of armed nation-state conflict into what they called "modern warfare." The military leaders in this tradition became convinced that war was a logical outgrowth of political and economic rivalry and an essential component of the United States' rise as a great power. And they believed that future conflicts, like those of the past, would require the mobilization of the entire nation. To prepare for these titanic clashes, the Managers encouraged the creation of a mass army, equipped with the best armaments, trained in large-unit operations, and controlled by educated professionals. At their best, the Managers provided the broad strategic leadership of a George C. Marshall or Dwight D. Eisenhower. But their fixation on future wars made this group indifferent to small outbreaks of violence, postconflict operations, and unconventional missions.

As consistently as each intellectual tradition has maintained its own vision of warfare, so each has invented its own rationale for failure. For the Guardians, war is best understood as an engineering project in which the outcome is determined by the correct application of immutable scientific principles. Strategic planning for future warfare is largely a matter of determining the correct national security policy and then totaling up weaponry and manpower and comparing it with that of potential enemies. Taken to extremes, this leads to the belief that the next war is predictable and its outcome predetermined. When conflicts do not turn out as planned, Guardians blame an irrational American society, through its political representatives, for refusing to accept the Guardians' logical and informed defense policies or for failing to allocate sufficient human resources and materiel. They reproach the army as an institution for not acknowledging their primacy in strategic direction and for pursuing risky military goals. When confronted with a war that fails to meet their preexisting convictions, their reinterpretation soon discovers that it actually confirms their beliefs.

For Heroes, war is simply battle—an extension of combat between individuals on both the physical and the moral plane. The side whose commanders and soldiers exhibit superior courage, strength, discipline, martial skills, honor, and so forth will inevitably secure victory, unless betrayed by other factors. In the face of evidence that charismatic leadership, tactical skill, high morale, and martial experience does not guarantee victory, Heroes blame their enemy for failing to fight honorably and their own civil and military leaders for wanting sufficient will to win. They often accuse American society of lacking the physical and spiritual qualities needed for warfighting. They have a similarly bad opinion of the institutional army. In their view, it is a soulless corporation in which warriors are subordinated to technicians and careerists. In their criticisms of the army, Heroes tend to make no distinction between Guardians and Managers—they throw them all into the same bureaucratic pot.

For Managers, war is fundamentally an organizational (as opposed to an engineering) problem—the rational coordination of resources, both human and materiel. Whereas the Guardians seek to make war more predictable, the Managers seek to make war more effective. They complain when Americans refuse to accept their guidance and instead champion irrational martial virtues, or (worse) defense priorities unfavorable to the army. In their internal assessment, Managers are contemptuous of the narrow technicism of the Guardians and the romanticism of the Heroes. Should overwhelming resources, superior administration, and detailed planning fail to secure victory, the Managers' response is to reorganize. Too often, this takes the form of what military personnel cynically term "moving the ravioli around": drawing elaborate diagrams to rearrange (and "re-acronymize") the chain of command, the force structure, and the budgetary priorities, while leaving the military institution and its fundamental problems virtually untouched. In the name of reform and modernization, Managers are perpetually engaged in the radical reorganization of administrative structures and tactical units, creating new concepts and buzzwords, and promoting their new, transformed military organization as superior to the one it replaced. Ironically, their reformist zeal is fed by historical lessons, so that an organizational scheme for the army of the future might claim as its inspiration a Roman victory two millennia ago.

Taken together, Guardians, Heroes, and Managers represent three distinct schools of thought whose influence continues to shape the army's vision and thus its conduct of warfare. But to study the army's way of war requires a clear delineation between the ideal of war and the practice of war. Peacetime military thought focuses on what the army thinks about past wars, how it interprets current threats of war, and how it anticipates future wars. From this perspective, the wars the United States has actually fought are important less for what happened than for what military intellectuals believed they had learned from them after the shooting stopped. The fact that much of American military thought has been narrow, contradictory, and logically suspect in no way diminishes its importance to the army's way of war or to the course of the nation's history. Today, more than ever, soldiers and citizens need to understand what the army hears in the echoes of battle.

1

FORTRESS AMERICA

During the Cold War, when many Americans believed they faced nuclear annihilation or communist dictatorship, the dangers posed a century earlier seemed insubstantial. But during this so-called "era of free security," the perils were very real indeed to those concerned with the nation's defense. Secretary of War John C. Calhoun warned Congress in 1820 that "however remote our situation from the great powers of the world and however pacific our policy," it was almost inevitable that the United States would be drawn into another protracted war.[1]

Calhoun did not need to remind his audience that the barely four-decades-old republic had already fought two wars with Great Britain, a naval quasi-war with France, and border skirmishes with Spain, or that a third Anglo-American war was widely anticipated. The United States also faced military challenges from opponents that would today be termed "non-state actors." A long-standing dispute in the Mediterranean with the corsair principalities continued to fester. In the Caribbean the nation's small navy hunted an assortment of maritime raiders, some of them agents of the various factions engaged in the Latin American wars of independence, some of them former allies, and some just pirates.

And always in the background were intermittent border conflicts with Native American peoples. However overblown these dangers appear to us today, the threat from such internal and external opponents remained ever present in contemporary military thought.

The absence of an American military profession prior to the War of 1812 makes it impossible to identify a distinct army philosophy or way of war at the time. Anthony Wayne's Legion of the United States showed considerable discipline and efficiency in suppressing Native American resistance at the Battle of Fallen Timbers in 1794, but it was soon broken up. The Corps of Artillerists and Engineers (created in 1794) supervised harbor defenses, but the organization was minuscule and much of its leadership foreign.[2] The Military Academy at West Point, the incubator of much of the regular army's professional identity, was not founded until 1802. First and foremost an engineering school, West Point would take two decades to develop the distinct educational and socializing methods that would separate its graduates from citizen-soldiers. Indeed, the early republic's military and civilian worlds were permeable, with men such as George Washington, Henry Knox, Alexander Hamilton, and Andrew Jackson moving easily from political to military duties and back.

Among these citizen-soldiers was a consensus that the European great powers were predatory and that military weakness invited attack. The War of Independence provided a graphic example of a primary danger facing the new republic—what one secretary of war termed "requisitional invasions" by European nations against vulnerable cities along the Atlantic coast.[3] Although the battles of Yorktown and Saratoga demonstrated the difficulties inherent in conquering the United States, Britain's capture of New York, Charleston, and Philadelphia, as well as its devastating naval raids up and down the Atlantic coast, were clear indications of the young republic's vulnerability. To the nation's

political and military leadership the solution appeared obvious—
to adopt a national defense policy that ensured domestic tran-
quility and avoided a military dictatorship while at the same time
deterring foreign aggression, protecting the borders, and avoiding
the appearance of threatening another nation. Washington's Farewell Address of 1796 captured the essential argument: the quar-
rels of Europeans were of no concern to the United States except
insofar as they threatened American interests or security, in which
case the nation must be strong enough to choose either peace or
war.[4]

The War of 1812 with Great Britain reinforced existing perceptions of the Hobbesian state of world affairs and provided tangible proof of the vulnerability of the nation's vital coastal ports.
Americans interpreted the war as proving the nation's inability to
defend its neutral rights or its territory. British maritime raids,
particularly those that sacked Hampton, burned Washington,
and attacked Baltimore and New Orleans, were a grim reminder
of similar incursions during the Revolutionary War. The lesson
was not lost on President James Monroe: it was necessary to "stop
the enemy at the coast. If this is done, our cities, and whole inte-
rior will be secure. For the accomplishment of this object, our
fortifications must be principally relied on."[5]

Monroe's peers shared his view of national security. In 1814
Congress created the Fortification Board to conduct a survey of
the United States' land and ocean frontiers and draw up a plan
for their protection. Even more extraordinary, it authorized significant funds for national defense even in the absence of an immediate crisis.[6]

The Fortification Board was composed of members of the
army's intellectual and technical elite, the Corps of Engineers. It
remained in permanent session until the Civil War and was the
nation's first military agency responsible for planning national security. Its 1821 and 1826 reports became the United States' only

coherent defense plan for the next six decades. This strategic vision was predicated on four essential Guardian presuppositions: that the fundamental mission of the armed forces was the defense of the continental United States; that national defense and warfare were governed by scientific principles understood only by a trained military elite; that these principles allowed warfare to be analyzed and even predicted; and that deterrence through overwhelming strength is the best form of national security.

Headed for most of its existence by the internationally renowned engineer Joseph G. Totten, the Fortification Board was in many respects an extension of his strategic concepts.[7] After Totten's appointment as chief engineer in 1838, the board's and the corps' perception of warfare were virtually identical. Totten's long tenure ensured a consistency of vision and direction, but it also contributed to the board's slide from innovation into reaction, and from strategy into self-interest. What started out as a defensible hypothesis about national security dwindled into a narrow dogmatism about the nature of future wars. The board's premises, assumptions, and penchant for institutional self-preservation proved extraordinarily influential.

In developing a plan, the Fortification Board assumed that the nation's next war would be much like the last; thus the War of 1812 became the model for future conflicts. But this template was based on a highly selective study of the lessons of the recent past. Virtually ignoring the aggressive military operations on the western and southern frontiers that broke the back of tribal resistance, the board focused solely on the British expeditionary raids along the coasts. In the board's view, these coastal attacks demonstrated that unless a hostile expedition could seize a port to serve as its base (as the British had done during the War of Independence), it could not sustain a land campaign or permanently occupy territory.

Indeed, without access to unloading and transportation facilities, the enemy would be forced to disembark troops in a difficult and hazardous over-the-beach landing. This would, in turn, impose severe constraints in the size, logistical support, and equipment (particularly artillery and ammunition) of the invading force. This relatively weak expedition would have to immediately march overland to seize a suitable harbor for the main force—in the process giving the regular army and militia time to prepare land defenses. As the battles in front of Baltimore and New Orleans had indicated, even untrained citizen-soldiers fighting behind earthworks could repel European veterans who were operating at such disadvantage.[8]

The board also concluded that Europe's great powers would threaten the nation for the foreseeable future, for both economic and political reasons. The United States' natural resources and expanding trade ensured economic rivalry, and European governments possessed large military establishments that were always eager for conquests. In the political realm, the board believed that struggle between "the personal ambition of kings" and the republican government of the United States—"the source whence all those principles adverse to their supremacy have flourished"— was equally inevitable.[9] Great Britain in particular possessed both the maritime power to launch a sudden raid and a demonstrated willingness to attack neutrals. The board implied that the foreign threat grew each day, for recent developments in weaponry, transportation (principally steam power), and military organization allowed enemies to strike with less warning and with far more power than in the past.

Given these assumptions, the board envisioned that future conflicts, though having much in common with the last one, would have far more horrific consequences. The memory of the burning of Washington and the plundering of the coast spurred the board's imagination. One of its scenarios was that an enemy might send an expedition to Louisiana, blockade New Orleans,

and ravage the area for 150 miles around, destroying plantations
and liberating slaves. Another was a raid on Philadelphia, with
enemy troops rowing ashore, cutting off the city, and then creating a swath of destruction across Pennsylvania and New Jersey.
Yet another scenario postulated 20,000 troops based in Halifax,
with expeditions sent out to menace the coast from Maine to
Louisiana, "ruin[ing] us by a war of mere threatenings. If the cities are not garrisoned they will become [its] prey at once, and if
they are the treasury will be gradually emptied, the credit of
the government exhausted, the wearied and starving militia will
desert to their homes, and nothing can avert the direful consum-
mation of tribute, pillage, and conflagration."[10]

To prevent such a dreadful fate, the board outlined a national
defensive scheme based on powerful harbor fortifications, an active navy, a small regular army, and a citizen militia. Reflecting its
members' scientific training, it proposed that these separate "elements" could be combined into a "reciprocal relationship" in
which the whole was stronger than the sum of its parts. The maritime component of this defense strategy was simple. Should
America feel that its political or economic interests were threatened, its warships would disrupt the enemy's seaborne communications and ravage its maritime trade. Rather than concentrating
on defeating the enemy fleet along the U.S. coastline—a risky if
not futile strategy—the navy "will be prepared to transfer the war
to distant oceans, and to the shores of the enemy."[11] But such a
maritime strategy required secure "ports of refuge." To provide
these, and also to protect the vulnerable coastal cities, the board
focused most of its attention on the main "element"—harbor fortifications.

Just as it had argued that recent improvements in weaponry
and military organization posed a new threat, so it concluded
that these same improvements could be used to protect the nation. In particular, it maintained that the improved design and

construction of masonry fortifications made them virtually impervious to ship-borne artillery while at the same time allowing the concentration of overwhelming firepower. Towering two or three stories high, mounting forty or fifty guns, protected from counter-fire by eight or more feet of bricks and stone, the forts would hurl crushing salvos into the vulnerable upper works of attacking ships.

Such fixed defenses would diminish the need for a standing army—the third element in the Fortification Board's strategy. The 1821 report calculated that fewer than 5,000 soldiers would be sufficient to maintain the works and repel a sudden and therefore relatively small-scale raid. The fourth element, the militia, would be called up only "to repel invasions," as the Constitution specified.[12] But in its discussion of both the third and fourth tier of the defensive system, the board was almost perfunctory, as if the soldiers and militia were little more than accessories of the fortresses themselves.

Central to America's national defense strategy was the principle of deterrence. Curiously for a group of officers with such ample evidence of American aggression in the form of Jackson's forays into Florida and the Southeast, the board clearly believed that the United States would not be the aggressor in future wars and that the nation's main concern was to defend itself against European encroachments. From the Anglo-American conflicts the board drew the lesson that if the nation was sufficiently prepared to withstand a sudden attack, the result would be a war of attrition in which "the advantage must always rest, everything else being equal, with the country which, from its geographical situation and its natural and artificial strength, is most secure from invasion." From this it followed that "it is this property of inaccessibility by land at which the United States should aim, and which it may attain by well contrived permanent works and by the gradual increase of the navy."[13]

The board asserted that once the fortifications were in place, the nation's territory would have absolute security. Indeed, "war, and all its terrors," would be "shut out from our territories by our fortresses, and transferred by our navy to the bosom of the ocean . . . Our wars thus becoming maritime will be less costly in men and money, and more in unison with our institutions—leaving untouched our domestic relations, our industry, and our internal financial resources."[14] Although the cost of this program was high—some $18 million or over three times the size of the national debt—it was cheaper and more effective than any alternative system, and represented a fraction of the financial loss that the destruction of even a minor port city would entail.

In the imagination of army officers, the War of 1812 also provided a template for fighting the next war on the Canadian border. Right after the war ended, President Monroe and Major General Jacob Brown had developed a plan for an attack up the St. Lawrence that probably would have failed for the same reasons that wartime expeditions had failed. But in the view of the Fortification Board, the Canadian border never loomed as large as the coast did, and board members devoted little attention to cross-border attack from either direction. Of the $8,250,000 dollars devoted to construction of fixed defenses between 1816 and 1829, only $200,000 went to the northern border.[15]

The Fortification Board's reports reveal a great deal about American military thought on a variety of levels. To begin with, they provide one of the first and most coherent summaries of the Guardian way of war. From 1821 on, particularly within the engineering and coast artillery communities, a strong contingent of strategic thinkers would focus firmly on protection of the homeland and would view the armed forces' mission as essentially deterrence. Of even more significance, the board's reports incorporate many of the basic strategic assumptions that would characterize later American military thought. It took as a fundamental truth that the nation would always be threatened by attack from a rival great power. It also believed this an imminent danger because of recent developments in military technology, organization, and methods. But it maintained that these same developments could be used to provide not just protection but absolute security. It bolstered this argument by conjuring up alarmist future scenarios and statistics, many of them counterfactual, to prove the strategic and financial benefits of its program.

Moreover, the board developed a military policy and a strategy that suited its narrow institutional self-interest. Dominated by engineers, it postulated a defense system it claimed was based on four mutually supporting elements, but in fact provided only vague guidance for the navy, neglected the rest of the regular army, and all but ignored the militia. Implicit in the board's view was the presupposition that the republic faced only one significant strategic problem, an enemy seaborne attack on a port, for which there was only one solution, harbor fortifications. By disregarding all ancillary threats in favor of this almost medieval worldview, the board was free to concentrate on problems that would yield to its expertise. But as a result, it created a program that was less a coherent plan of national defense than a series of disconnected strong points dotting the Atlantic coast. The board's insistence that the future would repeat the past—a conviction that owed much to its selective reading of the lessons of the War of 1812—made it blind to other strategic possibilities. Focused on the danger of invasion from Europe, it neither foresaw, nor made any provision for, offensive conflicts that might accompany frontier expansion. More illogically, the board simultaneously placed its faith in relatively new and unproven defensive technology while assuming that offensive technology would remain stagnant.

If with hindsight the Fortification Board's conceptual limitations appear obvious, nevertheless it was practically the only military agency to comment on national strategy. It occupied a unique place among military institutions, partly because of the respect accorded to the board and the Army Corps of Engineers both within and without the army. In Totten they had a worthy champion who was justly renowned as a scientist and engineer. During his four decades on the board, Totten's sustained, consistent, and unchanging articulation of the original defense plan was such that he often copied parts of it into his later recommendations for national defense. New information was assimilated only when it supported his preexisting views, as when he included in his 1836 report statistics to show that, at least hypothetically, in the event of invasion the United States could concentrate almost a million militiamen within ten days at its nine largest port cities. In the ensuing decades when others perceived in new technology or in their experience of war signs that the board's program—or at least its tactics and weaponry—needed to be revised, Totten saw only vindication of its prescience. His political superiors did not challenge his conservatism. Both the secretary of war and Congress deferred to the program and the corps, not least because of the substantial economic benefits the program's construction projects generated among constituents.

Within the army, the Fortification Board and the Corps of Engineers' interests were so symbiotic it was often hard to separate them. The board's program provided a justification for an educated officer corps, one whose expertise lay not in combat experience or political connections but in its grasp of "military art and science." Both an organizational philosophy and an effort to apply engineering precision to war, military art and science had its ultimate expression in the construction of fortifications. Moreover, both an officer's expertise and his ability to practice it was controlled by the corps, which governed the source of almost all post-1820 peacetime officers, the U.S. Military Academy at West Point. The engineers shaped the academy's curriculum and then drafted its top graduates, most of whom spent their careers carrying out the board's program.[16]

The board's authority was all the greater because the institutions that might have generated a critique were either nonexistent or intellectually moribund. Although after 1821 the army's senior officer was accorded the imposing title of commanding general, no one who held that office articulated either a concept of war or an alternative scheme of national defense. Commanding generals restricted their annual reports to Congress to pleas for more funding and personnel, administrative details, and brief references to frontier campaigning. Within the War Department, no agency was charged with developing or teaching strategy and doctrine, no professional journal existed to disseminate ideas, no planning staff prepared the nation for war, no agency systematically collected information on military developments. Military intellectuals probably had the most impact on national defense policy by indirect means, such as ghostwriting the secretary of war's reports to Congress and the President. But while such indirect influence could determine bureaucratic procedures, budgets, and the structure of forces, it seldom could define a national way of warfare. Even Calhoun's famous 1820 report, often cited as establishing the peacetime army's mission to prepare for war, interpreted such preparation almost entirely as a managerial task of administration and organization.[17]

Outside the Corps of Engineers, the army was divided by parochial jealousies among the combat branches of infantry, cavalry, and artillery (usually referred to as the "line"), who were united only in their mutual detestation of the "staff" bureaus composed of administrative and technical specialists. The army's small size—barely 6,000 in 1821, 8,500 in 1846, and 16,000 in 1860—its wide dispersal, and the lack of common schools or training facilities further inhibited the sharing of information. Those officers who served on the frontier failed to translate their experience into an organized body of military thought on warfare. Their combat service against Native Americans was episodic and varied greatly from officer to officer. But if creating a coherent corpus of military doctrine from these experiences was difficult, their shared belief that a commander's character and genius were more important than his education and that war was influenced as much by intangible moral forces as by scientific principles marked an important break with the Guardian way.

The Mexican War of 1846–1848 was a glorious victory that demonstrated, depending on the individual officer's perspective, the combat effectiveness of the regulars; the Corps of Engineers' expertise; the martial spirit of citizen-soldier volunteers; the poor discipline, political intriguing, and atrocious conduct of citizen-soldier volunteers; or the need for a commander to have charisma, experience, and intuition (usually referred to as "genius"). Winfield Scott's landing at Vera Cruz and capture of Mexico City were recognized in Europe as operations worthy of study. In turn, Scott declared that without "the science and skill" of his West Pointers he could not have succeeded with an army four times larger.[18]

Given the disparity of individual experience and the tendency of officers to interpret the war's lessons along rather narrow lines, it is not surprising that Mexico confirmed existing paradigms rather than providing new ones. In particular, it increased the already considerable conviction among West Point graduates that they alone understood the art and science of war. Only a few, such as Ulysses S. Grant, recognized that Brigadier General Zachary Taylor's dogged pursuit of his objectives, his refusal to panic, and his faith in his soldiers were more important qualities in a wartime commander than any science. The war also increased the regulars' profoundly ingrained distrust of citizen-soldiers, whom they viewed as undisciplined, insubordinate, and emotional. The belief that Americans were unfit for war without the regulars' scientific leadership and training, in turn, reinforced their preexisting convictions of the nation's vulnerability to attack and the consequent need for coastal fortifications. The army's failure to provide an institutional analysis of the war's lessons, or even a narrative of the military operations undertaken, only encouraged such narrow and parochial thinking. As a result, the Mexican War provided no challenge to the Guardians' strategic paradigm.

The navy also failed to provide an alternative strategic vision. It had no equivalent to a chief of staff or military advisor. Its cumbersome bureau system, which oversaw administration, supply, and construction, was not charged with developing a distinct vision of warfare appropriate for the navy. Nor did it produce a military intellectual of the stature of Totten or others to articulate a navalist strategy. Like the army, it was divided by personal rivalries, political factions, and deeply rooted antagonisms among the various branches; and it had no postgraduate service school, no professional journal, no planning staff, and no intelligence-gathering agency. Rather than developing its own strategic paradigm, the navy readily adopted the Guardians' way of war because it provided them with an offensive mission—to prowl the seas after enemy merchant shipping, free from the control of the army, a far better role than coastal defense or the "floating fortification" motif envisioned by President John Quincy Adams.[19]

The Fortification Board and the Corps of Engineers thus enjoyed a near monopoly on the development and dissemination of strategic discourse prior to the Civil War. As a result, antebellum military thought often displayed an engineer's tendency to seek precision, predictability, and order. At its most extreme, this led to an almost Panglossian confidence: "Modern warfare has attained such a degree of perfection, that nations no longer fear the inferiority of numbers. The science of fortification has furnished an effectual shield against the assaults of a superior force . . . so long as the science of fortification is studied and practiced, no nation can ever hope to gain much by conquest."[20]

Two of the army's most prominent pre–Civil War military thinkers, Dennis Hart Mahan and Henry W. Halleck, were among the leading exponents of the Guardians' scientific approach to warfare. West Pointers (first as cadets and then as faculty), members of the Corps of Engineers, and specialists in fortification, they accepted the intellectual paradigm of their branch without reservation.[21] Confronted with the problem of explaining the apparently chaotic, political, emotional, and unpredictable nature of war, both sought to impose order and predictability. In Halleck's view, "War is not, as some seem to suppose, a mere game of chance. Its principles constitute one of the most intricate of modern sciences. The general who understands the art of rightly applying its rules, and possesses the means of carrying out its precepts, may be morally certain of success."[22] He took a similar engineering approach to strategy, emphasizing the methodical seizure and control of decisive points rather than hazarding battle. In this context, Napoleon was no proponent of a revolutionary form of warfare but a conservative who returned to the "old and true system" of military operations based on "strategic points and lines."[23]

With a similar concern for predictability and precision, Mahan postulated that military science revealed principles of war that transcended time and space, as equally applicable in ancient Greece as in nineteenth-century America. He extolled Julius Caesar, who "by the development of gigantic plans, made and controlled by almost mathematical precision . . . fixed immovably those principles which, when acted upon, cannot fail to command success."[24] But it was Napoleon who had best put these principles into practice, leaving it to Mahan's generation to "systematize, and imbody in the form of doctrine" the great general's lessons.[25]

Both Halleck and Mahan anticipated the Managers' way of

war in their emphasis on military organization. Indeed, they approached the proper structure of military units, the correct hierarchy of command, and the delineation of staff responsibilities with far more passion than they regarded war itself. Halleck's 1846 book, revealingly titled *Elements of Military Arts and Science,* devoted four times the space to the arrangement and structure of military forces as to campaigning (strategy) or fighting (tactics). Mahan concluded that the primary lesson of the Mexican War was its demonstration that the United States had become "a powerful military state" and that "the military resources of this great Republic are no longer a question; a more thorough organization is alone waiting for their complete development."[26] Having summed up the recent war in barely a paragraph, he then devoted eleven full pages to advocating that the United States replicate Napoleon's Grand Armée down to the last hussar.[27]

The Crimean War of 1854–1856 only confirmed the wisdom of the Guardians' preexisting strategic tenets, at least from their own perspective. Almost immediately, Totten deduced from the Anglo-French landings in the Crimea further evidence that "great expeditions, greater than had ever been seen before . . . may be swiftly dispatched to the most distant lands" and that fortifications alone offered protection.[28] The service secretaries, or perhaps their officer ghostwriters, found further confirmation in long-held military views on the volatility of great power politics, the suddenness with which war might break out, the lack of national preparedness, and the necessity of continuing the board's program.

Evidence that did not fit into the Guardian paradigm, or contradicted it, was either dismissed or explained away. Thus one member of the Corps of Engineers cautioned against the popular perception that the fall of Sebastopol had proven that recent improvements in artillery made the corps' fortresses obsolete. The proper lesson was that if the Russians had but applied the sound construction principles that the corps practiced, Sebastopol would have withstood all attacks. It was therefore incumbent that the board's program be continued.[29] The report of the engineer who headed the three-officer observation committee to the Crimea, Major Richard R. Delafield, is particularly indicative of this mindset. As befitted an expert on fortifications, Delafield submitted detailed descriptions of the various shells and guns of both sides and the effect of artillery on fixed defenses. But when he witnessed a truly transformative technology that fell outside his professional expertise—the Prussian Dreyse breech-loading rifle—he dismissed it as an impractical novelty.[30]

That army engineers found in the Crimean War evidence that the nation must recommit itself to the program of the Fortification Board reflects their increasing frustration with how far the reality of harbor defense had fallen behind the vision. One problem, which would prove endemic, was the impossibility of fulfilling the board's promise of absolute security at low cost. The board's first report estimated that the nation's critical harbors could be made secure with 50 forts, to be built at a cost of slightly less than $18 million and manned by a peacetime garrison of 4,600. Fifteen years later, this level of security required 126 forts at a cost of over $31 million and 6,000 soldiers.

The expansion of the program in turn begat shortages, which were compounded by the army's own mistakes. In particular, the board devoted so much time to designing and building fortifications that it failed to provide sufficient artillery and gunners to defend them. By 1851, despite expenditures of over $20 million, only 59 sites were considered adequately fortified; of the 4,572 guns of all calibers needed to arm the main defenses, only 1,864 were actually mounted. As one secretary of war pointed out, some of these guns were more dangerous to their operators than to enemy warships.[31] Few forts had complete garrisons, and many were already in a process of deterioration that their small caretaker detachments could do little to prevent.

Fort Sumter in Charleston Harbor was a case in point. When

construction began in 1829, it was designed as a massive structure, its masonry walls towering over 50 feet high and supporting 135 guns on three tiers of casemates. But over thirty years later when the fort was finally called upon to fight, much of it was in disrepair. Only ten of the guns had been mounted, and the garrison consisted of some 80 soldiers. Despite the clear gap between ideal and reality, the board refused to consider replacing the enormously expensive and complicated masonry casemates with designs that were cheaper, easier to construct, and more in accord with recent developments in weaponry. Rather, it urged spending another $24 million building even more fortifications.[32]

The Guardian paradigm itself was so strong within the pre–Civil War army that criticism was not only rare but limited to discussing means, not ends. After a war scare with France, Secretary of War Lewis Cass argued that the defense system was too ambitious and expensive and was predicated on the unlikely scenario of an invasion. He urged that the construction of fixed defenses be scaled back and that new weapons such as steam-powered floating artillery batteries and mines replace them.[33] Four years later, the veteran frontier officer Major General Edmund Gaines echoed Cass in dismissing fortifications as obsolete and urging the adoption of steam batteries and mines. Gaines argued that his own defense system would not only present an "honest defiance towards the armies of Europe" but also provide internal security against the "home incendiary" and abolitionist.[34]

In response to these critics, Totten responded that these new weapons should be, and would be, incorporated into the board's harbor defense scheme, but it would be foolish to entrust the safety of the nation's cities to such unproven technology. In a report that Totten contributed to, and perhaps wrote, Cass's successor dismissed a purely maritime defensive strategy. No fleet, however powerful, could fully protect the coastal cities. If it concentrated its ships to guard one city, it would leave other cities vulnerable, and if it was destroyed in battle by the invader's fleet, the result would be catastrophic. It was foolish to suggest that the navy, the "Sword of the State in times of war," which should be "sweeping the Enemy's commerce from the Seas," would instead be "chained to the coast or kept within the harbors."[35] Thus, the Guardian theorists proved able to meld both the lessons of later wars and the challenge of new technology into their existing scheme.

Only in the years immediately preceding the outbreak of the Civil War did some members of the Corps of Engineers begin to seriously question its paradigm. In 1859 Lieutenant James St. Clair Morton wrote the secretary of war that the "revolution that strategy has undergone" rendered the board's program no longer valid: "When such extraordinary improvements are being effected in the means of destruction and of transportation, and such increase in the scale of warfare is observed . . . it is impossible that the art of war should remain stationary."[36] He believed that if the nation's most fortified city, New York, was attacked by a modern navy, "the ravage of shot and shell and of conflagration" would soon leave "the city in ruins, and reduc[e] its inhabitants to one common state of destitution."[37] Morton accused the corps of a "disinclination to the practical and a fondness for theory," which led it to continue to design and build grandiose fortresses predicated on dangerously obsolete European theories. His solution was to create a distinctly American defense based on a large army of citizen-soldiers and on cheap, easily deployable new technology such as mines that did not "require a lifetime spent in the ranks of the army, nor an education at a military academy" but were "essentially popular in . . . nature."[38]

Lieutenant Edward B. Hunt's 1860 essay entitled *Modern Warfare: Its Science and Art* also proclaimed an era of military transformation, and for much the same technological and military reasons. With European monarchies constantly increasing their armies, weapons, and fleets, the best "argument for peace" was the nation's coastal defenses whose "battlements go forth on no mission of attack; their vocation is to defend homes."[39] But Hunt broke from the board's orthodoxy by arguing that forts were not enough; the nation needed to develop a mobile force of citizen-soldiers who could repel any invader. Through training, innovative tactics, and a "complete system of military education" this national army would not only provide security against external foes but prevent the great danger of democracy: that "individualism will breed an anarchy more fatal, because more energetic, than the chaos born of obtuseness."[40]

Gaines, Morton, and Hunt objected to the board's coastal defense system as vulnerable to new technology, outdated by recent changes in military affairs, too costly, too inflexible, and too focused on one solution (the masonry casemated fortress) to every defense problem. They implicitly argued that for the corps—and by extension for the army's entire system of professional education—the design and construction of fortifications had become an end unto itself, divorced from the new realities of warfare and the nation's strategic needs. They criticized the board's scheme for its technological obsolescence, its failures to address land defense, and its exclusion of the militia.

Despite their vehement attacks on the Guardians' methods, these three critics still endorsed most of the group's assumptions. Indeed, for all their claims to innovation, Gaines, Morton, and Hunt were inherently conservative in their outlook. They accepted that the primary threat was from Europe, most probably Great Britain, and that it would come in the form of an attack on an Atlantic coastal city. They agreed that the nation's strategy should be defensive and deterrent. Like the board, they envisioned no scenario that required committing the army to combat operations outside of the North American continent. Where the board cited the War of 1812, its critics now cited the Cri-

mean War and other conflicts, but they shared similar conclusions about the hostile intentions of the international community
and the necessity for a coherent defense program. And, like the
board, its critics proved exceedingly poor prophets of the next
war. Indeed, writing two decades before the Civil War, Gaines
was more keenly aware of the danger posed by internal dissension
over slavery than were Morton and Hunt, writing barely a year
before its outbreak.

The surrender of Fort Sumter after just thirty-three hours of
ineffective resistance offered dramatic evidence of the limitations
of the nation's harbor defenses. In April 1862, almost exactly a
year later, Union warships steamed past the corps-designed fortifications guarding New Orleans almost untouched. That same
month Fort Pulaski at Savannah surrendered after being pounded
into rubble. As critics had predicted, new technology—rifled
cannon, steam-powered armored warships, and mines—radically
changed the dynamics of military fortification.[41]

Chief of Engineers Delafield concluded the war's three primary
lessons were that the corps' prized masonry forts could not withstand the new artillery, that mines were essential for protecting
harbors, and that much larger forces were needed for harbor defense. His successor, Brigadier General Andrew A. Humphreys,
found when he took office in 1866 that "confidence in the power
of existing masonry forts to resist the fire of the new artillery created in the struggle between guns and armor, was widely shaken;
while recent instances of the passage of land batteries by fleets
propelled by steam, pointed to the absolute necessity of devising
some effective obstruction to hold the enemy."[42] Thus, barely two
years after his death in 1864, Totten's system appeared completely
repudiated.

The first years after the war witnessed a strong effort to revive
the nation's harbor defenses. In 1866 Congress assigned to the
Harbor Defense Board the mission of reappraising the nation's se-

curity in the event of foreign attack. Its three committees, each consisting of one army and one navy officer, worked on an integrated defense plan that relied on long-range cruisers that would attack enemy merchant shipping and communications, and harbor defenses that would incorporate such new or improved technologies as mines, rifled cannon, and monitors.

By 1869 officers at the Artillery School had concluded that improvements in heavy guns made it impossible to build a fortress wall that could withstand sustained gunfire from either land or sea. To counter the increased range and power of naval gunnery, engineers and artillerymen began to design radically new fortresses camouflaged by the surrounding terrain when viewed from seaward. Instead of an overwhelming volume of firepower, they would mount a few rifled cannon whose shells could smash through any warship's armor five or six miles distant. These long-range guns would be supported by shorter-range heavy mortars whose shells would land on the unarmored decks, by minefields, and by mobile gun barges and monitors. With this layered scheme, enemy fleets would encounter a multitude of defenses; whether they attempted to force their way through with battleships or speed through with smaller vessels, they would be stopped.

In some respects, this new harbor defense system argues that responsible professionals assimilated the lessons of war, analyzed new weapons technologies, reassessed the threat, and incorporated their conclusions into a transformed military system. But such an interpretation fails to acknowledge the persistence with which military thinkers revived old arguments under the guise of new and innovative ideas. Once again, officers carefully selected incidents and data, ignored or explained away contrary data, and hypothesized counterfactuals. Thus, for example, one member of the corps argued that the true lesson of the Civil War was that whenever a corps-built fort fell, it was "due more to the weakness of the defenders themselves than to any essential damage inflicted by the shells of the enemy."[43] The forts themselves had not only fulfilled their mission, but the principles behind their construction were still valid. He closed by citing the 1826 Fortification Board as the most relevant guide for current defense policy.

The harbor defense community applied their professional expertise in testing and assessing new guns and construction materials, but their conclusions inevitably fit a broad strategic concept virtually unchanged from that of the antebellum Fortification Board. This was especially true of the Corps of Engineers, which continued to view itself as first among equals. In the decades after the Civil War, the corps tried to respond to a double challenge. One was intellectual and came from line officers such as William T. Sherman and Emory Upton, who sought to articulate a new version of land warfare. The other was methodological and came from Artillery officers asserting their branch's primacy in harbor defense.

The corps' response was perhaps predictable, and it incorporated many of the same arguments that succeeding generations of American military intellectuals would use. It created a fictive past. Disregarding three decades of complaints on the lack of support for the board's program, they now proclaimed that "General Totten was able to give the country what at their date were perhaps the most perfect sea-coast fortifications the world has ever seen."[44] Military intellectuals reiterated prewar arguments about the danger of foreign attack, the inability of naval forces to protect coastal cities, the need to rebuild existing defenses, and the failure of the population to comprehend the imminent peril. With martyred exasperation, one officer explained to his colleagues, "The great mass of our population is now, and from the nature of things must remain, ignorant of the requirements of National Defence. The duty of considering what should be done, and how it should be done, has been devolved upon a little band of professional Army and Navy men, largely graduates of West

Point and Annapolis, small in numbers and with no ready mode of interchanging views. Yet we are expected to elaborate a wise and comprehensive system of coast defence."[45]

Although the corps' senior leadership was the most consistently alarmist, it did speak for the army. As one essay pointed out in 1882, "The conditions of harbor defense have been revolutionized in the past twenty years" by the new "machine age of warfare."[46] Two years later, Commanding General Philip Sheridan told Congress that the nation's fortifications were "practically worthless against fire of modern heavy guns."[47] That same year, Lieutenant Arthur L. Wagner, soon to become the army's leading military theorist, reported the fortifications were collapsing and "we are destitute of heavy guns, and without the means of making them."[48] He claimed that the United States might soon be involved in a war to defend the Monroe Doctrine against aggressive European naval powers such as Great Britain, France, or Germany, any one of which could speedily transport tens of thousands of troops across the Atlantic and sack the nation's ports. Another officer wrote that "the defenceless condition of the sea-coast is well known to foreign powers . . . Before the important sea-coast cities could be prepared for defence, the ships-of-war of any second-rate power appearing in their harbors could exact all the tribute that the citizens might be able to pay."[49]

Against such a danger, the corps promised, as had the Fortification Board, that it could provide absolute security. In the words of its chief, "For the first time in the development of the modern art of war, the engineer has solved, with mathematical certainty, the problem of closing harbors and rivers against hostile ships."[50] After warning that a sudden attack on a port city by a modern navy might "paralyze" American resistance and force a humiliating peace, Lieutenant Tasker H. Bliss boasted that "our most skillful engineers have been engaged in devising a system of frontier defense that shall hold the enemy in check until the nation has had time to put forth its strength."[51] A few years later, an army officer lectured his naval colleagues that whereas in battles between armies "much is necessarily left to chance," in fortification "no such mistakes are justifiable." Because the direction of naval attack could be predicted, "we may with certainty foresee what [enemy] operations will be practicable, and by preparing to meet them we may compel him to either attack where we have carefully prepared a battle-field to give us every advantage, or, as has happened, to abandon his intention of attacking."[52]

Alternating warnings of imminent attack and assurances of protection persisted with the 1886 *Report of the Board of Fortifications or Other Defenses,* usually called the Endicott Board after the secretary of war who headed it. Like the Fortification Board six decades earlier, the Endicott Board portrayed an international climate in which war was ever present and an enemy might strike a coastal port at any time. As before, it saw current methods of waging war and new technology as having radically altered the military balance. New warship cannons were thirty times more powerful than those of the Civil War. It revived the specific scenario of a naval attack on a "defenseless" coastal metropolis and warned, "The plunder of one of our sea-ports might abundantly reimburse an enemy for the expenses of a war conducted against us."[53] It also revived its predecessor's argument that with the ports secure, the navy would be freed to attack enemy commerce, thus allowing the United States to wage a maritime war far from its coasts and at little economic cost.

If the strategic context and the nature of the threat closely followed that of the 1820s boards, so too did the solution: a layered maritime-land defense system to protect the nation's major ports against a sudden naval raid, provide secure harbors for the navy's warships, and protect coastal trade. Like the earlier Fortification Board, the Endicott Board promised that this security could be achieved at a reasonable expense if undertaken immediately. Although it estimated the total cost of the coastal defense system to be $126 million, an average of almost $10 million a year, the board claimed that this sum was actually cheaper than the earlier program. And, like the earlier board, it claimed its program would relieve the nation of the much higher expenditures and the implicit political dangers of a large standing army.

Where the 1886 study differed from the 1820s defense system was in its methods. Steam power, iron construction of warships, and above all improvements in artillery had rendered masonry towers more dangerous to their garrisons than to attacking fleets. But if military technology had created an imminent threat, it had also provided the solution. The Endicott Board advocated a comprehensive system consisting of deep-water warships to raid the enemy merchant marine and the latest coastal defense weapons—floating batteries and monitors, mines, torpedo boats, and new fortifications mounting new heavy artillery—all directed by an elite corps of specialists and backed up by a wartime mass army. A few long-range steel cannons (cast from a new $8 million foundry), dispersed behind cement-and-earth bunkers all but invisible from the sea, would replace the old batteries of dozens of smoothbore guns. So powerful were these new guns that they could sink a modern warship with a single well-placed shot.

Like the earlier Fortification Board, by outlining the threat and offering a plan of defense, the Endicott Board helped define the army's view of national security. Commanding General John M. Schofield told the secretary of war in 1894, "The situation of the United States is directly the opposite of that of the continental powers of Europe . . . Here there exists no necessity for great armies in the field. On the contrary, nearly the entire power of the nation is available for sea-coast defense."[54] A year later his successor, Nelson A. Miles, warned Congress that "war with any first class naval Power would result in a sacrifice of many of our most important cities, and ten days would be ample time to complete their destruction."[55] In subsequent addresses Miles claimed, "The unguarded condition of our coast is perfectly well known at the seat of government of every first-class foreign Power."[56] Revealingly, only a few months after this last jeremiad, harbor defense officers such as William E. Lassiter would mock the panicked demands from residents of the Atlantic coast—"who saw the seas filled with Spanish gunboats"—conveniently forgetting that for decades they had fostered such public hysteria.[57]

The Endicott Board report echoed the earlier Fortification Board reports in other ways as well. It supported the ascension of a new technical intellectual elite to leadership—the harbor defense artillery. Service secretaries, generals, and especially coast artillerymen waxed eloquent on the specialized skills required to coordinate the complex system of mines, machinery, rangefinding equipment, and armament. In the words of Captain A. D. Schenck, since the coastal artillery must defend "our banner on the outer walls of our land-defenses and maintain its honor in the face of an enemy's attack, it must be the first to meet him, and therefore should stand first in the order of readiness to resist such attack." Appropriating the elitist claims of the Corps of Engineers, he termed the gunners a "special and highly scientific branch of service whose modern enginery of warfare has become one of the wonders of the age."[58]

Like its predecessor, the Endicott Board encouraged the belief that its recommendations would not only protect the nation but also impose order and certainty in war. Its optimistic advocates found it "easy to assume that, in the near future, perfection will be attained and the maximum of power of guns and precision of fire will be secured," so that the "irresistible energy of the enormous projectile" would be directed with such "unerring" precision as to "annihilate" any aggressor "at a blow."[59]

But fissures soon emerged between the Endicott Board's plan and its implementation. Despite promises of perfection, the army had trouble with even the simplest technology. The cement in the new fortifications cracked and leaked, and the firing pits were too small to allow crews to load their guns. Casting gun mounts and cannon proved far more difficult than proposed. But even more seriously, the board's entire engineering solution to naval attack fell victim to technological change.

According to one member, the first principle of harbor defense was to estimate both enemy firepower and tactics and then ensure sufficient artillery "to overpower the enemy's fire."[60] And in some ways the Endicott Board was very forward-thinking. For example, it recognized that machine guns, then a relatively unproven weapon, could "concentrate within a small space the fire of whole regiments" and thus play a vital role in defending positions against attack.[61] But the core of the Endicott system relied on gigantic rifled cannon that could fire shells sufficient to pierce twenty inches of state-of-the-art warship armor at 1,500 to 2,000 yards. Unfortunately, by the 1890s, when construction on the first Endicott forts was just beginning, the standard Royal Navy warship carried two to four heavy cannon that could engage at over 3,000 yards. By the time the Endicott system was completed in the mid-1900s, warships like the HMS *Dreadnought* boasted ten twelve-inch guns with a range of 16,400 yards, firing five times faster, and far more accurately, than the original defense plan had envisioned. In short, like the 1820s Fortification Board, the Endicott members wrongly assumed that maritime technological development had reached a pinnacle, and that their system would be effective for decades. Instead, the pace of military technological change increased so fast that engineers and gunners were forced to revise the Endicott defense system even as they built it.

Other premises and assumptions proved equally faulty. Lieutenant Charles P. Summerall revived a criticism made of the antebellum defense system by noting that the Endicott plan devoted all its attention to the threat from the sea and glossed over landward defense with vague references to the militia.[62] The young artillery officer was correct. Although the board maintained that harbor fortifications could substitute for a large standing army, these forts would require 80,000 troops during wartime—or over three times the entire strength of the regular army. Yet it made no provision for mobilizing these forces; indeed, it did not address the problem of manpower at all. In a series of lectures, one board member devoted far more attention to such arcane issues as trench construction than he did to the size and composition of the wartime garrison.[63]

Even more ominous, the Endicott program was predicated on fortifications, guns, and garrisons ready to repel any sudden attack. But the Artillery branch itself was in a state of decrepitude. Few gunners, whether officers or soldiers, underwent more than the most rudimentary training. Lassiter, commissioned into the artillery from West Point in 1889, remembered it as being in "suspended animation," led by "Civil War veterans, the great majority of whom still lived in that period" and manned by soldiers who "kept their antiquated guns well painted."[64] Another soldier recalled his service in a coastal fort where, afraid to fire their ancient cannons, the officers prepared for martial strife by reading Kipling.[65] In 1900 the army's commanding general noted that the Artillery branch had less than half the troops required to provide one of the four shifts required for wartime, a third of its members were serving overseas, and of the 75 newly constructed forts only 43 were even partially garrisoned.[66]

Having secured approval for a new defensive program, the Guardians watched with approval the contemporaneous rise of "sea power" navalism in their sister service.[67] As late as 1855, Totten promised that if Congress would just continue funding his fortifications for a few more years, "we may go into war . . . confident that our frontiers are secure from devastation and insult, and feeling that our navy, not needed to watch our harbors, is free to traverse all seas in search of our foes, and our armies at liberty, in due measure, to attack our enemies as well as defend our own soil."[68]

Most army officers supported both the resurgence of naval construction that began in the 1880s and the increasing tendency for naval officers to define the navy's role exclusively as global, offensive, and directed at the destruction of the enemy fleet. In his 1886 essay on the nation's "military necessities," Wagner proclaimed, "The proper sphere of our navy is on the high seas, destroying the enemy's commerce, encountering *his* fleets, carrying alarm to *his* ports, and ravaging *his* coasts, rather than defending our own. The history of modern navies is a chronicle of successful offensive warfare."[69] Four years later, Commanding General Schofield told Congress, "An adequate sea-coast defense requires both the fortifications of each of the great sea-ports and the provision of an adequate fleet to take the part of the 'offensive defensive' in the event of war with any foreign power."[70] He emphasized that the national interests and security of the United States "require the maintenance of a first-class Navy that shall not be inferior to any other Navy of the world with which it may have to contend."[71] In these, and in other ways, army officers encouraged, and in some cases anticipated, many of the ideas soon to be associated with Alfred Thayer Mahan's strategy of "sea power."

But military intellectuals' support for an offensive global navy was based in part on a clear separation between the two services and their missions. In Schofield's words, "The purpose of the Navy of the United States is for operation beyond the reach of the guns of American fortification, while the object of the Army is to defend the sea-coasts against foreign attack, and any possible aggression from abroad."[72] In short, a naval war against enemy economic and maritime power was possible *only* if the army was first given the resources to protect the coastal cities. Such views, articulated barely four years before the United States undertook an offensive war against Spain, reveal much about both the Guardians' failure to anticipate the future and their narrow perspective on war. Even as the nation prepared for empire, they held to their conviction that the army's purpose was defensive and deterrent, that the most dangerous threat was a sudden attack, and that technology and the correct program could provide the nation with absolute security, if only its citizens would accept unquestioningly the guidance of its military scientist-strategists.

2

MODERN WARFARE

Both to the officers who lived through them and to later historians, the three decades between the outbreak of the Civil War and the end of the Spanish-American War were a period of profound transformation. Americans reeled from the effects of the Civil War and Reconstruction, especially in the South, from immigration and the settlement of the western frontier, and from industrialization and urbanization in the East and Midwest. As big business arose along a progressive middle class, the sheer rapidity of modernization threatened to tear American society apart. In the military services, advances rippled out and overlapped at a bewildering rate, not just in weapons, transportation, and communication but in doctrine, organization, and administration as well. To those American officers who had been taught—based on the dictums of Totten, Mahan, and Halleck—that war was a science with immutable principles of order and predictability, these changes were especially traumatic. Perhaps the coastal defense community could adapt the old Guardian paradigm to new technology, but for others the old way of war had been destroyed.

These army officers felt compelled to invent a new idea of warfare, and the process by which this doctrine evolved has had critical implications for the nation's military policy. Unfortunately, historians have often neglected this evolution in favor of the broader army reform movement, or have subordinated it to the study of "professionalism" in the officer corps. A good example is the influential 1957 work *The Soldier and the State* by Samuel Huntington. He argued that the post–Civil War era was "the most fertile, creative, and formative in the history of the American armed forces."[1] Despite widespread civilian indifference to military affairs, Huntington discerned in this period the formation of a distinct "American military mind," as officers began to probe the theory of war in order to sharpen their understanding of strategy and "military science." The development of a new philosophy of war provided the intellectual foundation this generation of officers needed to become competent and trustworthy practitioners of the nation's military policies—a competence ultimately proven by their outstanding leadership in World War II.

Huntington's thesis inaugurated a huge subfield of study in military professionalism. It also confirmed a deeply cherished belief among America's military personnel that, if left alone, the armed services would reform themselves, and their reforms would be vindicated on the battlefield. But as a historical explanation for the evolution of American military thought between 1865 and 1898, the thesis imposes a false coherence upon an era of confusion and disagreement, of many wrong turns and mistaken assumptions. Few army officers writing on military affairs after 1865 imagined they would be leading the nation's armed forces into a great war for empire before the end of the century. But they did know they were living in a period of military transformation that was both exhilarating and terrifying. As Captain A. D. Schenck marveled in 1895, just three years before the outbreak of the Spanish-American War, "Within a single generation . . . the art of war has changed more than it has ever changed since the advent of gunpowder."[2] They were a diverse and often factionalized assemblage, agreeing on one issue and emphatically disagreeing on another. Some focused narrowly on tactics or weapons, while others sought a radical revision of national security policy; some believed war was becoming more rational and humane, while others saw it as increasingly destructive and unpredictable.

But despite their many differences, military intellectuals shared certain assumptions. They all believed that a technological, organizational, and conceptual revolution in military affairs was under way. They were convinced that the United States was vulnerable to attack by its European rivals. They took as an article of faith that history offered clear lessons for current policy. And they all recognized that the American people required guidance or direction in preparing for the next conflict. These assumptions were interwoven in their efforts to develop a new concept of war.[3]

The term "modern warfare" appeared rarely in the pre–Civil War era. When it was used, it most often referred to integrating new technology into the existing harbor defense program. For example, an anonymous 1833 author declared, "Modern warfare has attained to such a degree of perfection" that it was "virtually impossible for an aggressor to secure victory."[4] In similar manner, Lieutenant Edward B. Hunt's 1860 *Modern Warfare: Its Science and Art* discussed the topic entirely in the context of the perceived lessons of the Crimean War and their application to fortifications.[5] But after the Civil War, "modern warfare" took on many different meanings, depending largely upon the divergent interests of the different services and branches. The harbor defense community continued to interpret it in reference to forts and artillery. But to officers of what would later be called the "mobile army"—infantry, cavalry, and field artillery—modern warfare encompassed a number of issues that went beyond the Guardian agenda.

One of the major differences between the Guardians and those who wrote on modern warfare was their approach to the past. Although the War of 1812 continued to shape the Guardian strategic perspective, the Civil War and the German wars of unification redefined warfare for this new generation of officers.[6] In contrast to the limited "cabinet wars" after 1815, the conflicts occurring between 1861 and 1871 had momentous political consequences. In just one decade, a united Germany emerged as the dominant land power in Europe, France was humiliated, Italy achieved independence, Austria-Hungary began its slide into client status, and the Confederacy was annihilated. These conflicts revolutionized the practice of war.

In 1846 the Americans had fought the first battles of the Mexican War with barely 2,000 troops, and in 1854 the allied expeditionary forces in the Crimea numbered 60,000. But by the 1860s the Confederacy, Austria, Prussia, and France each mustered over 500,000 soldiers, and some 2 million served with the Union. Battles were fought on a similarly colossal scale—160,000 combatants at Gettysburg, 320,000 at Sedan in 1870, and perhaps as many as 500,000 at Königgrätz in 1866. The numbers killed in combat, dead from disease, wounded, and captured were calamitous: 45,000 Austrians at Königgrätz; over 51,000 at Gettysburg; 435,000 French soldiers in 1870–71. Some 620,000 Americans died in the Civil War.

The size of the armies, the magnitude of the battles and casualties, and the immensity of their consequences all reflected the impact of industrialization. It would not have been possible to recruit, train, arm, transport, or direct these armies without the widespread adoption of telegraphs and railroads, or to support them without mass production of uniforms, munitions, weapons, and food. Organization and management were almost as important as industrialization. The Union victory owed a great deal to the application of industrial business practices to military challenges. Even more impressive was the Prussian system. Guided by its elite general staff, the Prussian army had organized and trained a large conscript army, adopted new weapons, developed doctrine, and drawn up strategic plans. When war broke out, it was as though a giant machine had been switched on. In a few weeks, tens of thousands of troops mobilized, trains deployed them to the front, generals coordinated the movements of their armies with the master war plan, and the enemy army was overwhelmed and smashed in a few battles.

The Civil War provided the army with the closest approach to a doctrine of war it had until 1905: General Orders Number 100 or *Instructions for the Government of Armies of the United States in the Field*. Written by the noted jurist Francis Lieber in 1863, the *Instructions* conferred both legitimacy and guidance to Union forces occupying the Confederacy during and after the war. The *Instructions* posited that in premodern conflicts, among "barbarous armies," and in "the internecine wars of savages," war was unregulated violence. Private property was wantonly destroyed, prisoners killed, and noncombatants slaughtered or enslaved. In contrast, what Lieber termed modern warfare took place within the community of "many nations and great governments," among which "peace is [the] normal condition" and "war has come to be acknowledged not to be its own end, but the means to obtain great ends of state, or to consist of defense against wrong." The great aim or "ultimate object of all modern war is a renewed state of peace," while "the destruction of the enemy in modern war, and indeed, modern war itself, are means to obtain that object." In sum, the Union cause was legitimate because as a civilized nation-state it was using military force only to secure a just peace.

Lieber may well have intended his code to provide both a rationale and a means to return to the limited conflicts of the eighteenth century in which, at least ideally, combatants would restrict military violence to one another's armies and avoid attacks on civilians. Certainly his definition of "modern regular wars" as those in which "protection of the inoffensive citizen of the hostile country is the rule; privation and disturbance of private relations are the exception" recalled the ideals of pre-Napoleonic limited conflicts. In this respect, the document was profoundly conservative. But in the face of massive popular resistance to occupation, the *Instructions* could also become a weapon for total war. Lieber maintained that "the more vigorously wars are pursued, the better it is for humanity. Sharp wars are brief." He gave wide latitude for violence based on "military necessity," defended retaliation, and insisted that "to save the country is paramount to all considerations."[7] All these justifications could be, and were, construed as a higher priority than the strictures against excessive force. Thus, the *Instructions* proved more than sufficient to legitimize the scorched-earth campaigns of Sheridan and Sherman.

None of the army's prominent antebellum intellectuals embraced the challenge of modern warfare. Totten died during the conflict, and Halleck—unpopular and virtually exiled—wrote no analysis of the war. Mahan was an anachronism long before his death in 1871. His 1863 edition of *Out-Post* largely ignored the Civil War and everything else that had occurred since 1815. Although he changed little of the original 1853 text, he almost doubled the length by adding a large section on principles of strategy and grand tactics. In this revision, Mahan noted that the outcome of war was not always predictable; he also acknowledged the existence of irrational factors such as chance or morale and admitted that generalship was often governed by instinct and expedience.[8] Except to his most discriminating contemporaries, however (or to later scholars predisposed to find them), such caveats were obscured by his emphasis on immutable principles, his geometric diagrams of operations, and his pedantic details of military organizations going back to the ancient Greeks.

Given the opportunity to analyze a truly modern war just a few hundred miles away, one that was cannibalizing his own nation (including many of his former pupils), his response was to chart the campaigns of Napoleon. Despite graphic evidence that war was becoming more violent and chaotic, Mahan still sought to deduce invariable paradigms and rules. And when a veteran commented that the tactics Mahan taught bore no relation to those the Union Army had actually employed, the enraged professor ordered him to be silent.[9]

A study of the military thinking of the army's senior leadership—commanding generals Ulysses S. Grant (1865–1869), William Tecumseh Sherman (1869–1883), Philip Sheridan (1884–1888), John M. Schofield (1888–1895), and Nelson A. Miles (1895–1903)—reveals a great deal of uncertainty, speculation, and erroneous conclusions about the lessons of the Civil War. With the exception of Schofield, this analysis was necessarily limited by its form and timing, being essentially four distinct narrative autobiographies, the first of which did not appear until 1885. Grant left the army so quickly that he had little lasting impact on the institution, as either commanding general or commander-in-chief. His memoirs are justly hailed as a classic of personal journalism, but they contain little on the Civil War's significance for future conflicts.[10]

Sherman's 1886 autobiography identified the four major technological changes that came to be associated with modern warfare—telegraph, railroad, rifle, and field entrenchments—but he was ambivalent about their impact and often contradictory in his predictions. Most of the guidance he provided suggests a return to the orderly and predictable form of warfare espoused by Halleck and Mahan.[11]

Sheridan was in many ways the most radical thinker. He foresaw war becoming ever more violent and total, involving not just armies but entire societies. He anticipated the collective impact of industrialization, entrenchments, new weaponry, and mass armies. He believed that in future wars, the cost of battle would be prohibitive; wars would become long struggles of attrition where economic and political strength were as important as military force.[12] But he made no discernible effort to shape army doctrine or education, change manpower policies, assimilate new technology, or in any other way incorporate his vision of future war into the army.

The only senior officer to contribute a serious analysis to the early debate over modern warfare was Schofield. Appalled at the cost, disorder, and social upheaval caused by the Civil War, he came to believe that only by limiting popular passion and military destruction could war achieve political objectives at an acceptable cost. This led him to seek what he termed a "science of war" to provide theoretical principles and allow for the integration of new technology, management, and tactics while at the same time limiting the escalation of violence.[13]

But Schofield soon discovered a fundamental paradox, expressed in this 1880 lecture: "Every progress made in the methods of war brings them more within the domain of science," even as science itself grew more complicated. Although "the art of war has already approached the margin of the exact sciences . . . the elements of the problems which war presents for solution are vastly more complex and difficult of exact measurement than those with which any other branch of science has to deal."[14] War, like all sciences, had "general military principles [that] like the laws of nature, of which they are in fact a part, are immutable." But applying these principles was ever more difficult because "no practical problem can be solved without an accurate estimate of the disturbing conditions. And since modern improvements in the methods and means of war have greatly increased the number, variety, and influence of these conditions, the labor of the military student has increased instead of diminished."[15] Schofield learned firsthand just how elusive an "accurate estimate of disturbing conditions" could be. Barely a year after he predicted that "foreign conquest and permanent occupation are not a part of the policy of this country," American soldiers were invading Puerto Rico, Cuba, and the Philippines.[16]

Nelson A. Miles, Schofield's successor, serves as a useful counter to the arguments that the period witnessed the development of a professional military ethos or the codification of a distinct American way of war. Miles' interest in technology rarely surpassed a fascination with gadgetry, as his effort to develop a special combat unit of bicyclists attests. Moreover, as a charismatic leader, he believed his genius transcended anything taught by military science. His view of warfare therefore stressed innate Heroic qualities. In this context, "drill, discipline, and instruction are but preparatory for the perfection and efficiency of the army," since what really mattered were an officer's "patriotism, untarnished honor, sterling integrity, impartial justice, obedience to rightful authority," and the "highest moral courage."[17] In April 1898 Miles correctly predicted the future struggle for Europe between Russia and Germany, but he failed to anticipate America's war with Spain that broke out that very month.[18] His inability to distinguish between military goals and personal ambition eventually led both President William McKinley and his own officers to regard him as an obstruction.

The senior leadership's failure to provide a clear vision of a new way of war was reflected at the lower levels as well. The army had no institution, whether staff or educational, charged with assessing the lessons of past conflicts or preparing for future ones. Nor did its school system provide a unified doctrine. After the Civil War, West Point declined into complacency and ritual, placing the burden of military education on a few branch schools and an individual officer's own academic interests. At the Artillery School, established in 1868, students spent some time studying the Civil War and European military operations, but their primary focus was on ordnance and gunnery. Sherman established

the School of Application for Infantry and Cavalry at Fort Leavenworth in 1881, but it provided only a rudimentary education
in tactics to lieutenants and captains. One student who attended
both schools recalled that "the commanding officer in each case
was a kindly, well-intentioned relic of the Civil War who, while
wanting his school to be a success, was frightened to death of the
innovations proposed by his subordinates."[19]

The majority of the officer corps, particularly in the infantry
and cavalry branches, had been commissioned for their Civil War
service, not for their professional training. Having learned to
fight by fighting, they were skeptical that the wisdom acquired in
the hard school of war could be imparted to others. For these veterans, Reconstruction and pacifying the frontier were full-time
occupations, and they had little inclination for theoretical speculation, much less the tedious work of turning speculations into
publishable documents. Even if they had been called upon to
write, it was not until 1880, with the founding of the Military
Service Institute and its journal, that a forum existed for officers
to provide detailed commentary on military issues. In the absence
of a single authority or vision, the task of interpreting modern
warfare fell to a variety of individuals and interest groups, few of
whom had much in common.

One of the first and most influential of these interpreters was
Emory Upton. A brilliant and opinionated officer, Upton rose
from lieutenant to brevet major general during the Civil War.
The appalling cost and duration of that war moved him to turn
his considerable intellect toward designing what he modestly
termed a "complete revolution" in tactics.[20] His drill manuals, the
first of which appeared in 1866, incorporated such lessons of
the Civil War as entrenchments, rifles, and a more dispersed or
"open" fighting order. His tactics could be applied to a variety of
formations, from squads and companies to brigades, divisions,
and corps. However, the regular army, which by 1877 numbered

less than 27,000 men, was clearly incapable of implementing them. Its infantry and cavalry were so dispersed in isolated companies along the frontier that they could barely manage rudimentary parade ground drill.

Upton was driven by a desire to make the army larger, more efficient, better prepared for war—and thus able to employ his tactics. His proposals for military reorganization, outlined in his 1878 book *The Armies of Asia and Europe,* borrowed heavily from the German example.[21] Like Mahan, Upton wanted to replicate another nation's military structure, but without transposing the underlying philosophy of war that had created these forces and guided them to victory. Like Mahan, he tended to fixate on the proper ordering of troop formations, the composition of the staff, the command hierarchy, and so forth. He was passionate in his plans for reorganizing the nation's military forces, but he devoted little attention to explaining how this new model army could serve national policy.

Like Mahan and Halleck before him, Upton tried to apply scientific precision to the study of history, deducing from the consequences whether various principles had been correctly applied. Also like them, he tended to disregard inconvenient variables, particularly such intangibles as morale, innovation, and technology, that did not lend themselves to scientific analysis. His Civil War experience convinced him that American wartime citizen-soldiers were the best troops in the world once they were properly trained and led. Why then had the war taken so long and been so destructive? Upton blamed the nation's shortsighted policies that all but precluded effective military forces until the Union was on the verge of defeat. He maintained that for a variety of reasons, most of them irrational, throughout the nation's history the American populace and its political leaders had persistently disregarded the sage advice of its military professionals. The resulting state of unpreparedness practically invited external attack and internal rebellion, and inevitably led to wars more costly in blood and treasure than necessary.

Upton's death interrupted the narrative of *The Military Policy of the United States* halfway through the Civil War, before he could analyze what had made it a distinctly modern conflict.[22] He did not discuss the importance of northern industry and finance, the shift in tactics caused by rifles, the suppression of guerrilla resistance, the use of African Americans as soldiers, the trench warfare of 1864, or Sherman and Sheridan's attacks on the Confederacy's socioeconomic structure.

Arthur L. Wagner, Upton's successor as the army's leading tactician, also based his critique of national military policy on lessons learned from history. In words Upton might have used, Wagner wrote in 1886, "The most prominent features of the military policy of the United States are a parsimonious and inadequate provision, in time of peace, for the necessities of war; an injudicious reliance upon raw troops; and a mischievous intermeddling by civil officials with the conduct of military operations."[23]

Wagner's 1889 book, *The Campaign of Königgrätz,* offered not just a detailed operational study but also a sermon that under the "new conditions of war resulting from the use of the telegraph, the railroad and breech-loading firearms," now "preparation for war is a more potent factor than mere numbers in computing the strength of a nation." In 1866 Prussia had been inferior to Austria in virtually every respect, except in "the organization, armament, equipment and *personnel* of its army," yet these were sufficient to ensure victory.[24] In this and other writings, Wagner provided a useful definition of modern warfare: it began rapidly and ended quickly; it involved large armies with the latest equipment; it made full use of industrial technologies such as the railroad and telegraph; it was fought at a furious pace; and it concluded with the complete defeat of one side. Thus, "It may be set down as an axiom of modern warfare that a nation without the power of prompt resistance is at the mercy of any well-prepared foe."[25]

Like Upton, Wagner was less interested in developing a theoretical paradigm of modern warfare than in creating the tactics and organization that would allow the army to practice it. Like Upton, he had no patience with those grizzled warriors who claimed their experience against the Cheyenne or Confederates fitted them for command in future wars. Assigned to Fort Leavenworth's School of Application in 1886, Wagner soon became its most influential teacher as well as a prolific writer on tactics and organization. A proponent of educating officers in what became known as "safe leadership," Wagner did not seek to discover a science of command that guaranteed its practitioner success. Rather, he accepted that the modern battlefield was chaotic and uncertain, and "to achieve success, a commander must have something of the gambler in his nature."[26]

Wagner believed that in the next war the small regular army would need to train, organize, and lead a hurriedly mobilized citizen-soldier army. The scale of industrialized warfare, the complexity of its weaponry, the coordination of transport and communications, the movement of tens of thousands of soldiers and their deployment into battle—all these required managerial skills equivalent to those displayed by financial magnates and captains of industry. He maintained it was folly to wait for a native genius of Washington's or Grant's skills to emerge. The nation needed a corps of commanders of sufficient education and ability to immediately command its armies. If all officers were taught essential tactical, organizational, staff, and other skills, they would be able to coordinate their activities and use their knowledge of past campaigns to wage war more effectively. To teach these skills, Wagner wrote a series of books on tactics and organization that educated a generation of officers into the complexities of fighting on the modern battlefield.[27]

John Bigelow, Wagner's contemporary, complemented Wagner's emphasis on tactics and organization with his own focus on strategy and operations in modern warfare. Like Wagner, Bigelow's initial writings were partisan, even reactionary. For example, he argued in 1882 that the "bayonet will be of greater use in the wars of the immediate future than in those of the recent past."[28] However, Bigelow's initial interest in European military history, particularly the Franco-Prussian War, soon found expression in his guide for large-scale military operations reflecting American realities.

The Principles of Strategy: Illustrated Mainly from American Campaigns, first published in 1891, proved Bigelow to be both insightful and original.[29] As his title indicates, Bigelow accepted the Mahan-Halleck dictum that strategy was governed by rules or principles. He used intricate diagrams to show their application in a number of campaigns. But he viewed strategy as more than simply moving troops from one place to another according to geometric formulas. He distinguished three types of strategy: tactical, or defeating the enemy in battle; "regular," or cutting the enemy's lines of communication and logistics; and political, or coercing the enemy government by threatening its control over the citizenry.

To Bigelow, the "primary object of military operations should be to overpower, and if possible, to capture or destroy, the hostile army." If defeating the enemy army failed to achieve the war's objectives, it might be necessary to capture the enemy's capital city and occupy key strategic points in enemy territory. Although Bigelow's focus was clearly directed against European opponents, he was one of the few officers who recognized that the army's next conflict might be in an "imperfectly-civilized country" in which "the only course to pursue may be that of carrying the war home to the people."[30]

American military intellectuals understood that history was not the only tool for understanding the dramatic changes in the conduct of war. Officers traveling to observe other armies and other wars also made significant contributions. Captain Francis V. Greene concluded that the Russo-Turkish War of 1877–1878 illustrated the way "a large army must always represent quite accurately the nation from which it is drawn." Although Russian soldiers were brave, hardy, and obedient, they were also illiterate and poorly trained; because so many were unable to read the numbers on the sights of their state-of-the-art rifles, in their hands a weapon with a range of 500 yards was accurate only at close quarters. Russian conscripts also lacked "the ready self reliance" and ability to adapt and innovate that American citizen-soldiers had demonstrated in the Civil War, and so they repeated the same tactical blunders on every battlefield.[31]

The Russian officers, uneducated and incompetent, did not understand weaponry and tactics, and callously squandered their troops in "rash murderous assaults."[32] The army's liabilities were paralleled by Russia's weak industry, primitive transportation system, and the absence of the civilian technical and managerial experts who had proved so crucial to the Union's victory. Despite its far greater manpower and wealth, Russia had been unable to take advantage of the changes wrought by modern warfare. The Turks—better prepared, more efficient, and fully attuned to new tactics and weaponry—were the victors.

The works of historian-policy advocates such as Upton and Wagner, and of observers and strategic writers such as Greene and Bigelow, expressed their conviction that in many ways the conduct of war had profoundly changed. These proponents of industrial warfare tended toward a total or absolutist view: war's objective was "annihilating the enemy's war power by destroying his armies."[33] They did agree with the Guardians that the major threat was a maritime attack on the coast and therefore supported the modernization of harbor fortifications, but it was an uneasy alliance. The 1886 Endicott Board and the harbor fortification program of the 1890s satisfied the service priorities of the engineers and heavy artillerists, aimed at deterrence, but provided no mission for the mobile troops in the infantry, cavalry, and field artillery save to passively defend the forts from land attack.

Not surprisingly, officers in these neglected branches quickly created scenarios in which the coastal fortifications failed, requiring land campaigns and large-scale battles. Thus, in 1884 Wagner postulated an invasion force of 100,000 men, a number soon to be accepted as a minimum. Within twelve years this had increased to 150,000.[34] With somewhat perverse logic, a handful of officers argued that the Endicott Board's program had actually increased the magnitude of the threat; by fortifying its harbors against a naval raid, the nation had forced its enemies to send sufficient forces for a land invasion. Commanding General Schofield, who had strongly promoted the harbor fortification program, claimed in 1894 that the nation's 10,000-mile coastline required "numerous small armies at suitable points near the seacoast throughout its entire extent, to prevent the landing of hostile forces."[35]

Like the Guardians' campaign for the construction of coastal fortifications, those in the mobile forces abstracted lessons from past and recent conflicts, speculated on potential enemies, and selectively interpreted historical evidence to justify a large land army. In 1898, with the nation only a few months from an offensive war against Spain, the winning essay on the topic "Based on present conditions and past experience how should our volunteer armies be raised, organized, trained, and mobilized for future wars?" called for a 460,000-man army to defend against a hypothetical British invasion.[36]

Some military intellectuals spoke out against these alarmist scenarios and tried to return discussion to a rational and practical analysis of the nation's real military needs. In his 1880 report, Sherman told Congress, "The idea of a hostile force landing on our coast is simply preposterous."[37] Bigelow demonstrated the mathematical impossibility of any nation's being able to land and support sufficient troops to invade the United States. A 1895 article analyzing European armies, transports, and fleets concluded that no European nation posed a credible threat to the territorial integrity of the United States.[38] But the majority of military officers who wrote on national defense agreed with Captain George P. Scriven that "the United States is by nature and by neglect one of the most vulnerable nations of the world, and that no great power has so vast an extent of frontier exposed to the attack of an enemy."[39]

In part because most modern warfare advocates viewed international relations as an amoral struggle in which a nation might invade the United States for the slightest of reasons, they were ambiguous about the moral implications of using the increasingly destructive products of industry. The army's accepted legal and ethical doctrine, the *Instructions for Armies in the Field,* hedged the question. "No conventional restriction of the modes adopted to injure the enemy is any longer admitted; but the law of war imposes many limitations and restrictions of justice, faith, and honor."[40] If, as the winner of an 1883 essay contest claimed, "the present, as the machine age of the industrial art, reflects more than any other the machine age of warfare," then the nation's survival might depend on its willingness to use weaponry that others would regard as indiscriminate and illegitimate.[41] As another author commented, "The weapons now issued to armies are of a more and more dangerous character, and they tend to make war even more terrible in the future than it has been in the past. The invention of formidable weapons of war continues to receive so much encouragement that only the most fearful carnage may be expected in the next great struggle as the result of various efforts to increase the efficiency of fire-arms."[42]

In 1880 Lieutenant Clinton B. Sears, a Civil War veteran,

West Point graduate, and engineer, addressed the issue of "the legitimate in war." Sears maintained that efforts to restrict military
technology were not only useless but also dangerous, since the
other side would inevitably use the forbidden weapon. He accepted Lieber's distinction that, unlike barbaric warfare, civilized
warfare did not kill noncombatants. But whereas Lieber had argued the "great object" of war was peace, Sears argued it was "to
destroy as effectually as possible the armed forces and military resources of the enemy."

In Sears' view, any weapon that accomplished the destruction
of the enemy was legitimate. This applied to a poisoned bullet,
"some effective projectile whose explosion will liberate a large volume of gas capable of producing asphysix [sic], say of a thousand
men at a time," or "balloons to rain upon the enemy from directly overhead every possible device for burning his buildings,
blowing up his magazines, and destroying his personnel." His
concluding argument, still heard today, was that the development
of ever more destructive weapons would deter future conflicts.
This prompted a rhetorical prayer to "save us, therefore, from the
cruel mercies of the weak. War, that splendid mistress . . . must be
given her full attributes and painted in her most deadly colors, in
order that the curses which undoubtedly she brings to the majority of the population may extend over as short a period as possible. Let us make her as deadly as we can in the name of humanity
and every good feeling."[43]

Sears' article drew an immediate response from Schofield.
Sears had envisioned a Hobbesian world in which every nation
would be driven to acquire and use the most deadly weapons.
Schofield argued that civilized nations sought prosperity and order, conditions that could only be achieved during peace. "War,
however frequently it may recur, is but a temporary interruption
of this desired condition . . . the necessary means of restoring
peace upon satisfactory terms." That weaponry was becoming

more destructive did not change the central fact that "the object
and end of war is *not* 'to kill.' This is but one of the *means* necessary to that end . . . The object of war is to conquer an honorable,
advantageous, and lasting peace." Therefore, it was of "the utmost importance to the future welfare of both nations that this
temporary passion of the people be not converted into lasting ha-
tred, by such acts of war on either side as the future sober judgment of mankind condemn as inhuman." Moreover, because civilized nations were a community, they were bound by shared
cultural values and "advancing civilization will, doubtless, more
and more emphatically condemn any wanton or unnecessary destruction of human life in war."[44]

The Sears-Schofield debate revealed a major division in military intellectual thought. Optimists believed that industrialization was making war more civilized, that "campaigns and battles
are shorter, more quickly decided and more decisive. Wars are
greatly reduced in length; theaters of war are consequently more
limited and the sufferings produced by wars are lessened. The
effects of war are not so disastrous."[45] But far more common
were terrifying and apocalyptic visions of the future. One officer
prophesized, "The storm of bullets which will sweep the coming
battlefield will allow no standing man to resist it, and yet the enemy must be reached, for he will remain in his position as long as
we stay at a distance, and we cannot have our attack demoralized
by fearful losses."[46]

In an 1890 article, Lieutenant John P. Wisser claimed, "In the
wars of to-morrow, where everything is to be on so grand a scale,
the separate scenes of the battle will be more terrific and their effects more terrible than ever in the past." He envisioned armies in
the millions, representing the totality of each nation's materiel
and psychological strength. Sped forward by railroads and covered by screens of tens of thousands of cavalry, the armies would
push onward until they collided. Then, as scattered forces began
to concentrate, "artillery battles with heavy siege guns, several

hundred on each side, will add a grander thunder to the storm of battle." Soon "a mosaic of innumerable smaller battles" would grow in fury as "whole battalions dwindle and melt in a few minutes," until finally one side managed to seize the advantage and break the enemy line, and then "with a grand 'hurrah!' the bayonet charge decides the final assault." Then would come a charge by thousands of massed cavalry to complete the work of "annihilation" and "produce a scene of havoc which we will not stop to contemplate."[47]

Soldiers recognized that, in Sherman's words, new developments in firearms had "revolutionized the equipment and tactics of armies," but the pace of change was so great that it frustrated even those who embraced it.[48] Even at its simplest levels—such as the four basic infantry weapons issued during a hypothetical soldier's thirty-year career—the implications of each change were so complex as to defy predictability. Joining the Union Army as a volunteer at the outbreak of the Civil War, a soldier might have been issued a .69 caliber smooth-bore musket, a muzzle-loading weapon that could be fired three times a minute and could rarely hit an individual target at over 100 yards. To compensate for its inaccuracy and slow rate of fire, officers kept their soldiers in compact masses for maneuver, deploying into one or two firing lines to deliver volleys at close range at equally dense enemy formations, and then closing with the bayonet. But by 1863 this soldier would be equipped with a .58 caliber rifled-musket. It had the same slow rate of fire, but intense training made it accurate out to 400 yards, thus rendering mass attacks against dug-in enemy defenders virtually suicidal—as the 7,000 casualties in one thirty-minute assault at Cold Harbor in 1864 illustrated. Largely as a result of innovation by the lower ranks, Civil War attack formations opened up: soldiers learned to avoid bunching, took cover until the last moment, and often maneuvered and fired as individuals.

In 1873 the army took a significant technological leap when it adopted the breech-loading Springfield .45–70 caliber rifle. This weapon could fire almost a dozen times a minute, was effective at 400 yards, and in tests could hit a target at 1,500 yards.[49] Greene calculated that whereas 400 soldiers armed with Civil War muzzleloaders could fire 1,800 shots in 12 minutes and inflict some 90 casualties, these same troops armed with breechloaders could fire 12,000 shots and kill or wound 1,200 in that time.[50] Equally significant, troops with the newer weapon could reload while prone or protected by shallow entrenchments. In 1892 the army made yet another radical improvement by adopting the .30 caliber Krag-Jorgensen bolt-action magazine rifle, capable of firing twenty times a minute with an effective range of 600 or more yards and a maximum range of 3,000. Moreover, it fired a smokeless-powder metal cartridge, thus eliminating the dense clouds of black smoke that impeded accuracy and revealed the shooters' location to the enemy.[51]

On one level, the army dealt with this transformation in weapons capabilities on very rational lines. The officer-specialists in the Bureau of Ordnance conducted exhaustive tests, and a series of boards composed of both technicians and combat veterans evaluated rifles, ammunition, and equipment. Upton's 1866 tactics were modified in 1874, in part to compensate for the adoption of the Springfield, and were later revised to take account of the increased lethality of weaponry. But as Greene had observed in the Russo-Turkish War, successfully adapting to modern weaponry posed challenges that went far beyond tactics. It required officers to balance current strategic demands against potential threats and to predict future technological developments. The War Department selected the Springfield not to fight its real battles on the western frontier but because it was better suited for the masses of untrained citizen-soldiers needed to repel a hypothetical invasion. Similarly, the Springfield was retained long after the great powers of Europe had adopted better weapons because, as Sheridan told Congress in 1884, it was adequate and "as danger of war with foreign nations seems remote, I think we can wait for still further improvements before finally adopting some good, reliable, standard magazine gun."[52]

The army's senior leaders were ambivalent about the effects of new weapons. "The only change that breech-loading arms will probably make in the art and practice of war," Sherman maintained, "will be to increase the amount of ammunition to be expended, and necessarily to be carried along; to still further 'thin out' the lines of attack, and to reduce battles to short, quick, decisive conflicts."[53] In contrast, Sheridan predicted that "if improvements in guns of every caliber continue to be as rapid as during the past fifteen or twenty years, and a good magazine rifle be finally attained, battles will become so destructive of human life that neither side in war will be able to stand up before the other. Armies will then resort to the spade, the pick, and the shovel; both sides will cover themselves by intrenchments, and any troops daring to make exposed attacks will be annihilated."[54]

Similar disagreements on the impact of modern armaments occurred throughout the officer corps, with positions reflecting equally personal visions of future warfare. "We are in the midst of one of the transition periods," concluded Captain Edwin Field, but the impact of modern weapons was "somewhat problematical" and the old principles of war still held true.[55] An 1880 article by cavalryman Brigadier General Wesley Merritt maintained that "a resolute charge leaves but a short time for the use even of breech-loaders."[56] But in the next issue of the same journal, Lieutenant Tasker H. Bliss argued "that troops will not endure a fire of more than a given intensity is a well-known fact; and it is also known that from the modern breech-loader can be obtained a fire much exceeding the required intensity."[57] Frank H. Edmunds, author of the manual that replaced Mahan's long outdated *Out-Post,* concluded in the 1880s that every war for the last four decades demonstrated the suicidal nature of frontal attacks against entrenched defenders armed with rifles.[58]

Many officers, most notably Schofield, could not make up their minds about the impact of weapons on war. In 1880 he observed, "Modern changes in the tactics of battle, due to the increased range and effectiveness of firearms, bring into far greater prominence than ever before the functions of a commander, which officers of all grades must exercise. Blind obedience, courage, and even discipline, however great, can no longer be relied upon to gain victories. Every captain and lieutenant should be, in no small degree, a real general." But in the same lecture, he also postulated that war was becoming more mathematical, and thus more predictable, and that a great general, such as Napoleon, could "eliminat[e] the factor of chance from the problems of war."[59] He returned to this theme in 1897, declaring that "the highest duty of a commander is to anticipate and provide for every possible contingency of war, so as to eliminate what is called chance."[60]

Military intellectuals who pondered the question of command tended to take one of the two positions Schofield had outlined. On one side were those who maintained, as did an 1879 West Point textbook, "that 'chance' as an element of a military problem can be made a very small factor, and as our knowledge of science increases, it may be possibly eliminated altogether. The master of the 'art of war' studies the science of war with a view to so thoroughly comprehending it, that he may from his knowledge thus acquired, be able to eliminate the elements of 'chance' from any military operation of which he has direction."[61] Officers who accepted this scientific view argued that the first step in imposing order on the modern battlefield was "to make the individual soldier act in accordance with the will of his commander even in opposition to his own."[62]

Schofield's other argument, that war was becoming more de-

centralized and that the commander's duty was to manage the
concentration and distribution of his troops but not to personally
direct every movement, also found considerable support. According to an 1882 essay on the most "important improvements in
the art of war" in the last two decades, "The essence of the modern system is to develop individuality, and to make officers and
men thinkers as well as fighters."[63] A year later, a textbook written
for students at the School of Application emphasized that in
modern combat soldiers needed to learn not only to act as part of
a unit but to have faith in their own individual abilities and to
initiate actions that previously commanders had ordered them to
do.[64] Captain Schenck sought to find a balance between control
and initiative. "An army in battle is no longer a mere mechanical
weapon in the hands of its commander"; for once a unit moves
within the killing range of rifles, "formal drill has vanished utterly." The solution was efficient training and command guidance so as to "make every officer and every man know almost
instinctively what to do and what decisions to form as each emergency arises."[65]

Schenck's effort illustrates a growing division within the officer
corps. On one side were Heroes, military intellectuals who believed that recent developments in technology, organization, and
tactics had revived traditional martial virtues such as character,
discipline, skill, experience, and élan. It was the individual, and
especially the individual commander, who was now the crucial
determinant. In the words of James Chester, "I am never so much
inclined to believe in born generals as when I get thinking about
the psychology of war. The ability to feel the pulse of a whole
army and count its heart-throbs in the heat of battle—to be able
to tell what it will do, and what it will not do—is a gift rather
than an accomplishment. It is a sort of inspiration. Men can
teach men how to obey, but God alone can teach them how to
command."[66]

On the other side of this divide were the Managers, who viewed modern warfare as an industrial process, much like the big businesses emerging in late nineteenth-century America. An army was a vast corporation that combined staff, command, and bureaucratic agencies to coordinate materiel and human resources to optimally execute war plans. The railroad, telegraph, and conscription had greatly expanded both the size and scope of war, making the ability to mobilize vast numbers of troops and communicate with them over large distances increasingly important.

Managers rejected the Heroes' belief that individual will and genius were the determining factors, and instead maintained that the nation's ability to mobilize its manpower, materiel, and popular support would ultimately decide victory or defeat. Schofield declared in 1897, "The valor of great masses of men, and even the genius of great commanders in the field, have been compelled to yield the first place in importance to the scientific skill and wisdom in finance which are able and willing to advance the most powerful engines of war."[67] Both Bigelow and Wagner stressed the importance of popular support, and Bigelow suggested a distinct form of strategy—"political strategy"—that targeted the opposing government and its population. In Wisser's view, war was now "a matter for the *people* to decide," and this "allowed the use of *all* available means" in securing victory.[68] To win such wars, the Managers emphasized, the army and the nation must prepare in peace. Their program included educating officers in their corporate responsibilities, adopting the newest technology, drawing up war plans, and training troops in large-scale operations.

The army's confusion over the meaning of "modern warfare" can perhaps best be understood by studying it in the microcosm of the Cavalry branch. In many respects, the last year of the Civil War was the highpoint for the cavalry and the benchmark by which it measured its mission, tactics, weaponry, and self-identity. Equipped with repeating carbines and pistols, the Union horsemen possessed formidable firepower and, in violation of accepted military wisdom, could not only seize terrain but also hold it. In contrast to contemporary European cavalry, which saw its mission as first and foremost mounted combat against other cavalry, the American horsemen fought dismounted as often as mounted. They were used both independently and with other combat arms for a host of missions: reconnaissance and security; screening; attacking isolated detachments; delaying enemy advances and harrying enemy withdrawals; seizing and defending strategic points; maintaining communications between separated forces; and raiding deep into enemy territory to destroy supplies and transportation.[69]

In the decades after the Civil War, the cavalry came under increasing criticism from officers who argued that modern firearms had rendered horsemen almost helpless against disciplined infantry and artillery, and recommended they be limited to reconnaissance activities far from the battlefield.[70] The cavalry's response was many-faceted. Some, such as Merritt, insisted the inherent martial virtues of horsemen outweighed the vagaries of technological development. "Who can doubt that determined, resolute, disciplined soldiers, who have confidence in themselves and their leaders, well armed and brave, can accomplish feats in charges in the heat of battle, such as have made and will continue to make the part of the cavalry glorious in all wars?"[71]

Citing the past exploits of horsemen as predictors of future trends, Lieutenant E. P. Andrus maintained that however much firearms had increased in range, accuracy, and rapidity of fire, "the man behind the weapon has not kept pace in improvement, in courage, confidence and consequent steadiness, with his weapon." The horrific sights of battle—now revealed by the use of smokeless powder—"will unnerve the ordinary man and thus render him an easy prey to cavalry."[72] Echoing this argument,

Lieutenant Charles D. Rhodes maintained that the new weaponry actually increased the "moral effect" of a mounted charge. "Men's nerves will fail them, and their firing grow wild, as the line of horsemen, the earth fairly trembling under the shock, come sweeping down on them."[73]

Cavalry advocates argued that since the nation's ground forces would never fight overseas, the army needed to prepare for war on the North American continent. A large mounted contingent was essential in any likely conflict, be it a quick offensive strike into a neighboring country or securing the border against enemy raids. And should the Endicott Board's scenario become reality and the nation be invaded, cavalrymen could conduct a fighting retreat while the regular army and militia gathered for the counterattack. Such operations required rapid and decisive action on every level, from driving off the enemy's pickets and gathering information, to reinforcing a threatened point or exploiting a breakthrough on the battlefield, to deep-ranging strategic raids that destroyed enemy industry and morale. Only mounted forces could provide such mobility and fighting power.[74]

With the benefit of hindsight, it is easy to dismiss the cavalry's response to modern warfare as self-serving and romantic. But those cavalry officers who wrote on warfare were active participants in the military debates of the time, and they included among their number prominent intellectuals such as Wagner and Bigelow. They believed themselves progressives readying the mounted branch for the wars of the future. In retrospect, they were reactionaries planning to fight the wars of the past.

This contradiction is nowhere better illustrated than in an 1891 article by Lieutenant J. Y. Blunt that argued, "In future we will have to reckon with troops handled according to the methods of modern scientific war . . . for whether we will have to meet the Canadians from the north or the Mexicans from the south, these nations have trained armies, better or worse, to be conquered at any cost, and as we are told that in future, wars will be 'short, sharp and decisive,' it behooves the army that would be victorious to be ready."[75] Blunt proposed that the Cavalry discard the obsolete dismounted, firepower-intensive tactics of the Indian wars and instead adopt new and innovative methods—massed charges of saber-wielding horsemen.

Blunt's startling conclusion illustrates the dangers of interpreting the period between 1865 and 1898 as one of evolution and progress in which a small group of enlightened reformers envisioned a professional army that would become a reality in the twentieth century. Such an interpretation imposes a coherence and foresight all too often missing in reality. Like the Guardians, the modern warfare movement was in many ways profoundly conservative. Even as they trumpeted the radical changes brought by new weaponry and industrialization, even as they prophesied horrific scenarios of future conflict, many theorists held profoundly regressive views. Just as the Guardians had been convinced the next war would repeat the events of 1814, so the post–Civil War theorists similarly failed to predict the future. Like the Guardians, they tried to create an army for a war the United States would never fight. And, like the Guardians in 1861, those who claimed to have seen the future of modern warfare were completely unprepared when their own nation went to war in 1898.

3

UNCONVENTIONAL
WARRIORS

In 1837 Major General Edmund P. Gaines unleashed a diatribe against military intellectuals who had "never seen the flash of an Enemy's Cannon" and who drew all their insight on war from "mazes of French Books." Instead, the nation should heed Heroes like himself, men whose long experience endowed them with a "common sense science of war" far superior to foreign theory.[1] Whatever the validity of Gaines' critique, it glossed over an important fact: neither the general nor his fellow officers had been exposed to hostile cannon fire for at least two decades. Their combat credentials derived almost entirely from their experience against Native American tribes, brigands, and other irregular warriors.

What contemporaries sometimes termed "minor warfare," and is today best termed "unconventional warfare," was a far cry from the great nation-state struggles envisioned by modern warfare enthusiasts. Encompassing partisan and guerrilla operations, punitive expeditions, small-unit raiding and skirmishing, counterinsurgency, and a variety of other forms of conflict, unconventional warfare was a continuation of America's long-standing struggle between colonists and native inhabitants.[2]

Although more common than the nation's great wars, and perhaps producing far greater political and economic gains, unconventional warfare received scant attention from Guardians and Managers. In 1860 a Corps of Engineers officer dismissed the rest of the army as engaged in "custodial duties, in small detachments on our Indian frontiers, where all its strength is expended in a disheartening struggle to hold fast to civilization in barbarous surroundings."[3] The great reformer Emory Upton believed that frontier warfare was ruining the army; he worried that when the nation ultimately faced a "first class power" its commanders would only be veterans of "action which will not merit the title of a skirmish."[4] The importance and the legitimacy of those waging irregular warfare were similarly dismissed in Mahan's declaration that a truly brave population would meet the enemy in battle rather than fight "a series of petty combats which only serve to exhaust the country without bringing about any decisive results."[5]

The Heroes' practical approach to warfare led them to adapt equipment and methods intended for European battlefields to frontier conditions. They reconfigured tactical organizations and modified transport to allow troops to campaign in all seasons and in all terrain. They created a disproportionately large cavalry force to match their opponents' mobility. They employed indigenous scouts. And they made a host of other improvisations. Experience taught individual officers to read the landscape for potential ambushes, to make use of local intelligence sources, to determine the size and composition of a war band, and to communicate with the indigenous populations.

In punitive campaigns against tribesmen defending their homelands, regular army officers discovered what their colonial predecessors had—the futility of chasing highly mobile bands of warriors. Frontier officers soon resorted to colonial methods of striking at the enemy's society by destroying foodstuffs and shelter and subjecting noncombatants to exposure and starvation.

One secretary of war described this warfare in 1858 as "beating their forces, capturing many prisoners . . . destroying large amounts of property, and laying waste their country."[6]

Unconventional warfare taught officers that military operations ended only when stability was imposed, and not with a decisive battle, a formal surrender, and a victory parade. Military success did not terminate resistance. With occupation came an equally long and arduous pacification process, defined by one officer as "all means, short of actual war, used by the dominating power in the operations of bringing back to a state of peace and order the inhabitants of a district lately in hostilities . . . It is not mere force; it is a judicious measure of force and persuasion, of severity and moderation."[7] Indeed, the term "peace establishment," used throughout the nineteenth century to describe the mission of the regular army, implicitly recognized that the military goal went beyond merely defeating opponents in battle and included the imposition of government, law, and order. What would now be termed "postconflict operations" required frontier officers to take on myriad roles having little to do with the technical warfare of the Guardians or the great nation-state struggles envisioned by the Managers. The frontier taught Heroes that although war was sometimes glorious, it was a complex and unscientific phenomena, and always contingent on the human element.

The Heroic officers who served on the frontier in the nineteenth century produced no military intellectual equivalent of Clausewitz to provide a theoretical understanding of minor warfare. They passed on Gaines' "common sense science" by various means ranging from official reports to memoirs. To those assigned pacification duties, the lessons of unconventional warfare—first in the West and later in the growing American empire—were handed down piecemeal. They could be gleaned from a variety of sources, such as field reports, articles, and books detailing tactical and logistical adaptations, field craft, command decisions, and other practical matters. Works such as Mahan's *Out-Post* or Arthur L. Wagner's *Service of Security*, although primarily designed for the European battlefield, did contain advice on small-unit formations, reconnaissance, patrolling, and intelligence gathering that could be adapted for Indian fighting. John Bigelow's *Principles of Strategy* provided examples of formations used on the frontier and even a brief study of campaigns pitting armies against rebellious populations.[8] There were also unwritten rules, such as tempering coercion with conciliation.

Some commanders did arrange training exercises to provide their troops with practical instruction in frontier operations. One example occurred in 1887 when Brigadier General Nelson A. Miles staged an exercise in which scattered garrisons of his Department of Arizona attempted to catch a detachment of soldiers acting as a "raiding party." This exercise provided more than useful training in tactics. It brought home to its participants the physical demands of desert campaigning, the need for accurate intelligence, and the importance of adapting to local conditions.[9]

For most officers, the continued failure to incorporate the lessons of frontier warfare into a formal written doctrine was not critical. They had such faith in their own leadership, their tactics and troop discipline, and their weaponry that they may even have welcomed the lack of overarching authority. Nonetheless, some warned that "the beginning of almost every Indian war has been marked by some disaster, due chiefly to ignorance of the country or the foe." Unless the army devoted more attention to passing on its veterans' dearly won knowledge of the "customs, signs, moral and intellectual traits, methods of chase, and warfare of each tribe," such early setbacks would be the pattern for the future.[10]

The attitude of army officers toward frontier conflict was complex, but the comments of one British traveler in 1833 describe the entire period of western expansion: "Officers seem to dislike Indian warfare very much; complain of the hardships attending 'bush expeditions;' the treachery of the enemy; their ambushes and surprises; and cruelty to prisoners."[11] The physical environment alone was daunting. Living conditions were primitive and brutal, basic necessities were often in short supply, and everything from the weather to the food to the insects could kill an unwary soldier. One officer recalled his service in the West as a "steady wearing, exhausting strain on the mind and physical system" and noted that, barely a decade later, more than half the officers he had served with on his first campaign were either disabled or dead.[12]

When to this physical and mental stress were added what General John Gibbon referred to as "the peculiar kind of Indian warfare in our country" in which "very few of the recognized rules of warfare are applicable, and the struggle degenerates into a series of operations in small detached parties in which exceedingly hard work and occasionally desperate encounters are the characteristics," the officer's life became even more hazardous.[13] The experience of soldiers in the Seminole Wars—"compelled to move their forces with the utmost caution, in the face of a bold, active, and wily foe . . . who hovered about their flanks, concentrating their numbers upon a point of attack with unexampled rapidity, and flying from the open ground with a swiftness that baffled the pursuit of the white man"—was a hallmark of frontier conflict.[14] Too often such warfare prompted cycles of retaliation, which then escalated into atrocities and the massacre of civilians—what Gibbon referred to as "the extreme logical conclusions . . . of a state of war."[15]

Frontier warfare brought out some of the worst characteristics of the Heroic martial tradition. General Ethan Allen Hitchcock noted the propensity of his fellow officers to treat all Indians in the same provocative and violent manner, seeking to cow them into submission through the most barbaric methods. Seminoles had been "treacherously slain and many of them captured under a flag of truce; some had been subjected to mutilation and torture; prisoners had been deliberately hanged," and the officers guilty of this misconduct were rewarded.[16] There was a strong punitive streak in pre–Civil War army thinking, a conviction that Indian tribes needed to be completely defeated before they could be made peaceful.

Paradoxically, at the same time it fostered a climate of barbarism and savagery, the Heroes' emphasis on individuality and martial virtues pointed to morality (often interpreted as the officer's personal character) as an essential component of warfare. Officers like Miles might believe that Indian–white conflict was unavoidable and the destruction of Native American culture inevitable, but once their opponents had ceased armed resistance, it was the government's ethical and legal responsibility to "devise some practical and judicious system by which we can govern one quarter of a million of our population, securing and maintaining their loyalty, raising them from the darkness of barbarism to the light of civilization, and put an end to these interminable and expensive Indian wars."[17]

Gaines employed harsh tactics against his Indian opponents, but he also publicly opposed their forcible removal across the Mississippi, urged that they be educated, and devoted considerable energy to protecting them from whites. In 1884 Colonel Albert G. Brackett noted that whereas in the past the army's task had been "to guard the infant settlements from the encroachments of the Indians on one hand, and on the other hand to prevent white men from trespassing upon the domain of the Indians," now "the trooper is called upon to shield the red man from the cupidity of the border settlers, instead of crowding him, as formerly, to the wall."[18]

A contractual view of war—that the hard hand of war should

be tempered by the benefits of peace—led Heroes to praise the courage of Native Americans and denounce their own government's duplicitous treatment. One officer declared, "The great mistake has been made by some of not considering them human beings, capable of the same feelings as the rest of mankind, the same passions, affections and hatreds. A people who can be crushed and exterminated but not enslaved, are certainly entitled to some respect."[19] Gibbon asserted, "From the time of the first white settlements . . . to the present day when treaties are made only to be broken by the whites, the history of the two races has been one continuous series of frauds and impositions."[20] Hitchcock wrote of the Seminole Wars, "The government is in the wrong, and this is the chief cause of the persevering opposition of the Indians, who have nobly defended their country against our attempt to enforce a fraudulent treaty. The natives used every means to avoid a war, but were forced into it by the tyranny of our government."[21] These officers, and others, believed the army should be the impartial protector of the Indians, not the agents of oppression. Thus, Heroic leaders found themselves having to resolve a number of contradictory positions, not least that their own belief in character and morality clashed with the obviously immoral means their government and its citizens were employing.

The army's constabulary duties on the frontier required officers to make both war and peace and to function as police as well as soldiers. Hugh L. Scott recalled one mission of pacification in which he swam icy rivers, braved a blizzard, marched almost 500 miles, and successfully arrested a few individuals who had fled their reservation. It was certainly hard, rigorous service that challenged an officer's endurance, adaptability, small-unit leadership, and field craft, but was it warfare? Even Scott accepted by the late 1880s that "a new era dawned for our army" and "the day of the Indian wars was over and . . . we must fit ourselves for war with civilized peoples."[22] Ironically, most of his efforts to master what he termed "civilized war" had little immediate benefit. Twenty years later, Scott, like many fellow officers, would be fully engaged in imperial missions of pacification thousands of miles from the western frontier.

The Heroes' emphasis on individual skill and adaptability and their broad interpretation of war allowed them to make a relatively easy transition to other irregular conflicts. So too, their contractual view of the relationship between the army and the populace ultimately became an essential part of army doctrine. During the Mexican War, General Winfield Scott was extremely sensitive to the threat of popular resistance. He decreed that his troops were to disturb the population as little as possible and to respect the inhabitants' religion and customs. He imposed draconian punishment on soldiers who committed crimes against civilians. Such measures had various goals: to limit armed violence to the rival armies and avoid popular participation; to control suffering and destruction; to impose discipline on his own troops; to protect his supply lines; and to provide order and control. But Scott insisted on equally good behavior from the occupied population. When guerrillas and partisans continued to attack his forces, Scott ordered them summarily executed and burned the villages of those he suspected as having aided them. Henry Halleck's *International Law* provided a cogent legal argument to support both Scott's policies and the contractual relationship between soldier and occupied population.[23]

The Civil War solidified the army's reliance on tactical adaptation to counter irregular warfare, but it produced no coherent pacification doctrine. Faced with widespread and violent resistance to federal authority, officers responded with a wide range of measures. In some districts, they raised local defense forces, paramilitaries, and elite counterinsurgent units from Unionists. In other areas, such as Missouri, they depopulated counties that aided and abetted guerrilla forces. They sent cavalry raids against suspected guerrilla hideouts. As the war dragged on, and as troops became more and more convinced of the implacable hostility of the southern populace, they turned increasingly toward destroying the economy and society that supported the Confederacy. Campaigns such as Sherman's march to the sea or Sheridan's destructive forays into the Shenandoah were only the most visible signs of a form of warfare very much akin to what the army had practiced on the frontier.[24]

As the Union army drove back the Confederate armies and occupied areas that had formerly been in rebellion, it faced a variety of postconflict problems that further reinforced its broad view that war did not end on the battlefield. Soldiers had to distinguish between partisans—Confederate troops detached for special operations—and guerrillas, who did not belong to a recognized military unit, wore no uniform, and raided or worked at civilian occupations as it suited them. Army officers witnessing the behavior of this latter group unanimously deplored their actions. In the words of General O. O. Howard, a man known for his piety and humanitarian instincts, "Guerrillas proper are those who are carrying on war without the pale of an army . . . they plunder and burn houses; they slay the most harmless non-combatants," and were no better than "organized mobs and robbers."[25] A further dilemma was the legal status of the occupied population. Officially, the war was a rebellion; ideologically, it was an uprising by the slave-holding autocracy. It followed that the majority of southerners were American citizens and had to be treated as such by the troops. Finally, as the designated agent of federal authority, the army needed to establish itself in all occupied areas as the legitimate government.

These concerns were addressed in 1863 with the proclamation of the *Instructions for the Government of Armies*. The *Instructions* made a sharp distinction between legitimate and illegitimate warfare, between "public war," defined as "a state of armed hostility between sovereign nations or governments," and "barbarous" war, insurrection, and criminal violence. "Partisans," or uniformed soldiers in authorized military units operating on special missions, were lawful. But "men, or squads of men, who commit hostilities, either by fighting, or inroads for destruction or plunder, or by raids of any kind . . . without being part and portion of the organized hostile army," and who alternately took up arms or became civilians, were "highway robbers or pirates."

The *Instructions* also outlined a social contract between the army and the population. Soldiers were held to a high standard of conduct, not only for the sake of military discipline but because as government agents charged with imposing order in the occupied area their behavior had to be orderly as well. They were expected to provide law enforcement, revive commerce, and improve public health, while at the same time interfering as little as possible with the lives, customs, and institutions of civilians. But this population had to accept the conqueror's authority. Continued resistance to lawful government made them "war traitors," "war rebels," and "armed prowlers." To crush such opposition and restore peace and order, the *Instructions* legitimized "protective retribution" such as confiscating or destroying property, imprisonment, and execution.[26]

For the Heroes, the *Instructions* provided a legal justification for methods already in practice. Implicit in the *Instructions* was recognition that the very nature of unconventional warfare, the problems of exerting command and control over dispersed garrisons and mobile forces, and the widely different levels of cooperation and opposition among the population necessitated delegating responsibility to the officer on the ground. It was up to the individual commander's judgment to determine what constituted the *Instructions'* definition of such phrases as "military necessity," "protective retribution," and "treated summarily" and then to assign an appropriate sanction.

Thus, both advocates of conciliation and of hard war could

find arguments to justify their positions, for the *Instructions* legitimized everything from burning homes to building schools. The
Instructions' very flexibility made them popular. It is little wonder
that, although intended as an emergency measure to provide specific guidance for Union troops pacifying occupied areas under
martial law, they became an essential part of army practice, regarded by many officers as the final word on occupation and pacification. Almost four decades later, when Filipino guerrillas
contested American occupation, officers would turn to the *Instructions* to meet the threat.

Some have seen close parallels between the Civil War and postwar army frontier campaigns, while others assert these conflicts
share few similarities. Both positions are correct, depending on
whose "way of war" is examined. Certainly, officers who had ravaged the homes of white Americans in South Carolina or Virginia
might have had few compunctions in applying equally harsh
measures against Indians in the West. And the tactics used were
similar—burning crops and homes, treating irregulars harshly,
and occasional resorting to the rhetoric of extermination. But the
number of differences is equally large. At roughly 27,000 officers
and men, the entire post-1877 regular army was much smaller
than the forces that Sherman, Sheridan, or Schofield had each
commanded in a single Civil War campaign. The scale of campaigns was also vastly different. The three-day Battle of Gettysburg involved some 160,000 troops and resulted in 45,000 casualties. The Red River campaign against the Kiowa took half a year
but involved no more than 2,000 soldiers, 25 skirmishes, and
fewer than 100 combat fatalities on both sides.

Not surprisingly, Guardians and Managers who believed the
army should prepare for war against a rival European power dismissed post–Civil War unconventional conflict as barely worthy
of note, an unpleasant reality that inhibited their efforts to transform the service. Upton declared to a fellow officer "that 'bush-

whacking' and Indian fighting with one or two companies do not qualify an officer for the position [of] General" when it came to "a great war."[27] In 1875 Sherman sent Upton and two other officers to study the Chinese, Japanese, and European colonial armies for possible lessons that could be applied on the western frontier. Instead, the group focused almost entirely on the organization and equipment of conventional forces, and pushed on to Europe as soon as possible to examine the armies of the great powers. In similar manner, American officers studying the 1882 Anglo-French expedition to Egypt concentrated not on its lessons for colonial war but on what it revealed about the danger of potential attacks on American seaports.[28]

The nation's heritage of experience from frontier warfare had little impact on the army's approach to civil unrest. All officers, whether Guardians, Managers, or Heroes, feared insurrections, riots, and other civil disturbances. Before the Civil War soldiers had been deployed to suppress sectional violence. During Reconstruction, service in the former Confederacy involved the army directly in restoring the South's economy and political system in what would now be termed nation building, and in extensive policing and counter-terrorism operations. But much of the South was reconstructed, by this definition, as early as 1870, and the political conservatism of most officers made them more concerned with securing stable government than instituting widespread social reforms.

With the onset of violent industrial strikes in the North—and particularly the Great Strike of 1877—some officers came to accept Sheridan's prophecy of future "wars of internal stress between capital and labor."[29] In an 1881 essay on America's military necessities, Wagner lamented, "Communistic principles have struck their roots into the social soil of the nation," and he warned that internal dangers were as great as any foreign threat. Indeed, a substantial part of the reformers' argument for increasing the regular army, closing small western garrisons, and transferring troops east to large posts for training stemmed from fear of "domestic warfare."[30] Schofield claimed that during the labor unrest of 1894 the army had faced a "widespread and formidable insurrection" and that "more than once . . . an infuriated mob in a single city was twice as formidable in numbers and capable of doing vastly greater injury to life and limb than the most formidable combination of Indian warriors that ever confronted the Army in this country." In the future, Americans must prepare "not only for defense against any possible foreign aggression, but also for defense against domestic violence in the form of forcible resistance to the laws of the United States."[31]

Some military intellectuals anticipated an international terrorist conspiracy dedicated to the destruction of Western civilization. According to one officer, "Recent events in Europe and America show that dynamite assassins do not hesitate to maim and kill women and children in their criminal efforts to overthrow governments that have become obnoxious to them."[32] In 1884 Sheridan cautioned that if attacked with newly invented explosives, the nation's financial and governmental centers could "be readily demolished and the commerce of entire cities destroyed by infuriated people with means carried with perfect safety to themselves in pockets of their clothing."[33] Captain John J. O'Connell commented that the deployment of a few companies of regulars during the Great Strike of 1894 had been "very much in the nature of a bluff." Had events gone differently, Washington might have been seized by agitators, the government expelled, and the city given over to the mob. He warned, "The next attempt at revolution . . . will be much more extended, formidable, and better organiz[ed]" because "the crying evil of the hour—unrestricted immigration—is leavening our American laborers with the principles of Socialism and anarchy, imported by the lowest and most vicious types of humanity."[34]

In retrospect, what is most interesting about the army's experience with unconventional warfare in the South, on the western frontier, and in northern cities is that it prompted almost no warfighting scenarios applicable to the nation's next great conflict—expeditionary warfare overseas. The service's resistance to the very idea of military operations outside the North American continent was long standing and based on both moral sentiment and a practical assessment of the nation's relative military strength. Many would have agreed with Hitchcock that "I might draw a line between my duty to remain in the army to repulse any attempt made from abroad upon us, and the questionable duty of going beyond our borders to inflict a direct wrong upon another people, with probable injury to us in the end."[35] After outlining his views on the best strategy in the event of war, Captain Joseph H. Dorst declared, "We do not need Mexico, do not want it and are better off without it. The country is not desirable and the absorption of its population will introduce a disturbing element into our political system that may threaten its stability."[36]

In an 1894 article entitled "Which Are More Needed for our Future Protection, More War-Ships or Better Coast Defenses?" George W. Van Deusen, a coast artilleryman, emphatically endorsed the latter on the grounds that it was "contrary to all the principles of our government to engage in foreign wars."[37] A year later, in an article entitled "If Attacked, Could the United States Carry on an Offensive War?" another officer, William R. Hamilton, doubted whether the nation could successfully mount an invasion of a lesser power such as Chile in less than a year.[38] Even discussions of occupying Hawaii or building a canal across the isthmus between North and South America were largely couched in traditional defensive rhetoric, though with the acknowledgment that it would "wrest from England a part of her carrying trade upon the ocean."[39] No discernible imperialist faction among army intellectuals urged configuration of the service for foreign conquest. As late as 1897, Schofield declared that "in special cases military forces may be needed to act in support of naval operations, or to hold for a time important points in a foreign country, but such service must be only auxiliary, not a primary object."[40] This isolationism contrasts sharply with doomsday predictions officers routinely made about enemy expeditions landing on American shores.

The outbreak of the Spanish-American War in 1898 was in some ways a major turning point, and in others a continuation of the army's way of unconventional warfare. The ensuing fifteen years of military operations encompassed not only distinct campaigns in Cuba and Puerto Rico (1898), the Philippine Islands (1898–1902), and China (1900) but also a decade of pacification campaigns in the Philippines (1902–1913), the Cuban Occupation (1906–1909), and various incursions into Mexico (1914–1917). As on the western frontier, soldiers faced a variety of opponents on even more varied terrain and were charged with a multiplicity of missions, ranging from the defeat of enemy armies to the creation of a colonial government. As on the frontier, military victory on the battlefield did not end armed conflict. This was especially true in the Philippines, where once the conventional war ended in late 1899, there was no centralized resistance, either political or ideological. As on the frontier, army officers relearned the Heroic martial tradition of initiative, morale, and adaptation of one's tactics to the environment and the enemy. And, as on the frontier, the army and successive presidential administrations steadfastly refused to dignify these conflicts as "war"— the Philippines were an "insurrection," the Chinese incursion a "rebellion," while Cuba had required "pacification."

Many veterans of Philippine campaigns shared the intellectual presuppositions of frontier Heroes. They too believed that the enemy must be totally defeated before negotiations were possible, but that military measures alone would not achieve the nation's goal of peacefully occupying the country and improving the lives and morality of the Filipinos. In the words of one officer, "The question of our policy is mainly a civil one. If we give the natives peace and prosperity, they will be content; and opposition will cease."[41] At the same time, officers viewed those who continued to resist occupation as illegal and illegitimate. According to Philippine commander Major General Arthur MacArthur, "The men who propose to lead small bodies for the purpose of guerrilla warfare must act without even the shadow of authority from a de facto government, and their operations from this time on will be the result of individual whims. In other words, men who try to continue the strife by individual action become simply leaders of banditti."[42] One officer fulminated, apparently without irony, that "if these people will only organize their forces into an army and get together in some number, and generally speaking, use modern, civilized methods of warfare, our task would be a simple one and comparatively easy."[43] Showing similar frustration another commented, "If our enemy possessed courage we would be compelled to use different tactics but if they had been courageous we should have killed or captured all of them before this."[44]

The imperial war experience further reinforced the Heroes' views on the importance of individual character. Officers frequently exhibited physical toughness, leadership, and indifference to danger, even at the sacrifice of military efficiency. General Charles King headed his brigade in the battle at Manila wearing his full dress uniform, riding a horse, and smoking a cigar—and soon lost control of his troops, who continued to advance miles past their objective. Captain Joseph B. Batchelor led a handful of soldiers across 200 miles of mountain jungle on an epic and purposeless march that almost destroyed his command and left him an invalid. A surprising number of senior colonels and generals, including some sexagenarian veterans of the Civil War, were killed or incapacitated while leading from the front. Journalist Frederick Palmer later contrasted the admiration soldiers expressed for their officers' public displays of bravery in the Philippines with the World War I doughboy's view that such conduct was both foolish and dangerous to others.[45]

Imperial warfare, like frontier warfare, was conducted in an atmosphere of confusion, violence, and moral ambiguity. Addressing a subordinate about his repeated use of the phrase "secured under pressure" and specifically about an incident in which a patrol may have tortured a guerrilla, Brigadier General J. Franklin Bell tried to explain the short- and long-term consequences of such actions. On one level, the patrol had been an outstanding success, the prisoner had shown them thirteen rifles, perhaps a tenth of the guerrilla armament in the province, and Bell believed "the end justified the means." But Bell also reminded his subordinate of the strict orders regulating troop conduct. However unrealistic their guidance was for the day-to-day business of counterinsurgency, such rules reflected the "temper of the American people."[46] Should the nation's citizens come to believe that the army was warring against the very people it was liberating, they would withdraw their support. The army would fail, even if it had won on the battlefield.

As Bell recognized, Heroic qualities such as adaptability, intelligence, leadership, and character were crucial in unconventional warfare. One observer commented that counterinsurgency operations in the boondocks did "a great deal to develop in all officers that most important quality, self-reliance, for with the defective communications, junior officers and their companies were often isolated for months from their headquarters and had to steer their own way as best they could. In the majority of cases they rose to the occasion, and the greatest credit is due to them for the manner in which they adapted themselves to circumstances."[47] Henry T. Allen put it even more simply: "It is a fact that the disposition of nearly every town in the archipelago depends upon the officer or officers who have been commanding in that town."[48] Thus, like their frontier predecessors, imperial veterans tended to take a broader view of war that went beyond the battlefield and included the restoration of law, order, and peace in the countryside.

Robert Lee Bullard was the closest thing to an imperial military theorist the army produced. His central thesis was this: officers must recognize that their professional duties extended far beyond the conduct of war. Imperial service had reconfirmed the experience of the frontier and Reconstruction, demonstrating that "if army officers and the army have had to know something of the art of war, they have had to know and use far more the art of pacification. In the Philippines the work was four-fifths peace and one-fifth war making."[49]

Although he shared the racist views of many of his contemporaries, Bullard believed an officer's "sense of superiority" conveyed "obligations and considerations toward those he regards as his inferiors." Those engaged in pacification must act in a way consonant with their national ideals, for neither the public nor political leaders would tolerate a military tyranny in America's colonies. Officers should appreciate how much "more bitter, perhaps, than defeat in war" occupation and pacification were to its subjects. It was inevitable they would resist, if only passively. Social relationships were crucial: when "the pacifier" dealt with the citizenry he must remain patient, empathetic, and calm, and he should learn the inhabitants' language and culture. He should avoid actions taken suddenly or in anger and refrain from any gratuitous interference in local customs or religious practices. But most important, he must remember, "Pacification is dual in its nature, composed of force and persuasion, severity and moderation." Being too lenient was as great a mistake as being too harsh. Should the occupied population offer violent resistance, officers must be willing to resort to a variety of "forceful measures," which might include "punitive expeditions, provost courts, military com-

missions, courts martial and reconcentration" (forcible resettle-
ment).[50] Bullard astutely noted that one of the consequences of
imperial rule was to break down regional and tribal loyalties and
create a national identity.

Though equally in the Heroic tradition, Major Augustus P.
Blocksom drew a very different lesson—that too many officers
lacked a "practical knowledge of the sterner features and necessities of war." Under a too-benevolent army rule, guerrillas could
live among the population, sneaking out to ambush and kill and
then returning to resume the guise of peaceful and friendly "ami-
gos." Only by employing the *Instructions'* full sanctions, which
Blocksom interpreted as torture and summary execution, was the
war won.

Blocksom defended the army against its critics, including the
"vicious hostility" of the press. The army was merely the instrument of its nation. "If inspired by military training with desire to
make war sharp and brief, they do not always conduct it in accord with the strictly moral point of the civil critic, the fault lies
either in the heart of the people from whom they spring or in the
war itself." He concluded with a self-justifying, simplistic, ethi-
cally suspect, and factually incorrect argument that has since been
echoed by many other military thinkers. "When war comes officers . . . will exert their power to keep its evils at the minimum.
But public sentiment will be morally responsible for its beginning, and should without cavil let the army and navy fight it to
the end, remembering that the larger the well-trained, properly
equipped fighting force sent early . . . the shorter will be the war
and the less liability to methods like those described . . . And
when things go wrong, the . . . blame for cruelty, privation, and
delay should be placed where it belongs—on war itself."[51]

Bullard and Blocksom were unique; most veterans of the imperial conflicts devoted little attention to retrospective analysis. Nor
did the army make much effort to incorporate the lessons of

its Philippine experience into training or professional education. The 1905 *Field Service Regulations* briefly covered guerrillas' legal status. The 1911 *Infantry Drill Regulations* discussed "minor warfare" only in terms of guerrillas on the battlefield.[52] At Fort Leavenworth and the newly founded Army War College, students studied European-based military science and large-unit conflicts such as the Civil War, the German wars of unification, and the Russo-Japanese War. But it is virtually impossible to find any mention in the curriculum of the lessons learned in the Philippines on counterinsurgency, peacekeeping, or occupation.

Instead of providing instruction for future counterinsurgency campaigns, many feared these imperial wars had taught all the wrong lessons. Living in isolated posts and fighting a distinctly local insurgency, officers had developed initiative and small-unit leadership. But they had also grown accustomed to an independence and individuality inimical to the discipline and doctrinal adherence required by large-unit operations. Modern warfare advocates worried that fighting untrained and poorly armed opponents had "played havoc" with these young officers' tactical judgment and "inculcated erroneous and regrettable ideas," including "impetuosity" and a "disdain" for the killing power of modern firearms.[53]

The imperial wars raised a larger question: was the army's sole purpose to prepare for, fight, and win the nation's wars, or was it also expected to secure the results of war? Bullard clearly favored the broader mission. "Our whole recent experience, then, our present duties and future prospects all point to the idea that by the study of war alone we shall be but little prepared for by far the greater burdens which are to fall upon us, which are the making of peace."[54] Major General Leonard Wood agreed. Writing to a colleague in the Philippines, he commented, "I don't think we have any moral right to go into a country, discipline a lot of savage people, a process which is generally accompanied by a great loss of life, and then put indifferent people in charge of them and permit conditions to rise which render the repetition of the process necessary. It is wrong."[55]

But prolonged foreign deployments, the public criticism of troop conduct in the Philippines, and particularly the increased likelihood of foreign attack on either the overseas possessions or the mainland United States had combined to dampen military enthusiasm for sustained peacekeeping. Responding to Wood's letter, his colleague noted that "the Army in its indifference to what is going on around it in the Philippines; in the way our officers isolate themselves on their reservations without keeping in touch with political or other conditions here; in their general don't-care attitude; and in their tendency to use the Philippine Islands as a place to wear out old clothes and save money, is a good deal of a joke to serious-minded people."[56] In 1915 the General Staff rejected the suggestion that American troops in the Philippines should receive special training for missions against "native uprisings and insurrections." The time allocated to this would interfere with the primary mission of defending the islands from foreign attack. Moreover, "the care of the natives" was best left to Filipino military and police forces.[57]

Such sentiments may explain most officers' lack of interest in irregular warfare. For a variety of reasons, many of them unsound, they agreed that if the army trained itself for modern warfare, it would be prepared to defeat any semicivilized foe. And indeed, although inevitably outnumbered and fighting on its opponents' terrain, the army subdued guerrillas, bandits, and sectarians with only slight adjustments to their weapons, tactics, and organization. No military intellectual believed the converse, that officers adept at small-unit tactics and reconstruction could easily adapt to the complexities of large-unit industrialized warfare. As Wood, himself a vigorous practitioner of imperial chastisement and social reform, put it, the "lessons" taught in such conflicts were "of little value and usually result in false deductions and a confidence which spells disaster when called upon to play the real game."[58]

What the army retained from its imperial wars were guidelines, small-unit tactical adaptations, and practical, if brutal, methods. These never coalesced into a formal doctrine based on a theoretical understanding of unconventional war. Where possible, American forces practiced conciliation, attempting to relieve, at least temporarily, the most obvious causes of public discontent. In what might be regarded as a textbook campaign, in 1906 the Army of Cuban Pacification flooded potential trouble spots with soldiers and overawed potential guerrillas while implementing an extensive program of road building, school construction, sanitation and medical projects, and legal reforms.[59]

When the Mexican Revolution broke out in 1910, the army again relied on tried and true but unwritten methods. Thus, in 1911 two officers returned from a secret mission to recommend that "the General Staff should at once begin a most careful, detailed study of the future occupation of Mexican territory, to include not only the military campaign whose objective must be the Mexican capital, but the subsequent military government of this vast country, whether such occupation be merely temporary as in the case of Cuba, or more or less permanent as in case of the Philippines."[60]

In 1914 a joint army-navy-marine force was sent into Vera Cruz. The military government sought to defuse resistance through a heavy troop presence and large-scale public works projects. But a survey of officers' experiences in street-fighting once again confirmed not only a host of ad hoc measures but also the old lesson that when it came to combating unconventional warfare, "no definite and rigid system is possible."[61] In similar fashion, Captain Frank McCoy's patrols along the Rio Grande taught him practical truths that any frontier or Philippine veteran would have known: the superiority of small and mobile forces; the importance of gathering intelligence; the necessity of understanding local customs and social relationships; and above all the need "to deal with both Mexicans and Americans with diplomacy and tact, to make them realize that the troops are their best friends and protectors, and thus to gain not only their sympathy but their active cooperation."[62]

In the period between the two world wars, the army continued to treat unconventional warfare as distinctly inferior to conventional battlefield operations. The *Field Service Regulations* of 1923, the keystone doctrinal manual, was written to prepare for "a war against an opponent organized for war on modern principles and equipped with all the means of modern warfare. An army capable of waging war under these conditions will prove adequate to any less grave emergency with which it may be confronted."[63] The occasional article on Indian fighting or imperial campaigns was more a historical or romantic vignette than an effort to impart tactical wisdom. At Fort Leavenworth and the Infantry School, instructors lectured briefly on counter-guerrilla tactics, expeditionary warfare, and civil affairs. But their subject was World War I or the postwar colonial struggles, particularly the French operations in Morocco, and almost never the American experience. In 1922, when the army added a short training section on "minor warfare" to the *Field Service Regulations,* it simply plagiarized British doctrine. Similarly, in 1937 a Cavalry School instructor proposed a section on "guerrilla warfare" based on German operations in Belgium and France.[64] Throughout the interwar era, practical instruction in unconventional war was limited to field problems such as avoiding ambush, using local auxiliaries, and gathering intelligence.

Army planning for counter-insurgency campaigns continued to rely on earlier tenets. War Plan Brown dealt with potential uprisings in the Philippines, ranging from minor violence to full-scale insurrection. The troops assigned to implement Brown were to be trained in "guerrilla warfare" and in "attack, defense, mopping up, and control of towns."[65] But no such training was ever implemented. The Mexican military was considered so weak that in 1922 the army's War Plans Division urged that War Plan Green be retitled Special Plan Green because "it is really not a war plan but a plan of occupation . . . for occupying a country incapable of serious military resistance."[66] After expeditionary columns seized and occupied most of the country, the army would establish a government, reform the education and legal systems, employ honest police and civil servants, and make it clear to the Mexican populace that the "intention of the United States is to bring about peace and good order."[67]

In 1924 the War Plans Division staged a war game for Green. The staff concluded that the Mexicans would launch guerrilla attacks on isolated units, raid the border, and cut the expeditionary columns' vulnerable logistical lines. Despite claims by aviators on the staff that air power could protect communications and shatter enemy resistance, the division's director believed that the occupation would turn into a long, slow, and frustrating unconventional war. Reflecting these concerns, the revised 1927 Green Plan called for a single rapidly moving column to depose the government and then immediately withdraw. The director made it clear that the plan "does not envisage a military occupation of Mexico, nor of operations against the Mexican nation as distinguished from the Mexican government."[68] For at least one veteran of both earlier Mexican and Philippine interventions, the whole concept was flawed. "We ought to realize that punitive expeditions, or expeditions to dispossess the government in power are worse than useless and are not to be undertaken."[69]

Unconventional warfare has often been the army's task but seldom its calling. This is not to say that soldiers were ineffective in the pacification of the frontier—whether in the American West

or the Far East. Nor is it to say that over the years military intellectuals have ignored the problem of defeating irregular opponents and restoring peace. The army's operational reports and
journals provide a legacy of practical advice on everything from
packing mules, to training native soldiers, to dismantling a guerrilla network in an occupied village. They even yield rules, or
principles, for the army's practice of unconventional war. These
include seeking combat at whatever the odds (a rule that Custer
followed to his disadvantage), striking at the irregulars' supply
system, even if it means operations against noncombatants, developing intelligence networks, and preparing for a variety of civil
and military duties. Underlying all of this is a view that successful
counterinsurgency must balance coercion with conciliation.

But the vast majority of writing on unconventional conflict reflects the distinct Heroic tradition. Across the decades, veterans stressed the importance of character, intuition, experience,
courage, honor, and other intangible attributes. They have approached war in a broader, if less precise manner, as encompassing not only the destruction of the enemy but also the winning of
the peace. For those military intellectuals who followed this way
of war, the key question was how these individual qualities could
apply to the industrialized process that had defined great power
conflict since the Civil War.

4

PROVIDING FOR WAR?

The war with Spain in 1898 revealed the army's unpreparedness for modern warfare, and subsequent imperial commitments in the Caribbean and the Pacific stretched it to the breaking point. Appointed in 1899 with a mandate to reform the nation's scandalously weak land forces, Secretary of War Elihu Root declared, "The real object of having an army is to provide for war."[1] His annual reports outlined a comprehensive reorganization that included the creation of a chief of staff and a General Staff, a command and staff school, and the Army War College to educate officers in war planning. For the first time in its existence, the army had formal institutions to design a distinct body of theoretical knowledge of warfare and to apply it to the nation's strategic problems. Instead of individuals such as Mahan, or branches such as the Corps of Engineers, imposing their personal or parochial visions, the possibility now existed of a distinct and unified army way of war.

The secretary's remodeling was so sweeping, and so central to the army's self-identity as a "warfighting" organization, that a century later reformers would invoke Root's legacy as justification for the service's transformation program for the post–Cold War world.[2] Yet, although the Root era may have been a radical break with the past in terms of military administration, in the realm of military thought it represented evolution, not revolution. The army's three traditional ways of war continued to shape the service's interpretation of the lessons of the past, its assessment of the present, and its predictions for the future. Influenced by the contemporary Progressive Movement, they found new rationales for old prejudices. Post-Root Guardians, Heroes, and Managers adopted new weaponry, new opponents, and new military methods into scenarios remarkably similar to their nineteenth-century predecessors. Like their forebears, they bemoaned their fate, to "face a discouraging situation, working for the best interests of the country . . . but believing that only a national calamity would awaken the people to the necessity of proper defense."[3] Perhaps even more pessimistic than their predecessors, the beneficiaries of Root's military transformation were convinced that this calamity would soon occur.

Moreover, Root's injunction to provide an army for war came at a substantial cost. Both the service and the nation sacrificed much that had served them well for a century, not least a small and inexpensive military establishment. The regular army increased from less than 27,000 before the war with Spain to 75,000 in 1903, and to 105,000 in 1915. Appropriations quadrupled from their pre-1898 level. Whether the service's efficiency increased proportionately to the financial and human resources lavished on it is less clear. Such factors as recruitment and retention, officer resignations and absenteeism, courts martial, desertion, and troop health might lead one to argue—as many officers did—that in its first decade of existence the post-Root army was *less* prepared for war than the pre-1898 army.

By some standards, the likelihood of war actually rose after 1898. Although the imperial conquests of 1898–1902 increased the nation's prestige, they burdened it with overseas territories far from the mainland, which could be reinforced only with great difficulty and, in some cases, were well within the range of powerful enemies. Presidents, no longer constrained by minuscule defense establishments, dispatched troops and warships to enforce their particular economic or moral agendas. And despite the creation of planning staffs, the improvements in military education, and the supposed professionalization of the officer corps, in 1917 the army was no better able to predict the next great conflict than it had been in 1898, or to envision how it would be fought. Instead, contemporaries often contrasted the nation's supposedly secure past with the dangerous present, seeming to forget their predecessors' dire predictions even as they repeated them.

In his 1910 annual report, Chief of Staff J. Franklin Bell claimed that "with modern ocean transportation facilities . . . it would be easier to conduct a campaign from Europe against New York than it was for General Grant in 1864 to conduct his campaign through Northern Virginia."[4] As Bell's warning makes clear, despite the Root era's alleged transformative role, some military intellectuals continued the Guardian tradition, repeating the familiar litany that "the safeguard of isolation no longer exists."[5] Advances in technology, the volatile international situation, and the nation's weakness all invited imminent attack. In 1898 the specter of Spanish squadrons raiding Atlantic cities once more incited public hysteria and released a flood of spending on continental defense. Within two years, half of the Endicott fortifications were completed. But a 1905 fortification board headed by Secretary of War William H. Taft grimly concluded that not only were the Endicott guns outranged by modern warships, but the nation's increasing wealth and global involvements made a maritime attack even more likely. In response, the Taft Board reconfirmed the essential strategic principles of the Totten-Endicott system, albeit with bigger guns and better mechanisms for accurate firing, and extended it to the newly acquired territories.[6]

Despite the nation's latest effort to protect its borders, many military intellectuals claimed the threat to them grew every year. In 1908 General Thomas Anderson warned of "a world in arms" in which Britain, Germany, and Japan might land over a million troops on American shores before the army could mobilize for defense.[7] That same year, Lieutenant Hugh Johnson outlined two possible future wars. In the first, "a superb army of 200,000 seasoned Germans" captured New York, while in the second Japan conquered the West Coast.[8] Bell's 1909 report predicted that without a considerable military buildup, "portions of this country may be overrun by the enemy, important places captured, and contributions levied upon our great cities, sufficient to defray the expenses of the war."[9]

The expenditure of $144 million on harbor defenses did not allay the military's fears. Far from applauding the program, some now argued it was almost irrelevant because no modern fleet would attack a fortified port. One officer informed readers it would require 270,000 coastal defenders to repulse an invasion and an additional one million soldiers for the mobile army. Even worse, the fortifications' very existence lulled the public into a false sense of security. The same year he announced the completion of the Endicott system, the chief of engineers requested funding to build entrenchments and provide artillery for their landward defense. Perversely, the more Americans spent on defense, and the more the army made preparation for war its primary mission, the graver the threats and the weaker the nation appeared.[10]

Guardian strategists not only maintained a drumbeat of alarm to justify ever-greater expenditures but also showed remarkable flexibility in reconciling the acquisition of an overseas empire with their traditional deterrent philosophy. With relatively little opposition, Guardian doctrine was adapted to include preemptive expeditionary intervention in the Caribbean to forestall a European attack. Surveying the new empire, officers made an alarming discovery: fortifications were either obsolete or nonexistent. Until the ports were protected, an enemy fleet might easily steam in, land an expeditionary force, seize the capital, and assert its legal right to rule the entire territory. Since the United States had done precisely this to Spain at Manila Bay in 1898, this scenario resonated among military planners.

To their frustration, the American public would not support an army sufficiently large to ensure the protection of overseas territories. Officers considered the empire's indigenous populations far too untrustworthy to play a role in their own defense. Nor was the army willing to sacrifice its institutional commitment to modern warfare for the unpopular task of imperial policing. As it had done when it faced a similar problem in the nineteenth century, the army turned to the greatest "force multiplier" of the era: the heavily armed strategic harbor.

The investment in building fortified keeps at Pearl Harbor, Manila Bay, and the two entrances to the Panama Canal was enormous, but the army hoped to reap two long-term benefits: to defend the possessions themselves and to keep the majority of its troops within the continental United States to prepare for a putative European invasion. But by 1915, when these fortifications were almost complete, the Philippine Defense Board concluded that not only were those in Manila Bay vulnerable to land attack, but they would serve little strategic purpose in a Pacific war. This finding reflected a growing consensus among Guardian strategists that the overseas possessions, and particularly the Philippines, were valuable only to facilitate the army's traditional mission of protecting the continental United States.[11]

Decades earlier, military intellectuals had defined modern warfare as the adaptation of industry and technology for military purposes, the rapid mobilization of enormous armies, rapid military operations, a few titanic battles, and complete victory or defeat. They only disagreed on the details. Their Root-era successors adopted their predecessors' definition and their fears of invasion, but they disagreed vehemently about what the future would bring and how best to provide for it. Many military writers believed that the pace of change, particularly in weaponry, had altered the conduct if not the very nature of war. Some postulated military technology would lead to shorter, less bloody wars and help the West spread civilization to the benighted portions of the earth. Trucks could replace mules and horses, allowing armies to campaign over much greater distances, while machine guns, magazine rifles, and quick-firing artillery amplified the deadliness of the battlefield. Aviation was of special concern, prompting some to warn that the nation's cities were vulnerable to attack by airplanes and dirigibles; they thus married new technology to the century-old Guardian scenario.

Other officers were equally certain that technology was overvalued. Machine guns, one officer sniffed, had "kept up a terrible clatter on San Juan Heights" but had killed no Spaniards and were in all respects "very inferior engines of war."[12] The airplane, a 1910 editorial declared, had limited use as a scout and no role as an offensive weapon.[13] An observer of the Russo-Japanese War concluded, "What counted most were not new-fangled devices" but training, tactics, leadership, and administration.[14] In 1915 William "Billy" Mitchell denounced those who foolishly placed their "reliance wherever possible on machines or new inventions to do the work which only human blood and bone is capable of doing. This is particularly true of a non-military nation which is constantly looking out for some invention or marvelous thing which shall be so deadly and destructive as to make war impossible." The future prophet of air power cautioned against "the tendency to exaggerate the importance of materiel in modern war and to underrate the personnel."[15]

Branch interests also shaped military intellectuals' concepts of modern warfare. Members of the Coast Artillery Corps, which separated from the Field Artillery branch in 1907, argued that since they alone were expected to go instantly into action against enemy attack, they should receive first priority in resources and manpower, even if it meant neglecting the rest of the army. But their peers emphatically repudiated this claim, so much so that coast artillerymen soon complained that post-Root schools all but ignored the topic of harbor defense. A few members of the corps actually questioned its self-identification with fortifications and fixed guns, urging preparation for mobile warfare even if it required their subordination to nonspecialists on the battlefield.[16]

Similar disagreements characterized the wartime role of cavalry. To some it was obvious that "the use of cavalry . . . [on] the actual field of battle has been made impossible normally through increased effect of infantry fire."[17] But others still maintained that recent wars showed either what cavalry could accomplish (the Boer War) or what it might have accomplished (the Russo-Japanese War). Moreover, mounted service imbued an intangible warrior spirit, so that "good cavalry . . . when dismounted for attack or defense, is equal to, if not superior, to the best infantry, man for man, on account of a confidence inspired by the knowledge of its power as a mounted force."[18]

Even among themselves, cavalrymen could not reach a consensus on such basic issues as pistols or sabers, much less on the nature of the next war. The 1906 Cavalry Board declared, "The charge is the decisive and most important and characteristic cavalry movement," and predicted the next war would be characterized by "great cavalry combats, taking place far in advance of the main body" that "must be decided largely by shock action."[19] That same year, Major James Parker claimed that the future of mounted warfare lay with "initiative, speed, surprise, the power of the horse, the magnetism of the assault and the terror of cold steel."[20] But by 1912 Parker, although now a member of a new

Cavalry Board, reversed himself. New weapons made mounted combat almost impossible; the future belonged to those who rode to battle but fought as infantry.[21]

In addition to their branch disagreements, officers differed on one of the Root era's most desired, and most unsuccessful, reforms: the creation of a mobile army. This organization would fuse the regular infantry, cavalry, and field artillery into large-scale formations (brigades and divisions) that could train, and, if necessary, fight the armies of another great power. As envisioned by one chief of staff in 1909, it would be "a first line of offense or defense, behind which the [wartime citizen-soldier] army can be organized, properly trained, and molded into an efficient force."[22] Like the navy's new steel battleship fleet, the mobile army's mission was to seek out and destroy enemy field forces, but only within the continental United States or possibly as part of an expeditionary force sent beyond the borders to defend the Monroe Doctrine. However, as so often happens with military reform, the mobile army's strategic mission was soon mired in arguments about organization, manpower, and force structure. Virtually all proposals for its force structure were far too ambitious for the American public to support; even senior military officers viewed them with skepticism. When the United States went to war in 1917 the mobile army was such a dead letter that the regular army could barely dispatch a single infantry division to France.

Those who wanted to prepare the army for modern warfare were not only divided by branch interests but by their adherence to the army's three martial traditions. Managers perceived war as essentially an industrial process directed by a trained corporate elite. Heroes interpreted it as an extension of individual combat, and therefore determined as much by skill and mental preparation as by mass and organization. This tension contributed a curious, almost schizophrenic quality to military theory and practice. At the same time that military intellectuals contemplated the effect of rapid-fire artillery and machine guns, they also urged the retention of the saber and bayonet. They worked out schemes to raise armies in the millions while at the same time insisting that the regulars' rigid peacetime discipline must apply to wartime cit-izen-soldiers. They trained officers as scientific practitioners of "safe leadership" while simultaneously stressing the commander's intangible, God-given qualities of character and determination.[23] Unable to resolve these paradoxes, which only multiplied over time, the army eventually applied a dysfunctional doctrine in the trenches of France—on the one hand centralizing control through huge staffs and meticulously planned battles, while on the other extolling "open warfare" predicated on the individual soldier armed with a rifle and bayonet.

These contradictions permeated the extended debate over the nature and future of war, often flavored by a Social Darwinist in-sistence that human progress and war were interconnected. One military intellectual deduced from recent conflicts that "the im-proved weapons and implements of war have given the nations of the earth the power to preserve order throughout their extensive domains, to curb and restrain unruly elements, to force respect everywhere for law, and to strike swift and telling blows against lawlessness, crime, and rebellion."[24] War's civilizing influence, and the nation's security, demanded military preparedness and constant vigilance. Peace was always at the mercy of the "brigand nation" whose people, "trained and equipped for plunder, find no law to deny the indescribable exhilaration of that, to them, the greatest of all human sports—appropriating quickly by force what others have accumulated patiently through years."[25]

Oddly mixing with this Social Darwinism was a nostalgic ro-manticism. Officers regretted the pernicious influence of indus-trialism and corporate organization on the martial spirit. "War has become a business, like any other business, where sentiment has little value. It has but one watchword—efficiency. Glory is no more the soldier's dream, but only success . . . The hero who in scarlet and bearskin strode so picturesquely across the field of battle and drove the enemy at the bayonet's point, now lies on his belly in the dirt and shoots at an unseen enemy a mile away."[26]

The prevalence of Social Darwinist thought may explain the profound pessimism that any review of their nation's martial past imbued in Root-era military intellectuals. They interpreted the Spanish-American War as vindicating army warnings about the dangers of unpreparedness. Had the opponent been anyone other than Spain, the result would have been a disaster. Officers criticized the "yellow press," politicians, the militia, and a belligerent and unreasoning public for rushing the nation into war. A General Staff report concluded that at the outbreak of the war the United States' lacked a strategic plan, an efficient organization, modern weapons, trained soldiers, and virtually every other military necessity.[27]

The army's interpretation of the Spanish-American War was notable for what it omitted. In 1898 the inefficiency of the War Department and the bungling of regular officers had greatly contributed to the war's confusion and its casualties. Time and again, the army's senior leadership failed to anticipate or execute President William McKinley's decisions. The staff and technical bureaus—bastions of regular army elitism—proved astonishingly unprepared: the ordnance department could not even place a sufficient number of modern weapons in the hands of the troops. In the hastily organized mobilization camps, thousands of volunteers sickened and died, most because of indiscipline and poor sanitation but many because of the regular army's inefficiency. In Cuba, commanders demonstrated great physical bravery but scant tactical ability, leading one officer to complain, "We are now and have been handled by incompetent men and I sincerely hope that they be made [to] suffer some day."[28] Thirty years later, a veteran bemoaned the "useless slaughter of our men at San Juan through the worst possible mismanagement" and complained, "The blunderers were promoted with indecent haste, while most of the Army thought they would be court martialed."[29]

Beyond their own brief conflict with Spain, military intellectuals looked to the Russo-Japanese War of 1904–1905 for inspiration. This was the first major post-Root reform conflict and the first to be systematically studied by the newly created General Staff, which assigned observers to report on the combatants' weaponry, tactics, and equipment. On a variety of levels—by destroying the Russian Pacific and home fleets, by transporting and sustaining large armies in hostile territory, by demonstrating their ability at maneuver and siege craft, and by the prowess of their senior commanders—the Japanese made the Cuban campaign look amateurish. Observers were impressed by the Japanese soldiers' martial spirit. They were, one concluded, "the finest fighting machines made."[30]

The war dramatically changed the strategic balance in the Far East, making Japan the dominant military and naval power. The concurrent completion of much of the Endicott coastal defense program had convinced many that no fleet would risk a direct attack on a fortified harbor, thus resolving the tactical problem that had so engrossed American military thinkers since the War of 1812. But Japan's capture of Port Arthur by a landward siege showed some American coast artillerymen that "without the co-operation of mobile forces our seacoast defenses cannot endure."[31]

The Russo-Japanese War had the clearest application in the Pacific. By 1907 the General Staff had concluded that Japan could transport sufficient expeditionary forces to besiege and capture Pearl Harbor and Manila before a relief force could arrive. In 1912 a lecturer at the Army War College drew a direct analogy between Pacific defense and recent historical experience when he argued that "distant overseas possessions can be defended effectively only on the high seas; sea power, and not local armies, will determine the ultimate fate of such possessions. The United States [is] in much the same situation as Spain in 1898, being involved in the defense of a dependency, fairly well-garrisoned, but distant, against attack by a nearby strong power."[32]

The Russo-Japanese War also confirmed modern warfare dogmas. It began suddenly and ended decisively; it had been decided by titanic battles; and a smaller nation with better military organization, leadership, and training had overcome one much larger but unprepared. But the Russo-Japanese conflict highlighted the differences within the army between Guardians, Managers, and Heroes. For Guardians, the war demonstrated that although the tactics of coastal defense had changed, the nation's traditional deterrent strategy was even wiser than had been recognized. The overseas territories should be regarded not as springboards for further empire but as outlying bastions for the defense of the continental United States. The Managers drew the lesson that the weaknesses of Russian society, its corrupt administration, and its inability to mobilize its industrial or human resources played as large a role in Russia's defeat as the failings of its commanders and troops. In contrast, Japan had not only trained a mass conscript army and a professional officer corps but had infused a martial spirit in its population, creating enormous war industries and mobilizing the entire nation. Downplaying the importance of firepower, staff work, and entrenchments, Heroes credited Japan's success to its offensive tactics, its soldiers' high morale, and their willingness to close with the enemy and use the bayonet.[33]

The differing interpretations were symptomatic of a growing division between Managers and Heroes. Drawing their inspiration from the "managerial revolution" in American business, the Managers sought to apply the "principles of large-scale corporate organization and expertise . . . to the rapidly expanding armed forces of the industrialized powers."[34] The commander needed to be a competent executive, able to delegate and coordinate, and to ensure his "team" worked toward a common end. The individual recruit was comparable to a worker in a factory, whose "duties though varied are simple and can be measured and defined in works and his proficiency in them can be classified. Therefore every duty of the individual soldier must be surveyed, defined and standardized for the entire army and he himself must be classified in his skill and proficiency."[35]

Heroes were not hostile to technology or organizational reforms, and often supported Managerial programs. But they believed that "in estimating military efficiency more weight should be given to personal characteristics and demonstrated ascendancy over the minds and wills of men and less weight should be attached to mere professional knowledge and the ability to pass good examinations."[36] Yet they disagreed with one another on whether soldiers' martial virtues were encouraged through unquestioning obedience or through decentralized command, internal discipline, and self-motivation.

The development of doctrine—defined as "the core statement of the army's view of war" and "a common guide for the conduct of operations"—provided further evidence of Manager-Hero differences.[37] For Managers seeking to impose rational order over large-scale combat operations, doctrine was an essential tool. But in practice, doctrine reflected the values of Heroes. The first combined-arms manual, the 1905 *Field Service Regulations,* concluded that the offensive's key advantage lay with soldiers' "moral superiority. When the die is cast and the attack is on, they no longer meditate upon the consequences; they look forward, nor backward."[38] The 1911 *Infantry Drill Regulations* reiterated, "Modern combat demands the highest order of training, discipline, leadership, and morale on the part of the infantry. Complicated maneuvers are impracticable; efficient leadership and a determination to win by simple and direct measures must be depended

upon for success."[39] They downplayed the importance of entrenchments, logistics, and firepower; field artillery was of minor importance and machine guns no more than "weapons of
emergency."[40] In contrast, the *Regulations* promised, "an attack is
bound to succeed if fire superiority is gained and properly used"
and "confidence in their ability to use the bayonet gives the as-
saulting troops the promise of success."[41]

The 1914 *Cavalry Service Regulations* placed even more emphasis on Heroic values. The "general principles" for the employment of cavalry in combat began with the assertion, "Mounted
action is the principal method of Fighting of Cavalry. Animated
by an aggressive spirit, it will seize every opportunity to attack
with the horse and the saber." Fusing character with tactics, the
manual declared that "a bold leader" always sought "opportunities for mounted attack, which will produce more rapid and decisive results than can be gained by the most skillful use of the
rifle."[42] Cavalrymen should "cultivate the habit of prompt decision" and "lean always toward the aggressive" since "undue caution . . . forfeits the advantages of surprise, which is an influential
factor in the success of a charge, since the moral element is combined with the effects of the weapons."[43]

The army's emphasis on offensive doctrine clashed with its pessimistic appraisal of the nation's preparation for war and its citizens' martial spirit. Mitchell began his 1915 General Staff study
of "our nation's faulty military policy" with an almost obligatory
condemnation of the American people, who foolishly clung to
the belief that the navy and the oceans removed any need to prepare for war. Calculating military forces and merchant tonnage,
Mitchell estimated that Great Britain might land up to 200,000
troops in two weeks; Germany 750,000 in three months; and
even Austria-Hungary could send 150,000. The United States'
defenses against such numbers were pathetic. Mitchell dismissed
the navy as "entirely incapable of taking up the offensive in Euro-

pean waters." At best it could serve as "a delaying force" for a few months at the cost of its complete destruction. Within the continental United States there were but 35,000 regulars and 116,000 national guardsmen, none of them sufficiently organized, equipped, or prepared. The result was inevitable: destruction of the nation's cities, military defeat, and a humiliating peace.[44]

Similar fears of imminent threat and deep gloom about national preparedness permeate the plans drawn up by the first peacetime strategic planning agency, the Army War College. Accepting the premises inherited from military strategists since the nation's founding, the planners identified Great Britain's navy as the most dangerous threat. The college's 1904 scenarios for an Anglo-American war ("Red-Blue" in military parlance) anticipated British naval attacks on the Atlantic coast and an incursion from Canada.[45] Its 1909–1910 problem envisioned a British expeditionary force of 166,000 men occupying most of New England, linking up with forces from Canada, and then striking for New York City. Although the student planners estimated it would take more than six months for the United States to mobilize even a fraction of the required forces, they nevertheless urged an immediate offensive into Canada. They acknowledged, "The clamor of public opinion may demand the diverting of our main army eastward to assist in the defense of Boston" but insisted that "the surest way to protect that city . . . is to vigorously attack Montreal."[46]

A similar mix of frustration, doubt, and fantasy characterized army war planning against Japan, or "Orange." A 1906–1907 diplomatic crisis, more accurately described as a war scare, led to a dramatic shift in army strategic thought. Japan's propensity to attack prior to a declaration of war, its ability to transport tens of thousands of troops overseas, and the effectiveness of its armed forces in both mobile and siege warfare—all these demonstrated the vulnerability of isolated garrisons in Hawaii and the Philippines unless the American battle fleet could rapidly relieve them. But the navy, following its own sea control doctrine, insisted its battle fleet must be free to hunt down and destroy Japan's. It re- fused to commit itself to the defense of the Pacific territories. Moreover, until the Panama Canal was complete, it would take at least six months for warships to steam from their Atlantic ports to the West Coast and then on to the Philippines. Only if the coastal fortifications in Manila Bay and Pearl Harbor held out for this long would the fleet arrive to find a safe anchorage.

When the army tested these distressing scenarios, it discovered they were actually optimistic. Maneuvers in both Hawaii and the Philippines revealed that even if the forts withstood a siege, the harbors could be shelled by land-based artillery, making them in- accessible to the American fleet. Reflecting these grim realities, in 1908 students played out a hypothetical war in which the Pacific possessions fell in less than a month. The next year's problem added a Japanese expedition that landed near Seattle and ravaged the Columbia River basin. This scenario, repeated in 1910 with even more disastrous consequences to the West Coast, demon- strated once again that in the Pacific "the role of the United States is defensive, and will be so for a long time."[47]

War planning against Japan reinforced the army's ambivalence about the navy's role in national defense. In 1910 Chief of Staff Leonard Wood told a journalist, "A navy is primarily a factor of offense, rather than defense. The Navy can be used advanta- geously only when operating on the offensive and to chain it, as a police force, to the approaches of the Canal would be to deprive the nation of the most valuable service it could render in time of need. The Navy should be at all times free to operate against the enemy wherever he may be."[48] In many respects this navalism was simply a revision of traditional Guardian arguments. Some of the most vocal supporters of this strategy, members of the Coast Ar- tillery Corps, recognized that with the fleet far from the nation's coasts there would be an even stronger need for harbor fortifications. A 1912 General Staff report qualified its support of naval independence with the caveat that "a fleet unsupported by an army is unable to secure the fruits of naval victory; a fleet defeated at sea is powerless to prevent invasion."[49] A later study described the army-navy "co-ordinate relationship" as a formula for giving each service essentially separate roles.[50] As before and later, army support for navy expansion was contingent on there being an equally large increase in land forces.

A World War I general recalled that the prewar "plans were not worth much, for they did not accept conditions as they actually existed in the U.S. at the time . . . they envisioned the use of troops that did not exist and could not be expected except after long delay."[51] Taken as a whole, plans focused on large-scale conventional operations—battles and campaigns—and neglected economic, political, and social factors. Not until 1915 would the War Department put together a committee to study industrial mobilization. Far too often, military intellectuals simply totaled up respective military forces and drew up a plan that would allow the regular army the opportunity to win the war, or at least the decisive part of the war, virtually on its own. They considered warfare only within the narrow range of their professional expertise—operational doctrine, force structure, weaponry—revealing just how narrowly they interpreted Root's mandate.

One notable failing in the war plans—and, indeed, in most post-Root military thought—was any recognition that the American people, either as militia or citizens, might contest the invasion of their nation. Instead, strategists assumed popular participation would be almost entirely negative and take the form of panic and interference in sound military policy. Should the long-expected invasion occur, "The newspapers would call for battle, the people would demand it; our 77,000 regulars would be forced to attack, and would be wiped out of existence . . . [and the] invaders would have a free hand in our coast towns."[52] The army's bleak predictions were predicated, in part, on its widely held belief that American society might prove incapable of the necessary preparation and sacrifice needed to secure victory, and thus national survival, in case of war. "Our people, although aggressive enough, are not a military people," commented General Fred C. Ainsworth, and only a "national disaster and humiliation" would ever teach them "that the effective maintenance of an army of professional soldiers is absolutely essential to the preservation of the national honor and life."[53]

Many officers embraced the concepts of modern warfare while simultaneously rejecting modernization, particularly industrialization, urbanization, and immigration. Major John H. Parker found evidence in all social classes of a "progressive deterioration of Americans in suitability for emergency material out of which to make volunteer soldiers."[54] Captain William Wallace's article, "Our National Decline," postulated that "modern business and social life, combining, as they do, to over or under indulgence in work or play, in appetite or sleep, have keyed up our nerves to a point where in battle, if they do not snap, they are likely to tingle so as to destroy the calmness and deliberation under fire that is undoubtedly the main ingredient of the white man's battle courage."[55]

Captain LeRoy Eltinge's *Psychology of War* declared, "The people and the army are so bound up together that unless the military virtues of courage, mutual confidence and self-sacrifice for the good of the state are developed among the people they will not exist in the army." As a result, "modern wars are expected to be short. A big reverse and both army and populace lose their nerve."[56] Unfortunately, America's Anglo-Saxon population had been diluted by immigration, so that "a big war will now make it necessary to combine all these unfusible [sic] elements into one another."[57] Ironically, military intellectuals whose forebears had excoriated the nineteenth-century citizen-soldier now mourned his passing. Posthumously transformed into a rugged fighter and natural marksman, he sparkled as a diamond when compared to the human lumps of coal produced by the industrialized metropolis.

The military intellectuals' bleak view of American society enhanced their conviction that the regular army should not only organize and command the nation's land forces but direct national strategy as well. To Captain Carl Reichmann, "It is self-evident that no one is so qualified and capable of imparting the intelligent, common sense discipline of the regular army as those who have been brought up in that discipline. The logical deduction is, that in the creation of volunteer regiments the important places should be filled by officers drawn from the regular army."[58] Another officer urged the creation of a "Minister of War" on the grounds that "the practical and theoretical knowledge of the professional soldier should determine the ways and means" necessary for the nation to protect itself.[59] It might even be necessary for the military to take temporary power, for "war is despotic; an army is a despotism; and a monarch who is himself a soldier and commands his own troops, has more than double chances of success."[60]

Officers also assumed that the nation's institutions, and even its citizenry, needed to be radically reformed. As one officer exhorted, a popular army, whether filled by volunteers or conscripts, "would direct the military enthusiasm of our youth into the right channels" and teach them patriotism, obedience, discipline, cleanliness, and subordination. The nation must undertake a radical shift in its values, starting with the complete re-education of its youth to "impress the truth that military obligation to the Government is at all times a higher and nobler duty than the pursuit of wealth and political honors."[61] Much of the impetus for military training camps, a reserve officers corps, and other programs associated with the post-1915 preparedness movement had at their core a desire to impose military discipline on what officers perceived as an unruly, diverse, and potentially disloyal citizenry.[62]

The last and least clearly articulated assumption was that both the politicians and the populace itself were fundamentally unworthy of their army. The American people, sniffed one officer, "were busily engaged in making money and pursuing the arts of peace and not one in a hundred thousand gave any thought whatever to the urgent needs of his country should it ever become involved in a really great war."[63] When it came to preparing for national defense, James Harbord explained, "you can never expect any initiative from Congress unless pushed by people from behind. To tell the honest American voter that he is worthless as a soldier without training does not win votes like telling him that the citizen soldier of America can win over the brutal hirelings of any other land with or without training."[64] Writing to a colleague in 1912, Wood declared, "The country is thoroughly unready. The people are filled with ignorance and a cheap conceit as to their military ability, which has been catered to and built up by fakers of the [William Jennings] Bryan type, and I am sorry to say by a number of college presidents."[65]

The regular army's critique of American society was both self-serving and shortsighted. In criticizing civilians, officers too often overlooked the service's own internal problems: the ongoing attritional warfare between the technical bureaus; branch parochialism; the incessant bickering over promotion; careerism; the high desertion rates and other signs of enlisted discontent; and the often-expressed sentiment that the army was in decline. Officers boasted of their professional ability, but there was scant evidence to support this. The army established boards to weed out the old and infirm—not an inconsiderable number in an institution where the average captain was forty—and routinely declared the vast majority of officers proficient. But in 1910 a senior general complained of the "detriment and menace to the service" posed by "officers utterly incompetent for the commands they exercise [who] have clearly demonstrated their inefficiency, yet under existing regulations . . . it has been found impossible to get rid of these officers."[66] A year later the chief of staff confessed in his annual report, "There is much deadwood in the army."[67]

Similar problems plagued other symbols of Root's reforms. In 1911 the mobile army took three months to assemble a single division on the Mexican border, and was "thoroughly disorganized and scattered" in the process.[68] The manpower reserve system showed little sign of improvement; its movement to the southwestern border was almost as chaotic as the mobilization of 1898. The General Staff, and especially Chief of Staff Wood, so alienated the War Department's bureaucracy, Congress, and President Woodrow Wilson that their authority was increasingly circumscribed after 1912. And despite the urgent warnings of military intellectuals that war was imminent, one officer's 1915 diary noted, "Our army hasn't begun to grasp the idea of preparing to work together as a whole in real serious business. Having no objectives in view, we expend our energy on details . . . A little work in the morning. Golf, polo, tennis, riding in the hills in the afternoon. The Club at sunset. Dinner in the evening. A lazy man's paradise."[69]

The army's inability to predict World War I reveals the shallowness of the Root-era transformation. Examples of this myopia are legion, represented by Wood's 1914 declaration "that no modern war between first class powers will last for one year."[70] One popular explanation for the failure of foresight is Wilson's opposition to any hint of preparation for war prior to 1917, which prevented realistic contingency planning. But this argument is specious. Far from being constrained, many officers, especially Wood, skirted dangerously close to overt denunciations of the president and the political system.

Nor were officers circumspect in discussing the possibilities of war. In writing for their colleagues and the public, military in-tellectuals lamented an America invaded, its cities burned, its women ravaged, and the nation forced into debt and decline. As the world war continued, and the mutual slaughter virtually ended any possibility of attack from Europe, officers created ever more fanciful scenarios. A 1916 War College study warned that countries as diverse as Russia and Germany had the potential to invade with overwhelming numbers; even Italy could land more than 200,000 soldiers in little over a month.[71] In 1917 one officer anticipated a sudden German attack, the rapid capture of New York City, and a ransom demand of $10 billion. "What would our Country do? For three days there would be an outburst of in-dignation, especially through the West, and a popular demand that New York be sacrificed and an army raised to drive the 'inso-lent' invader from our shores. Then the voice of 'big business' would be heard, and the cry of the populace drowned. The city would pay ransom and Congress would make the nation pay for it."[72] That same year, Lieutenant Colonel Henry Jervey's *Warfare of the Future* made an impassioned plea for continental defense on the grounds of imminent attack, while simultaneously insist-ing, "The United States, if drawn into a conflict with a first-class power or combination of powers, is not likely to send expedi-tions across the seas to invade the territory of a distant power."[73] Within a few months of both these predictions, the United States dispatched the first of over a million soldiers to France.

The wartime performance of General John J. Pershing and the American Expeditionary Forces (AEF) epitomize the ambivalent legacy of the Root era on the army's way of war. Pershing was a firm believer that war was a struggle of individuals in which morale, will, charismatic command, discipline, and aggressive-ness were more important than weaponry or management. Yet, Pershing's own staff were the beneficiaries of Root's reforms: rela-tively young officers who had graduated from Leavenworth and the War College, served on the General Staff, and been actively involved in institutional reforms. But neither Pershing nor his staff appreciated that modern warfare required a national effort, in which nonmilitary factors—industrial production, popular support, international relations, business and labor—demanded as much attention as strictly military ones. Instead, they viewed battle operations as the center of the war effort and insisted that everything else be subordinate. As one prominent staff officer recalled, "The fact is that those of us serving in Europe . . . had no adequate conception of the difficulties encountered in the United States when this mighty task was in progress, or of the splendid work actually done to overcome them and make possible the brilliant accomplishments of our forces on the European battlefields."[74] Shaped by Heroic concepts, the army tried to fight World War I with a doctrine of "open warfare" suited for well-trained regulars campaigning on the plains of Luzon or the Mexican border. But it was a doctrine applied only with great difficulty, and much bloodshed, by the mass army of citizen-soldiers on the Western Front.

In the two decades between the splendid little war of 1898 and the war to end all wars in 1917, the army underwent profound transformation under Root's directive that it "provide for war." But despite the completion of the harbor fortification program, the creation of institutions charged with planning and preparing for conflict, and a tripling in manpower, along with other improvements, the army did not believe that the nation was more secure. Both planners and individual officers outlined alarming and quite improbable scenarios of national defeat while producing equally dubious solutions. As they had prior to 1898, military thinkers continued to draw both from the past and from current events only those lessons that confirmed their cherished beliefs.

5

DISSENTING VISIONS

A decade after serving as a chief of artillery for the American Expeditionary Forces and directing the AEF's titanic bombardments on the Western Front, Major General William E. Lassiter recalled his observations of a recent war exercise: "Fine body of men, the 1st Cavalry Division. Excellent esprit, lots of vim—but operating as if they had been to sleep like Rip Van Winkle and knew nothing of machine guns, aeroplanes, etc. Obsessed with the idea that they must charge, and that modern weapons will not permit them to charge . . . And so they go careening over the open plains . . . waving their antiquated sabers and yelling at the top of their lungs. Stirring to the senses in peacetime, but murder in war." The experience led him to reflect, "It is terribly difficult for military men to keep their methods adapted to rapidly changing times. Between wars the military business slumps. Our people lose interest. Congress concerns itself more with cutting down the Army than with building it up. And the troops . . . find a large part of their time and energy taken up with caring for buildings, grounds, and other impedimenta. In view of all the inertias to be overcome, and in view of the fact that our lives and honor are not in peril from outside aggression, it is not likely that our

Army is going to be kept in an up-to-the-minute state of preparedness."[1]

Lassiter's pessimism was shared by others. One veteran bitterly commented, "In that interim between wars, many of the top men in the Army had made their success in war, but were not looking forward to any future war."[2] This criticism, and much that has followed, reflects a perspective shaped by the army's frenzied preparation for World War II, by the humiliations of early defeats such as Pearl Harbor, Bataan, and Kasserine Pass, and by the often-expressed sentiment that victory was due less to military skill than to allies, firepower, and industrial might. It reflects fore-knowledge denied to those military intellectuals who wrote during the period between the wars. For these officers, the question was not how to prepare for blitzkrieg and amphibious warfare but how to reconcile the army's three traditional visions of war with the lessons of the great war to end all wars they had just won.

In the immediate aftermath of World War I, most uniformed commentators believed it was still possible and even desirable to return to the nation's historic continental deterrent strategy. Only a few urged an active international role, warning that Europe's unstable borders and the nation's global interests made a retreat into isolationism untenable, and a virtual guarantee of future war. The 1920 War Department's directive that the army make "the adequate defense of all permanent fortified or garrisoned possessions of the United States the top priority" received little challenge within the service.[3]

The shift into isolationism and protection of the nation's territory did not mean that military intellectuals believed the nation no longer faced the threat of war. Although their arguments were often wrapped in idealistic oratory, they maintained that the predatory nature of human and international relations was unchanged. In fact, the postwar world promised to be even more violent. The four War College students who submitted essays on

"The Causes and Prevention of War" in 1926 were unanimous that aggression and violence were endemic to both mankind and the international system. Only armed force could protect the United States from a host of grasping rivals.[4]

To army strategists in the immediate postwar era, the primary threats were, in order of magnitude, a two-ocean war with an Anglo-Japanese coalition, a Pacific war with Japan alone, and the ever-turbulent Mexican border. This was virtually the same strategic situation that prewar planners had faced, and it is not surprising that their solutions were also familiar: continental defense, a mobile horse cavalry component on the border, and the means to mobilize a large field army in the event of a major conflict. Although the army was less preemptive than the navy, which developed war plans against Great Britain even while the United States was allied with Great Britain against Germany, by 1922 it had completed war plans against Mexico, Great Britain, an Anglo-Japanese coalition, and Japan.

The 1920 National Defense Act seemed to address this multiplicity of dangers. Rejecting army manpower schemes dating back to Upton, the act incorporated Brigadier General John McAuley Palmer's vision of a trained citizen-soldier defense force. It authorized a unified "Army of the United States" with a peacetime strength of 288,000 regulars to provide training cadres, to man overseas garrisons, and to serve as an immediately deployable expeditionary force. In the event of a great war, the regulars would be reinforced by a 435,000-man National Guard and a potentially larger federal Organized Reserves, both trained by the regular army. The act divided the continental United States into nine administrative corps, each of which could mobilize one regular, two guard, and three reserve divisions, which together would form three field armies immediately upon the declaration of war.

The act also addressed some of the specific lessons of World

War I. Recognizing that modern warfare required the concentration of all elements of national power, the act established an assistant secretary of war to oversee the procurement of military supplies and the mobilization of industry. The importance of new technologies was acknowledged with two newly created combat organizations, the Air Service (to become the Army Air Corps in 1926) and the Chemical Warfare Service. For better or worse, the act did not accord mechanization—the use of armored vehicles for combat—the same status, and it rejected proposals to establish a separate tank corps. Instead, it assigned tanks to the newly formed Office of the Chief of Infantry, and scout or combat cars to the Office of the Chief of Cavalry. Army service journals lauded the 1920 Defense Act as the first formally authorized national security policy in the nation's history.[5]

But Congress soon gutted most of Palmer's plan. It rejected universal military training and cut the regular army to barely 130,000; not until 1940 would it approach authorized strength. Materiel suffered from similar shortfalls. The spit-shined troops and gleaming equipment the army displayed on parade made up its public image. But for over a decade after the armistice, soldiers lived in rotting wartime barracks, wore war-surplus clothing, fired increasingly dangerous war-surplus ammunition, and ate increasingly suspect war-surplus provisions. Without resources to accomplish any of its missions, the army pretended to do them all, with the result that in both the overseas possessions—the Canal Zone, Hawaii, and the Philippines—and the continental United States, it was little more than a collection of skeleton units devoting their time to maintenance, administration, and the desultory training of the National Guard and reserves.

Despite these setbacks, and in contrast with the aftermath of earlier conflicts, the army set out to make a comprehensive study of the lessons of World War I and their application for future military contingencies. This process occurred on a variety of levels, from the War Department down to the individual military officer. In 1920 the service secretary, proclaiming that the conflict "marked the beginning of a new era in the military art," instructed the army "to study the records of the World War, with a view to extracting from them all the lessons they contain."[6] Among these lessons were: that the immense size of modern armies imposed logistical demands met only by the mobilization of domestic industry and transportation; that size, logistics, and fortifications rendered armies immobile; and that war was increasingly dominated by technology such as artillery, airplanes, and tanks, all of which required highly specialized operators.

The commander of the AEF, John J. Pershing, had already established a series of boards to study the war's lessons and their application for future organization, logistics, equipment, and doctrine. These culminated in the April 1919 *Report of the Superior Board on Organization and Tactics,* which recommended that the postwar army be restructured for trench warfare. Pershing, in turn, submitted his own report, which declared, "Our army is most likely to operate on the American Continent and mobility is especially necessary under all probable conditions of warfare in this theater." The general concluded that World War I had been an anomaly; he therefore rejected many of the Superior Board's recommendations on the grounds it had been too influenced by "the necessities of stabilized warfare in Western Europe rather than upon the requirements of warfare of the character and in the theater upon which we are most likely to be engaged."[7] Such disagreements over the war's lessons would prove all too common over the next two decades.

World War I only strengthened the Guardian dogma that "our national policy [was] one of non-interference in the affairs of foreign nations" and its "military policy [is] purely defensive in character."[8] This was supplemented by another lesson, one shared with the Managers, that the scope of modern warfare was so great it required the resources of the entire nation. But while the Managers studied how best to mobilize the nation's industry and manpower for both an offensive and defensive contingency, the Guardians fiercely opposed anything other than a defensive war. By the late 1930s this credo would prompt some officers to join the America First Committee or even to publicly criticize what they viewed as a provocative American foreign policy that would cause "another useless, fruitless, foolish, utterly unnecessary war."[9] Major General Johnson Hagood's 1937 diatribe *We Can Defend America* advocated reorganizing the army so as to make a large-scale overseas war all but impossible. A year later, Major General George Van Horn Moseley declared, "Let us mind our own business as to the family life and internal affairs of our neighbors. It is very clear that the thinking American citizen wants us to mind our own business. Very definitely they do not want war. Soldier that I am, I believe they are right."[10]

The Guardians' influence on national strategy may be seen in the War Plans Division's 1924–1925 Special Plan Blue: The National Position in Readiness. Blue was intended to provide the military force structure, organization, command system, and tactics "for defense against an enemy coming from any or all directions."[11] It assumed a combined Anglo-Canadian-Mexican-Japanese coalition defeating the navy and sending 100,000 soldiers across the nation's borders on the first day of war. Although Plan Blue never progressed past increasingly vitriolic correspondence between Washington and the various corps commands, the fact that the army's only over-arching national defense scheme prior to 1939 was based on protecting the continent from invasion reveals how much the Guardian tradition influenced army strategy.

If World War I had little influence on the Guardians' strategic paradigm, it had a far greater impact on the harbor defense mission that had defined their existence for over a century. The AEF Superior Board recommended shifting responsibility for the sea-coast fortifications to the navy—in effect abolishing the Coast Artillery Corps—and attaching all artillery to mobile combat units.[12] Although this initiative fell short, it illustrates one senior commander's complaint that "within the Army itself there is little liaison between the Coast Artillery and the so-called Mobile Army. A rivalry has sprung up between them."[13]

The point was driven home when harbor defense was excluded from the army's manual for warfighting, the 1923 *Field Service Regulations (FSR 1923).*[14] The branch that had prided itself for decades on its superior education, technical sophistication, and scientific skills—all necessary for the complex task of hitting a rapidly moving target at 35,000 yards—was now dismissed as a bunch of pseudo-soldiers who had never fired a shot in anger. Groups that had previously supported harbor fortifications—the public, the press, and Congress—now accepted their dismantling. The Coast Artillery Corps' proportionate strength within the regular army establishment shrank from 28 percent in 1907 to less than 10 percent by 1928, leading one officer to describe it as "a mere skeleton," noting with alarm that within the entire continental United States there were fewer than 4,000 troops assigned to fortifications.[15] Armament was so deteriorated and so rarely inspected that no one knew whether it would work under wartime conditions. In one test, ten of eleven mines failed to function after barely three months in the water.[16] All of this indicated that the fortifications upon which so many officers had defined their professional identity were irrelevant.

The harbor defense community responded as it had when threatened in the nineteenth century. It argued that new technology would soon restore its primacy, and it resurrected old scenarios as modern threats. The airplane, which could both identify and bomb harbor defenses designed to be invisible and invulnerable to ship bombardment, was initially hailed as a valuable ally. The chief of Coast Artillery led the chorus: "Never in the future will fortifications be independent of another branch—the air service."[17] In particular, gunners hailed the ability of aircraft to spot the approach of enemy fleets and to direct artillery fire at over-the-horizon targets. By the 1930s some Coast Artillery officers were proposing an integrated sea-air-land defense system with a unified command structure and inter- and intra-service training.

The Coast Artillery's enthusiasm for aviation was predicated on their confidence that the airplane posed no threat to their branch's primacy in defending the nation's shores. To the editor of the *Coast Artillery Journal,* it was obvious that "the chance of an enemy bombing fleet putting out of commission a modern harbor defense is absolutely nil."[18] With similar assurance, in 1925 the journal boasted of the newest antiaircraft weaponry, "should this country be invaded tomorrow and such guns be furnished for the defense of our principal cities, the inhabitants thereof would be adequately protected from the horrors of a bombing raid."[19] A year later, an officer writing on the defense of Washington claimed that with these new guns any antiaircraft battery "can confidently expect to prevent a bomber from successfully attacking a limited target such as the Capitol building, the Navy Yard, or the railroad terminus."[20]

The Guardians alternated these sanguine proclamations with shocking new versions of century-old specters arising from insufficient harbor defense. In 1924 the *Coast Artillery Journal* predicted, "One hour of bombardment and New York would be in flames, and amid a fleeing, panic stricken populace, the enemy transports would quickly unload their hundreds of thousands of troops at the multiple docks, and our principal city, the very heart of our country, would lie stricken in the hands of the enemy . . . A great nation would at last awaken to the undefended condition of its harbors only to find itself the slaves of a ruthless enemy."[21]

As had so often proved the case in the past, both the danger of the threat and the promise of the future were greatly exaggerated.

In 1919 the corps unveiled its new sixteen-inch rifled cannon, a weapon that could fire a one-ton shell over twenty miles and destroy a battleship with one well-placed shot. But the construction and emplacement of these guns went so slowly that in 1926 the chief of Coast Artillery estimated the last one would not be ready until 1961.[22]

The nation's defenses against aerial attack were no better. Little of the new antiaircraft weaponry that had so excited the *Journal*'s editor was ever purchased. Even if it had been, it would have soon become useless, since by the mid-1920s the army's World War I–era sound-ranging equipment and searchlights could not track most military aircraft. Field tests showed that few antiaircraft crews could protect even themselves, much less the heavy artillery they were supposed to guard. In 1924 an antiaircraft regiment stationed in Hawaii fired some 25,000 machine gun bullets at a target towed slowly through a prescribed course—and hit it 191 times. Abysmal as this was, it outscored the regiment's three-inch guns, which fired 2,000 shells and recorded only two shrapnel holes. These same guns were still in use almost two decades later, which may help explain why on December 7, 1941, army antiaircraft may have inflicted as much damage on American airplanes as on Japanese. Indeed, by the 1930s one coast defense officer publicly acknowledged that harbor fortifications were "wholly exposed and vulnerable to attack from the air, and there is no protection from gunfire from the rear."[23] Those who had once so proudly protected their nation now themselves needed protection.

Although the harbor defense community was increasingly demoralized, other intellectuals, including reformers within the Coast Artillery Corps, inherited the Guardian mandate. The lesson these reformers took from World War I was that their branch must abandon the "concrete pedestal" of stationary fortress defense and instead serve as mobile heavy artillery for the great field armies that would fight the next war.[24] They cited the 1915 Dardanelles campaign as proof of the danger of expeditionary attack and as a template for successful beach defense. They were inspired by the Joint Army-Navy Board's May 1920 redefinition of coast defense to include the entire seaboard, not just protected harbors. To officers such as Lieutenant Colonel Homer R. Oldfield, the corps was still first among equals: "The chief reason for the maintenance of an army in this country is to render our territory secure from invasion. The whole of our army is then a coast defense force."[25]

Perhaps the most significant Guardian military thinker of the early postwar period was Major General William G. Haan, whose Positive System of Coast Defense was approved by the Joint Board in 1920.[26] Haan, a Coast Artillery officer who had commanded an infantry division in France, recognized that, at its simplest, an amphibious landing resembled a World War I offensive. The attackers not only had to cross the equivalent of No Man's Land (the water) but had to bring with them sufficient manpower and supplies to withstand counterattack until reinforcements could expand the salient.

Haan's Positive System applied the defense-in-depth tactics that had turned so many assaults into bloody failures on the Western Front. As the enemy fleet approached the shoreline, heavy railroad and tractor artillery would be rushed to the threatened area and begin shelling the vulnerable warships and transports at distances ranging up to 25,000 yards. This would force the enemy to disembark their landing craft far from the shore, and as their troops approached the beach, they would be blasted by beach cordons of machine guns and artillery. Those disorganized and demoralized survivors who struggled ashore would be struck by a violent counterattack launched by the main force of infantry and artillery, rushed forward just in time to drive the invaders into the sea. Conceptually, the Positive System was a radical innovation: simultaneously breaking from the fixation on harbor defense that had dominated Guardian thought since 1821 and ending the coast defense community's equally long separation from the mobile army. Not surprisingly, it provoked resistance from the harbor fortification community, which claimed it substituted an unproven theory for a defense policy that had deterred invasion for over a century.[27]

Haan's Positive System required large numbers of highly trained troops, even larger amounts of firepower, excellent communications in the rear, and a command that could rapidly coordinate men, weapons, and transportation. All of this existed only on paper in the 1920 Defense Act. It was all very well for coast artillery officers to proclaim that the "final defense of the coast . . . rests in the bayonet of the infantry."[28] But the unpleasant fact remained that there were insufficient infantry—or artillery, aviation, communications, or much else—to implement the Positive System should an enemy attack. Indeed, the army never even attempted the first step of the scheme, a national survey of potential landing sites. In the overseas commands, which were even more directly threatened by an amphibious attack, the situation was little better. The Hawaiian Department conducted a series of maneuvers in the 1920s that demonstrated both the inherent soundness of the Positive System and the inability of the small garrison to put it into practice.[29]

In addition to their dominance in the traditional coastal defense constituencies, Guardian ideas were assimilated by others, particularly in the aviation community. The insular and doctrinaire approach of air force historians has led them to interpret airpower doctrine in the interwar period as directed toward "the effort to establish an independent air force; the development of a doctrine of strategic bombardment; and the search for a heavy bomber by which this doctrine could be applied."[30] But in fact, the Guardian way of war permeated much of the discussion about aviation in the immediate postwar military intellectual community. Several air officers agreed with their coast defense colleagues that the two branches should cooperate to form an integrated air-land defense system. In championing the airborne bomb over the land-based gun they were not challenging the deterrent objectives of the nation's continental defense strategy, only the means by which these objectives were achieved.

In common with earlier Guardians, aviators were preoccupied with both the imminent danger posed by technology—in their particular case the bomber—and a technological solution, the air defense pursuit airplane. Predictably, aviators revised the century-old scenarios of apocalyptic attack. "Out of the dawn behind a cloud of smoke there may come the sound of great guns firing at an important harbor. Overhead will be the whir of aircraft. Now and then the terrific bursts of aerial bombs of great size exploding near the forts . . . Other squadrons of planes and fleets of airships will be dropping men, and munitions and food at vital points . . . We may expect to see whole hamlets along the shores captured and their inhabitants held as hostage."[31] Aviators also shared with earlier Guardians the faith that if the nation committed itself to an appropriate military policy—in their case a massive air force— then not only would such horrors be prevented, but war itself would never touch the nation's shores.

William "Billy" Mitchell was the best-known aviation spokesman to adopt the Guardian strategic paradigm, as both the title and content of his most influential work, *Winged Defense*, testify.[32] In 1915, before he ever took a flying lesson, Mitchell had written a grim if improbable jeremiad. With dexterous statistical manipulation, he argued that the United States could be attacked by a multitude of nations ranging from Japan to Italy.[33] In 1919 he drew up a complex defense plan reminiscent of Totten's scheme but with airbases and antiaircraft defenses, not fortifications and guns, protecting America's cities. His 1926 article,

"When the Air Raiders Come," which had New York City reduced to "a heap of dead and smoldering ashes," invoked traditional Guardian scenarios.[34] Although he advocated an offensive
operational and tactical role for the air force, on the national level
he favored a defensive, almost isolationist strategy, as even his putative opponents on the General Staff recognized.[35]

Mitchell was not alone. In the early 1920s the army conducted
extensive experiments with both aircraft and antiaircraft technologies, while the General Staff, the Army War College, the Coast
Artillery Corps, and other agencies tried to implement what one
reviewing officer termed "an elaborate system of antiaircraft defense along our coasts and extended inland to the probable radius
of enemy aircraft operating from floating bases." Commanders
dutifully submitted extensive proposals for airbases, early warning stations, and antiaircraft positions until it was concluded
their combined requirements were "so tremendous" that "there
can be no possibility of their fulfillment."[36] Protection for New
York City alone required twenty-five full-strength regiments (or
much of the regular army's combat manpower) and almost as
much money as the service's annual research and development
budget.[37]

The Guardian legacy remained the dominant influence on
the nation's security policy, which until late in the 1930s was
noninterventionist, deterrent, and focused on continental defense. Far from being discredited by World War I, the lessons of
that conflict were interpreted to show that the increased power of
defense could provide a new measure of security. The Guardian's
traditional constituency, the fortress defenders, was joined by reformers within the Coast Artillery Corps in advocating a new and
expanded doctrine of coast defense. Other groups, most notably
from the aviation community, also adopted Guardian arguments
to articulate a way of war that conformed to traditional American
military thought.

While the Guardians were shaping the army's postwar strategy, Heroes were influencing the army's approach to fighting the next war. Like the Guardians, most Heroes regarded World War I less an indicator of future warfare than a confirmation of traditional beliefs. Like the Guardians, they selected lessons to validate their presuppositions and disregarded any that did not. For example, Pershing, the AEF Superior Board, and *Field Service Regulations 1923* all advocated offensive infantry operations that had proven impossible on the Western Front; all three still insisted that decisive battles more reminiscent of 1870 than 1917 should remain the military objective.[38]

World War I inspired a nationalistic romanticism among some Heroes. In the words of Captain Paul S. Bond, "We went to Europe with knapsacks filled with foreign trench warfare manuals, and came home with sound American ideas and doctrines based on our own war experiences and our *own* tactical conceptions, which in principle had proven sound."[39] What were these sound American doctrines? They consisted mostly of vague references to the "open warfare" that the AEF had allegedly practiced in France, less a doctrine for conducting battle than what Major General Charles P. Summerall termed an "offensive spirit . . . a desire to close with the enemy and engage in personal combat."[40] This emphasis on character over technique was shared by a member of the Superior Board, who praised "those stalwart men . . . who insisted upon an *open warfare* doctrine. Only by it were we saved from the horrors of loss of morale and the failure of our troops to fulfill the demands made upon them."[41]

In 1921, perhaps to give the Heroic creed as much substance as spirit, the army adopted nine "Principles of War": objective, offensive, economy of forces, superiority, fire and movement, cooperation, surprise, protection, simplicity of movement. These principles were in line with Heroic priorities, not least because they championed a method of warfare far removed from the trenches of the Western Front. They defined the objective of military operations as the destruction of the enemy army in battle, and they prescribed its accomplishment by maneuver, surprise, simplicity, and above all offensive action. Notably missing were principles addressing such factors as weaponry, firepower, attrition, field fortifications, logistics, and mobilizing the national industrial base. Echoing Mahan's earlier efforts at precision and predictability, some maintained that "the proper application of these principles of war comprises the whole art of war."[42]

As some officers noted, there was an inherent contradiction between the rote application of the Principles of War and the traditional Heroic emphasis on the "the human element"—the amalgam of such qualities as experience, morale, aggressiveness, and innovation. In his 1921 War College lecture on the principles, Colonel William K. Naylor emphasized, "We must never imagine that we can induce infallible rules nor reduce war to an exact science."[43] In Naylor's opinion, intangible factors like discipline and morale were more important than weapons or rules. Major E. S. Hughes criticized not only the rote learning and application of the principles in the schools but their entire premise as alien to "the true nature of war." In his view, "war is just another of life's activities. It is an art like painting or sculpturing, but a million times more intricate. It has rules, but they are elastic . . . The statement that a principle of war, as a guide to action, is infallible and immutable is nonsense, an insult to an intelligent man, and a dangerous doctrine for an unintelligent one."[44]

Heroes emphasized the human element over the principles, or, to quote the title of one 1933 article, "Men Make War; Men Must Fight It."[45] According to one officer, World War I had shown that "spirit maintains fighting force, and war is more a clash of will than it is of armament, for the minute a side decides it is beaten and it is useless to fight, it ceases to fight, no matter how much armament is available."[46] Colonel Robert McCleave agreed. "There is no limit save in the moral[e] of the troops and their leaders and . . . no troops are beaten until they admit the fact . . . *War is the shock of two wills . . . Moral force is the soul of battle*."[47] In 1923 Colonel Frank Parker, lecturing on "The Psychology of the Battlefield and Management of the Crowd Mind," told his audience, "We make war primarily with men. They give the energy and cohesion to the weapons which destroy our enemy and gain the victory."[48] Similarly, in 1934 Major General Hanson Ely harangued officers at the Army War College: "It is the mind that wins battles, that will always win them, that always has won them throughout the world's history. The spirituality, the moral quality of war, has not changed. Mechanics, modern arms, all the artillery, gas, tanks, aircraft, etc., invented by man and his science, will not make an end to this thing, so lightly considered at the moment and called the *human soul*."[49]

To mobilize these souls was the task of the Heroic leader. World War I had proved it. The Superior Board proclaimed, "All the activities of a separate military organization, large or small, must be controlled by the mind of the commander. It has not always been understood that much of the power and force of a military unit rests in the will, personality and character of the commander."[50] The 1923 *FSR* were filled with exhortations such as, "It is the special duty of the higher command to stimulate and cultivate fighting spirit, aggressiveness, and initiative of the infantry soldier."[51] Throughout the 1920s the Army War College taught that education and managerial skill was secondary to a commander's "morally strong character."[52]

Heroes distinguished the "science of command," which dealt with mastering the "mechanics" of organization, from the "art of command," which derived from will and personality.[53] A great commander such as Pershing or Robert E. Lee could impose his character or will on an entire army down to the lowest private and "arouse, mold, control, and direct the minds of his men to attain a desired military end."[54] Lieutenant Colonel Jennings C. Wise dismissed officers who based their authority purely on rank. "The control which they exercise" over the "human machine" of their combat unit "knows nothing of psychological ascendancy over the minds of the component individuals."[55] Pershing's AEF deputy, James G. Harbord, whose World War I combat leadership had usually been from well in the rear, declared "the greatest fighting machine" was the individual soldier with rifle and bayonet. "A little foxhole in the ground was an effective defense against artillery fire, even when the cannons were hub to hub. A wet handkerchief overcame gas."[56] As long as the spirit remained, the flesh would continue to fight. Yet tensions would soon emerge when new armaments, especially the airplane and the tank, challenged traditional Heroic concepts.

The army as an institution was not hostile to aviation. Surveying the lessons of World War I, the AEF Superior Board made the confident prediction, "Undoubtedly aviation will affect to a greater and greater extent the tactics of future warfare."[57] It delineated four crucial missions: reconnaissance for both information and artillery spotting (observation); aerial combat (pursuit); supporting combat operations (attack or close air support); and attacking military and industrial targets (bombardment). The *FSR 1923,* subsequent army and War Department boards on aviation, and even many aviators confirmed these same categories and emphasized the importance of integrating airplanes into combat operations.[58]

Where officers disagreed with one another was on whether the airplane was a revolutionary weapon that could achieve victory by bombarding enemy cities and factories, thus rendering armies irrelevant. Those opposed to this view echoed Stephen O. Fuqua's claim that "the best use of our aviation is to confine it to the battle front as a part of the attacking mass to win the battle."[59] Reflecting both anticivilian bias and branch elitism, one officer declared confidently, "The air service may whip the statesmen and the non-combatants gathered into cities, but never the Infantry in the field."[60] That same year Summerall complained, "The most extravagant dreams have been entertained for the airplane, none of which have ever approached realization." Meanwhile, "the public is being deceived and misled by loose, fanciful, and irresponsible talk."[61] Military intellectuals quite correctly noted that the limited range and load capacity of contemporary airplanes made a cross-ocean attack impossible. And as one sarcastically observed, "To create a defense system based upon a hypothetical air attack from Canada, Mexico, or any of our near neighbors would be wholly unreasonable."[62] Nor would airplanes allow the United States to wage short, cheap, long-range wars. Bombing cities might damage structures and kill civilians, but only the occupation of territory would force an enemy to surrender. Just as aviators had borrowed from Guardian debates, so ground officers appropriated claims from aviators in the pursuit community that a well-developed air defense system could destroy attacking bombers.

In their discussion of mechanization, and especially the tank, Heroes showed a similar ambivalence—impressed with the weapon but disputing its revolutionary potential. By the late 1920s virtually all agreed that "in any future war we shall witness a decided increase in the use of highly mobile, armored forces."[63] But how would they be used? British armored theorists such as J. F. C. Fuller and Basil Liddell Hart frequently contributed to service journals, and, as one friend of Liddell Hart noted, the reaction of army officers ranged "from almost fanatic devotion to acute hostility."[64] Some viewed the tank as a weapon whose chief attributes were mobility and striking power. They wanted to create armored spearheads to range far in front of the main body of the army, or behind enemy lines, disrupting enemy communications and logistics and attacking strategic points.[65] Others, recognizing that in World War I the "Infantry advanced with heavy casualties or not at all," viewed tanks as support vehicles, mobile armored fortresses that would accompany the advancing foot soldiers and destroy machine gun nests and pillboxes and "deliver most of the shock action against an enemy."[66]

The Heroes' effort to incorporate technology into warfare was hampered by a variety of factors, not least their casual approach to the complexities of industrial mobilization and their disdain for technical specialization. As chief of staff, Douglas MacArthur proclaimed that future conflict would be waged by elite mechanized armies whose speed and mobility could out-maneuver enemy trench lines and strike at the vulnerable flank and rear areas. But in 1931 he told President Herbert Hoover he opposed the research, development, or purchase of tanks and other "expensive toys" because in wartime the automobile industry could easily provide vehicles for military use.[67] And when congressional reformers tried to cut personnel and obsolescent organizations in order to fund tanks and airplanes, MacArthur fought them with a crusader's zeal.

Branch identity also shaped the Heroes' perception of technology. In 1930 the chief of infantry dismissed "schools of thought [that] visualize a war of machines" and declared, "The very weapons and methods—motorization, chemical agents, automatic weapons, and tanks and armored vehicles—that some claim may replace Infantry, will be used by the Infantry to perform that very necessary object of battle—to gain and hold ground. The Infantry may be reinforced but not replaced."[68] In urging his fellow horsemen to embrace the tank, one Leavenworth student urged them to "imagine a cavalry regiment or even brigade attacking in open order in successive waves preceded by a battalion of light fast tanks! What a combination! The moving fortresses of fire followed by the horseman with cold steel! What troops would stand against it?"[69]

As this sentiment indicates, some of the most extreme proponents of the Heroic view were in the Cavalry branch. On the
Western Front, mounted combat had played virtually no role after 1914. The only American unit of horsemen to be sent to
France spent most of its time managing a remount depot. Small
wonder that by the end of the war, mounted forces were perceived both within and without the army as an anachronism; morale sank precipitously.[70] During the next two decades, horsemen
reinterpreted the lessons of the Great War. In addition to contributing a two-volume history of wartime cavalry operations, the
Cavalry School published a study of the campaign of Field Marshall Allenby in Palestine, with the admonition that future wars
"will approximate much more closely to those in Palestine than to
those in France, and until we can produce machines that can go
wherever cavalry can go, and that can achieve everything that
Cavalry can achieve, we must depend on the man and the horse
to obtain really decisive results."[71] By the late 1920s the cavalry
had convinced itself that "any unprejudiced study of the last war
will show that no decisive results were obtained without the use
of cavalry."[72]

While extolling their branch's accomplishments, cavalry intellectuals also dismissed World War I as a useful guide for the future. Its search for the true principles for waging mounted combat led the Cavalry School to reject recent history and declare,
"The primary source was the Civil War."[73] Lieutenant Colonel
J. D. Pillow lectured in 1927 that "no nation and no military
leaders will voluntarily submit to a war of attrition behind barbed
wire, with all its attendant evils of inordinate length, immense casualties, great cost, and probably indecisive results . . . An army
exists for war of maneuver . . . and in mobile warfare cavalry en-
joys the use of its prime characteristic—mobility."[74]

Historical lessons aside, throughout the interwar era the
United States had a practical need for a large mounted force. In

the succinct words of Chief of Staff Summerall, "Our Army is maintained for purely defensive purposes. Any campaign along our border or in the continental United States would particularly favor the extensive use of cavalry."[75] As late as 1940, and despite graphic evidence of blitzkrieg in Poland and France, true believers like Patton remained convinced that "in the next war . . . we will need horse cavalry and lots of it."[76]

Both their perception of the lessons of the past and their view of the future shaped the cavalry's preparations for the next war. Alongside the intra-branch debate over tanks and mechanization, this debate took place within a larger discussion on technology and mobile warfare. Many who opposed mechanization did so because they believed they had an alternative, and better, solution.

In the interwar period the cavalry, responding to criticism that its units lacked combat power, dramatically increased the number of automatic rifles and light machine guns in its regiments until they exceeded those of the Infantry. This, when combined with the ability to rapidly shift positions, was believed sufficient to allow mounted units to deliver a heavy volume of fire—and at the crucial time and place. It also incorporated the gasoline engine and motorized transport to drive "portee" units to the area of operations, where they would mount their steeds and deploy.

Predictably, these efforts to incorporate technology were not completely successful. In combat against infantry, the cavalry's sole firepower advantage was machine guns. Its troopers lacked virtually every other supporting weapon, from mortars to anti-tank guns. And porteeing exhausted both horses and men, all but incapacitating mounted units. But by nurturing such rationalizations, which persisted into World War II, the cavalry could claim that it was both progressive and sensible, assimilating the latest in technology while at the same time retaining the methods of fighting that had made it so successful in the past.

Cavalrymen, and Patton in particular, were among the most vociferous proponents of the supremacy of the "human element" in battle. As early as 1921 he abandoned his support for tank warfare and began attacking what he perceived as an army-wide emphasis on technology, over-centralization, and technical specialization. In Patton's view, "The bayonet charge and the saber charge are the highest physical demonstration of moral victory. The fierce frenzy of hate and determination flashing from the bloodshot eyes squinting behind the glittering steel is what wins."[77] In a 1931 *Cavalry Journal* article entitled "Success in War" he repudiated the century-old tradition of scientific warfare first articulated by Totten, Halleck, and Mahan. "War," Patton emphasized, was "an art and as such is not susceptible of explanation by fixed formula." Yet "wormish men" sought to impose rationality on war and "to make tangible its intangibility." The "truth" was that "the history of war is the history of warriors; few in number, mighty in influence. Alexander, not Macedonia, conquered the world. Scipio, not Rome, destroyed Carthage." Returning to an earlier theme, he concluded that "the fixed determination to acquire the warrior soul, and having acquired it, to conquer or perish with honor, is the secret of success in war."[78]

A similar faith in the human element, and a similar rejection of trench warfare, is seen in Colonel Joseph Marius Scammell's 1934 article "Some Comments on the Caribbean War." Scammell was a brilliant if inconsistent thinker who in 1922 mapped out a Japanese-American war using Sun Tzu for strategic guidance. Assuming the pen name of Brigadier General Elmer Zilch, Scammell foretold an invasion by a European coalition, whose combined fleets blocked the Panama Canal and trapped the American battle fleet in the Pacific. The invaders then landed a large army equipped with the most modern weapons and began the conquest of Mexico.

In a direct swipe at the Managers, Scammell denounced the

General Staff for having "failed to develop a distinctly American theory of war." Instead, by conforming to the "influence of the materialistic age," the army had made "logistics instead of the human and intellectual factors the basis of our war plans." Burdened by artillery, transport, and all the paraphernalia of trench warfare, the American field force was quickly routed by the invaders. Fortunately, in the nation's darkest hour, a native martial genius, General Caldwell, appeared. Out of castoffs and rejects he created an elite force with the simple philosophy: "I make warriors first, then soldiers . . . and then I can make technicians and tacticians over night." Like Caldwell, his troops "mysteriously appeared from nowhere" to strike devastating blows on the coalition's supply line and its isolated detachments, and then disappeared. Harassed and demoralized, the invaders were soon routed. Caldwell, the penultimate warrior, not only saved the nation but created a tactical revolution. The chastened army abandoned its earlier "European" emphasis on logistics and organization and became "100 per cent American. It took tactics from the Red Man, the Minute Man . . . even our modern racketeering gangster . . . Fighting, not administration, became the main business of our army."[79]

Scammell's article displayed another facet of the Heroic way of war: the virtual absence of anyone but military personnel. The Heroes' elitism and belief in martial virtues caused them to place the citizenry in two camps, as either potential soldiers or as a weak, emotional, irrational mob. As before the war, Heroes still criticized the public's apathy toward national security issues, its hostility to anything that resembled militarism, its bland assurance that war posed no threat, and above all its acceptance of civilian interference in military affairs. A 1923 book on United States' military history presented a litany of "mistakes, deficiencies, and abuses," of which the most egregious were "ignorance of and lack of interest in the national defense by the American people

and their representatives in Congress" and "failure to hear the repeated warnings of our greatest and wisest rulers and leaders."[80]

To military intellectuals in the Heroic camp, the pacifist was
not just misguided but a hypocrite, "without loyalty to that government that permits him to enjoy the blessings bestowed upon
him."[81] The political radical, seeking to subvert the army's professional expertise with the revolutionary credo of class warfare, was
even more dangerous. In 1920 the War Plans Division began
drawing up Special Plan White to deal with the threat of internal subversion; corps commanders assessed the dangers posed by
unions, radicals, and ethnic groups. The judge advocate issued a
pamphlet in 1922 claiming that while "apparently suppressing an
isolated disturbance arising from industrial disagreement," the
army was "in reality facing the problem of resisting foreign invasion, political in nature and designedly entered upon to destroy
our form of government."[82]

The Heroes' distrust of civilian society further convinced them
that the techniques of World War I, and the mass army required,
must not be the basis for future warfare. Technology in the form
of the armored fighting vehicle, the radio, motorized transport,
and the airplane offered an alternative to the trenches while restoring maneuver, individual martial ability, and morale to war.
But it also threatened to remove the human element, reduc-
ing war to a battle of machines. The Heroes' response combined
tactical reform with appeals to valor. When the Field Artillery
branch developed new methods of fire control and indirect fire, it
insisted it was doing this only to better practice "open warfare." The Infantry branch, like the Cavalry, experimented with
new weapons and technology, but did little to develop the combined arms system of artillery, tanks, and infantry that ultimately
proved most successful. For most of the interwar period Heroes
still maintained that "battle is normally determined by physical
encounter with the bayonet or the fear thereof; all other agencies

of destruction, as artillery, machine guns and aircraft, are auxiliary in their effect, however potent, and serve to make possible the advance of the foot soldier to hand-to-hand encounter."[83]

The strategic school most influenced by World War I was the Managers, who considered it a revolutionary event. Colonel C. M. Bundel summarized their position: "A few generations ago war was merely conflict between armed forces, and when the forces of one side had been overcome the war was over . . . Now, however, war . . . means a whole nation engaged in a struggle, with every agency, civil and military, involved and every individual doing his part to make the effort effective."[84] Such views were manifest in the provisions of the National Defense Act of 1920 that created both an assistant secretary of war for industrial mobilization and the Industrial War College.

Managers believed that to play its part in the national war effort it was imperative that the army plan ahead, anticipating warfare far into the future. In the words of the 1936 Draft Mobilization Plan, the army must avoid the mistake it had made in 1917, when the nation had "drift[ed] into war without having made provisions for prompt mobilization of industry" and "improvised methods were unable to prevent extravagance and delays in procuring munitions or to prevent profiteering in some quarters and unnecessary suffering in others." World War I had taught one essential lesson. "War is no longer simply a battle between armed forces in the field—it is a struggle in which each side strives to bring to bear against the enemy the coordinated power of every individual and every material resource at its command. The conflict extends from the soldier in the most forward line to the humblest citizen in the remotest hamlet in the rear."[85]

Lieutenant Colonel Hjalmar Erickson's 1922 essay "War, Its Nature, Doctrines, and Methods" sought to provide a conceptual framework for the organization and planning of American wars. Erickson, a War College instructor, believed, like most military intellectuals, that "man has always lived and always will live in a state of constant friction with his fellow men and with nature."[86] Like other Managers, he took as a cardinal tenet that "all people, all activities, and all resources of a nation are required for the prosecution of modern wars . . . and that the military plans are only a part of the whole war plan of the nation." This national war plan required a distinctly American "doctrine of war . . . *a theory of using a Nation's force under particular conditions*" based on two fundamental principles: "*to fight future wars to definite conclusions*" and "*to carry war into enemy countries so as to avoid hostile occupation of our own.*" It followed that although in future wars the United States' war aims would be defensive—"No one conceives that our country would enter upon a war of conquest and aggrandizement"—the nation's armed forces must take the strategic and tactical offensive.[87] Erickson's essay neatly linked the Managers' plan of national organization for modern warfare, the public's isolationist mood, and the army's faith that World War I had vindicated offensive "open warfare."

Managers naturally disputed the Heroes' focus on the individual commanders' will, arguing that "we have passed from the age of great captains to an age of nations in arms . . . A modern nation must rest its faith, not in the trust that a deliverer will be raised in time of need, but in training the composite mind of its regular army to think in terms of the next war."[88] Their view on leadership was captured in a 1925 lecture subtitled "The Machine Which the Army Commander Operates."[89] As Summerall emphasized, military command had to be exercised through a staff organization resembling a modern corporation. "If we conceive that the leader is only for war, then we shall have no leaders in war . . . the nearest analogy to war, for us, is the business or industrial leader in peace."[90]

In the Managers' view, army schools should teach military command with the same thoroughness they taught technical and tactical skills, and senior officers should adapt the latest "theories of the psychology of leadership" from the commercial sector.[91] Whereas Heroes referred to the commander's will as an unstoppable spiritual force, Managers saw it as the intelligence guiding a corporate organization. One of their central tenets was that individual military genius was rare and unpredictable, but even mediocre commanders could achieve solid staff work and organizational efficiency.

Both Managers and Heroes recognized that the world war demonstrated the importance of popular support. But they differed markedly in their approach to the American public. The Heroes tended to view patriotism, national will, and sacrifice as emotional connections supporting the military in war. They distrusted most aspects of American society and were acutely sensitive to any perceived challenge to the military ethos. In contrast, the Managers believed that "morale is a basic factor in the conduct of war and is largely a civil function."[92] The "tendency of modern war to extremes of destruction" made it necessary for "a partnership between the statesman and his military commanders, the statesman being the senior partner, each having confidence in the other, understanding the needs and difficulties of the other."[93]

But Managers joined with Heroes in rejecting civilian authority over what they viewed as areas of military expertise. Reflecting on excessive patriotic zeal during World War I, Major L. B. Magruder concluded the average citizen was "unreliable, a source of danger and a drag upon the smooth functioning of the war machine."[94] Remediation, Managers emphasized, relied on the army. Fortunately, the 1920 Defense Act insured that many officers would be assigned to National Guard, Reserve, or teaching assignments and would thus have an opportunity to inform the citizenry about military concerns. War Plans Director Briant H. Wells suggested that instead of discussing important issues such as national security or trade, leaders emphasize "a sentimental catch word" such as "the slogan of Freedom." With considerable candor, Wells noted this had proved successful in the past: "The United States has fought six wars with Freedom as the catch word; the economic questions were kept in the background."[95]

Perhaps no military intellectual personified the Managers' position better than Dwight D. Eisenhower. In two 1931 speeches written for the assistant secretary of war, Eisenhower argued that "modern war" was "essentially dual in nature—combatant and industrial."[96] Therefore, "to meet the demands of armed conflict every material resource, and every individual in the state must be called upon to bear a proportionate share of the burden."[97] Eisenhower's experiences in the Philippines in the 1930s trying to build an army for a financially weak government reinforced his conviction that national defense expenditures must be *provided without wrecking the very thing* [they] *are appropriated to secure, the stability and security of the nation.*"[98]

The Managers' approach to the technology of warfare was significantly different from the Heroes. They believed that "so costly and destructive are modern wars that every mechanical means will be resorted to in the attempt to successfully terminate the contest. Faster moving armies, more powerful in striking energy, equipped with every instrument that modern science and ingenuity can devise will be the contending forces of the future."[99] A 1922 article "What of the Future" argued that the world war had made "the question of armament into an element of strategy."[100] Managers proposed that in peacetime the army prepare to adapt a host of civilian technologies ranging from radios to engines to wartime production methods. Openly mocking the Heroic ethos, Captain Bonner Fellers declared, "The day is gone when, for purposes of morale, one must assume the offensive with foot troops against modern weapons . . . today it is dead as slavery. If a commander is able to inflict heavy slaughter on the enemy and at the same time suffer few losses himself; if he can strike the heart of the nation with machines, morale will take care of itself."[101]

Whereas some Heroes viewed mechanization as a means to

restore martial skills and mobility to war, Managers saw it as the logical result of the industrialization of warfare. Major John Burns urged his fellow officers to shake off the "dead hand" of the past and recognize the implications of the "machine age" in which they lived. "We have industry changing the tools of war with lightening speed; and society shaping our human material—the basic weapon of war—to a different, untried pattern . . . It is a revolution, if we could but see it. Yes, a new technique of war is ready to break from the egg—a war of machines and of science; a war in three dimensions."[102] Tank pioneer Colonel S. D. Rockenbach maintained that "muscle appears to have reached the limit of its efficiency. The only way to supplement it is by machines, and there can be but little doubt that as the navy eventually abandoned sails and took to steam, so will the army abandon muscle as the motive force and take to gasoline or electricity."[103]

The army was only marginally better at predicting the nature of conflict in World War II than in World War I or the Spanish-American War. Despite the creation of a War Plans Division, despite the presence of arguably the greatest generation of American military leaders, despite a far better military intelligence system to monitor foreign developments, and despite an extensive internal discussion on the nature of the next war, the army lagged behind the other services, and even its own Air Corps, in providing a coherent doctrine for warfare. Instead, as Hagood commented, too many plans were "drawn with no knowledge of our enemy, and with practically no knowledge of what our own Navy proposes to do."[104] He might have added that the army seemed ignorant of even its own resources, for as another officer commented, the plan to defend the Atlantic seaboard was based on nonexistent fortresses, troops, and guns. This problem, this officer believed, arose from army planners' obstinate tendency to develop an "ideal" scenario rather than base plans on "the actual armament that will be available."[105]

With the possible exception of the Orange Plan against Japan, which was not finalized until the late 1930s, all the war plans for World War II date from 1941. Even the Orange Plan, generally conceded to be the only remotely plausible plan drawn up during the entire interwar period, was scarcely respected by contemporaries. In 1925 the assistant chief of staff noted that the plan completely ignored the unpleasant reality that Japan's probable course of action made it irrelevant. A decade later, the head of the War Plans Division stated that for the United States to follow the Orange Plan would be "literally an act of madness."[106]

Ironically, the Guardians played a crucial role in the realm of Pacific strategy, which for decades had been virtually synonymous with war plans against Japan. Since 1907 army planners had wrestled with the dilemma of protecting the overseas possessions, and particularly Manila Bay, against an opponent with the potential to land overwhelming forces three months before the first American relief expedition could arrive. For most of those years, planners in both Washington and Manila had focused on the tactical defense of Manila Bay. They ignored the navy's oft-repeated declarations that its fleet would never be shackled to a geographical objective—not even to a naval base which the navy demanded that the army protect. Further complicating the picture, while everyone recognized that Hawaii, or at least Pearl Harbor, was crucial to protecting the nation's western coast, there was no consensus on the strategic role of the Philippines. Imperialists like Leonard Wood and Douglas MacArthur bolstered their demand for a military presence with such nonmilitary arguments as America's duty to civilize Asia.

From the earliest days of empire, a succession of Guardian strategists had raised uncomfortable questions about the army's commitment to Philippine defense, and in the process presented practical military reasons for withdrawal. They had noted that ultimate possession of the islands depended on winning the naval war; winning the land campaign was therefore irrelevant. The Manila Bay fortifications were vulnerable to both air and land bombardment, and Guardians protested that defending the Philippines tied up essential resources needed elsewhere. But most important, as early as 1916 they had raised the specter of what might happen if, whether by its own skill or the design of the enemy, the Manila Bay garrison was able to hold out. The nation's precious battle fleet might be forced to undertake a hastily planned relief mission into the Far East where, at the end of a long and debilitating cruise, it would encounter the Japanese fleet. The result would most likely be a devastating defeat and complete Japanese command of the western Pacific. Unable to accept this grim prognosis, the army produced a series of unsatisfactory Orange plans, including MacArthur's bizarre 1933 scheme to ship virtually every regular soldier in the continental United States to the Philippines at the outbreak of war.

In the 1930s a core of Guardians in the War Plans Division—most notably Brigadier General Stanley C. Embick and Colonel Walter Krueger—urged that the United States reduce its military forces in the Philippines to the minimum needed to maintain public order. Establishing an impenetrable Alaska-Hawaii-Panama defensive perimeter would protect the continental United States and lessen the possibility the nation might be drawn into a great power conflict in the Far East. Krueger declared that both militarily and economically the United States was "virtually invulnerable" and exerted "virtual hegemony" over the Western Hemisphere. The only danger of war came from its "bungling policy" of provocation in Asia, itself based on a "dogma" that combined naked greed for Far Eastern resources with moralistic platitudes about the Open Door and uplifting Asians. He accused the navy of exploiting this dogma to justify an offensive mission while proclaiming itself "the first line of defense."[107] Supported by Chief of Staff Malin Craig, the Guardians made

Embick's perimeter the basis of Pacific defense, and in the process reconciled military with foreign and domestic policy. But they were not strong enough to prevent MacArthur's cavalier disregard of these plans or the futile effort to reinforce the Philippines in 1941.

While the Guardians' contribution was primarily strategic, the Heroes provided a concept for combat. They recognized the danger implicit in the organization-and-materiel-driven Managerial way of war, which reduced the soldier to the least important cog in the vast national war machine. The Heroes insisted that warfare was above all a human activity. Their study of the past convinced them that "the tide of battle in the future, more than ever before, will be in the hands of each soldier at the front. The bravery and intelligence of each man is more than ever of primary importance."[108] Although this belief often took the form of absurd declarations about mind overcoming matter, on the whole it was a positive development, leading to the crucial observation that "whatever the science of the superior commander, the genius of his strategic combinations, the precision of his concentrations, whatever numerical superiority he may have, victory will escape him if the soldier does not properly conduct himself without being watched, and if he is not personally animated by the resolution to conquer."[109]

Heroes recognized that in modern warfare soldiers were exposed to terrifying barrages of artillery and machine guns. They moved through an environment both deadly and empty; they had to overcome the instinct to flee from this carnage and instead advance into it. Walter Wheeler commented, "It would be impossible to pay men to do what they have to do in combat; war is not a matter of commerce. Men can be ordered to do these things, but military service is not slavery. Men have to desire to enter combat; their desire must arise out of conviction."[110] In short, soldiers were not naturally heroes. Each had a "nerve-breaking point," and victory or defeat often rested on the morale of "a few brave men, each of whom in his little sphere steadies his group."[111]

Although inclined to overvalue the charismatic commander's ability to impose his will, Heroes did recognize that confusion and uncertainty, chance and friction were inherent in combat. In this environment, a soldier's morale was as vital as his technical expertise; he needed to remain calm and focused, to improvise and adapt, and above all to continue to move forward against all difficulties to achieve the objective. This very adaptability in all ranks allowed soldiers to resolve problems and to learn from mistakes, and proved critical for American combat success in World War II.[112]

Given both the minuscule numbers of regulars and the nation's often-declared isolationist stance and deterrent strategy, the army could have easily focused on perfecting the techniques of beach defense. But partly from their own bellicosity and faith in the human spirit, Heroes confidently predicted that "attrition will be eliminated as a major instrument of strategy, and battle for decisive effect will become once more the main object of military operations."[113] Most counter-intuitively, they argued that the next war would be waged on the strategic and tactical offensive. In practice, their faith in the offensive may have led Heroes to minimize the horrific effects of weaponry both on the battlefield and to civilian society in future warfare. However, it also contributed to the army's ability to adjust to a variety of tactical and operational challenges in World War II, from fighting in the jungles, to the arctic, to the desert, to the beaches of Normandy.

The Managers' view of war was summed up by Major St. Clair Streett in 1932: "The aim of the nation at war is to subdue the enemy's will to resist with the least human or economic loss to itself. The destruction of the enemy's forces is but a means to the attainment of this goal. All such acts, such as defeat in the field,

propaganda, blockade, diplomacy, or attack on centers of industry, population, or government, are but means to this end."[114]
They drummed home the dogma that the nation needed to create a "military machine" that ensured a "balanced distribution of brain and brawn, both in the field armies and the supporting industrial organization."[115] From World War I they drew the conclusion that wars were more than just military struggles; they involved all aspects of national life. This shaped their view of the future and helped create an army in which some of the best and brightest officers, such as Eisenhower, devoted much of their peacetime careers to industrial mobilization. In many respects, from the 1941 Victory Plan to Eisenhower's conduct of operations as supreme commander, the Managers had a decisive impact on the army's way of war in World War II.

The army faced a considerable challenge assimilating the lessons of the first world war in preparation for the second. With hindsight, it is easy to spot crucial decisions made or unmade, branch parochialism crushing technological or tactical innovations, reactionaries dismissing visionaries, and a host of other errors and missteps that led to the defeats at Pearl Harbor and Kasserine Pass. Yet this same period produced the army's greatest generation of strategic and operational leaders—Marshall, Eisenhower, Patton—who would lead the service to its greatest victories. The interwar era witnessed enormous divides between military intellectuals over strategy, technology, the nature of war, and a host of other subjects. Guardians, Heroes, and Managers developed radically different interpretations of the past and visions of the future. Each school played an important part in preparing the United States for the challenge of World War II, but their stubborn disagreements and lack of consensus inhibited their collective effectiveness.

Yet, if a military institution's wartime success is the ultimate vindication for its peacetime preparation, the interwar period was clearly a high point in the history of American military thought. Indeed, compared to what has happened when the army shared a single vision of war—and then found that the enemy it was fighting was not the one it had prepared for—there is much to be said for the interwar era's vibrant if discordant debate.

6

ATOMIC WAR

World War II proved to be the army's finest hour. The defeat of
Germany and Japan was a titanic military triumph, calling forth
the service's greatest effort since the preservation of the Union.
The army's recruitment, training, equipping, and transport of
millions of citizen-soldiers across the globe, its development and
production of weaponry, and the strategic insight and operational
leadership of its commanders all proved its professional expertise.
Yet at this moment of greatest triumph, the explosion of the
atomic bomb at Hiroshima dramatically redefined modern warfare, making both the army and "conventional warfare" seem irrelevant.

Just when momentous changes in international affairs—the
Cold War, the Communist victory in China, decolonization, the
Soviet military buildup, the Warsaw Pact, reconstruction of Europe and Japan—required equally momentous changes in U.S.
national security policy, the army's status plummeted. The nation's military missions (and the bulk of funding) went to those
services that promised to project power globally—the navy and
the newly independent U.S. Air Force. Presidents Harry S. Truman and Dwight D. Eisenhower both sought to cut land forces

to the bare minimum. Pundits prophesied an era of "push button warfare" waged by a few scientists. A new breed of civilian defense and security studies analysts challenged the military's claim to expertise in strategy and defense policy. According to many in rival services, the media, politics, and even the general public, ground combat was obsolete.

Against this tide of neglect, military intellectuals struggled to prove the relevance of the army and of land warfare. They relentlessly attacked a national strategy based on all-out Soviet–American nuclear war, and they resisted the defense reorganization plans that grew out of this strategy. In opposition to "general warfare," they championed such notions as "limited warfare" and "flexible response." They argued that only land power could prevent Soviet aggression across what General Maxwell D. Taylor called "the spectrum of possible challenges" from brush fire wars to atomic war.[1]

Ironically, and with no apparent recognition of the contradiction, the service's own definition of war shrank to a single colossal land campaign against the armies of the Warsaw Pact in Europe. Struck by this vision, in the 1950s the army radically transformed itself, acquiring new weaponry and a new tactical organization but in the process losing much of its ability to fight in any conflict except atomic war. In the short run, the army's attempt to redefine national security strategy was apparently vindicated in 1960, when President John F. Kennedy repudiated, at least verbally, Eisenhower's vision and committed the nation to a strategy of flexible response in the Cold War. But this proved a Pyrrhic victory. What one officer termed the "army concept" of war directly contributed to the Vietnam debacle.[2]

In the immediate aftermath of the surrender of the Axis powers, the army endured what its deputy chief of staff termed a "destructive demobilization" that left it "relatively impotent."[3] Too often, poorly educated, badly trained, and ill-disciplined misfits whom one officer characterized as "the dregs of humanity" replaced combat veterans.[4] Regular army manpower shrank from some 8,000,000 in September 1945 to 700,000 in 1950. Much of this force was stationed overseas in occupation duties, and realistic preparation for land warfare came to a standstill. A 1947 feasibility study for intervention in Greece determined that only by completely disrupting its entire recruitment and training system could the army commit the two divisions that were supposedly its rapid deployment force, and even then it would take almost three months.[5] Not only manpower was affected. The government slashed military research, development, and procurement funding so deeply that by 1950 the soldiers of World War II's "Arsenal of Democracy" lacked tanks, antiaircraft guns, and ammunition.

Small wonder that collectively the postwar army suffered from malaise. Unsure of its future, bitter at its sudden decline, its intellectuals lashed out at rival services, politicians, the fickle public, and occasionally their own seemingly ineffective senior leadership. This last group proved an especially tempting target, since some generals had contributed to the trauma. Perhaps still influenced by wartime Chief of Staff George C. Marshall's record as "the organizer of victory," his successor, Eisenhower, continued to focus on priorities that far transcended specifically army concerns. During his 1945–1948 tenure as chief of staff, he and the General Staff immersed themselves in managerial issues such as grand strategy, national security, budgets, defense organization, service unification, universal military training, international relations, alliances, industrial production, domestic security, and so on. Each of these problems had important military ramifications, and collectively their resolution was essential for the nation's security; but they were far removed from the emphasis on ground warfare that had historically been the army's first priority. Moreover, Eisenhower and his staff were unable, or unwilling, to prevent the relegation of their service to secondary status, far below that of the air force in budgets and prestige.

In their efforts to organize the nation's industrial and manpower resources, the army's high command downplayed, if it did not forget, their service's self-defined reason for existence as fighting and winning the nation's wars. Lieutenant General James M. Gavin succinctly observed, "The army's big problem in the postwar era was learning how to live in the nuclear environment."[6] The service had to justify its role as the decisive means of combat in an age that saw the atomic bomb as the ultimate weapon. Complicating this problem was that, at least initially, many of its own strategists agreed with an Army Field Forces' study that "the possession of the atomic bomb and the facilities for its production is the most vital factor in United States strategic security."[7] In a 1946 briefing to President Truman, Major General Lauris Norstad predicted that "by 1951 atomic warfare, guided missiles, biological warfare and extended capabilities of air power will bring about changes in the composition and equipment of our forces as well as our strategy." The nation "must prepare for a total war" initiated by a "heavy surprise attack . . . designed to destroy or paralyze our abilities so as to force quickly a favorable decision."[8] Another army study provided a grim corollary: "This country must be prepared to employ instantly all means and methods for the total destruction of the enemy."[9] The army role in such a conflict was unclear. In 1948 Deputy Chief of Staff J. Lawton Collins frankly declared, "We couldn't possibly embark on large scale land operations against Russia."[10] Far from taking the offensive, some strategists feared the army would be hard pressed to defeat a Soviet invasion of Alaska.

The nation's war plans acknowledged that American superiority in airpower and atomic weaponry made it logical to strike immediately at the Soviet heartland and avoid bloody land campaigns on the Eurasian periphery, particularly when enemy

ground forces enjoyed overwhelming manpower and materiel superiority. Plan Pincher, developed in 1946, assumed the outbreak
of war in mid-1947. It estimated Soviet forces at the outset of
war at 4,500,000, of which over 3,000,000 were ground forces
organized into some 208 combat divisions. Within four months,
these would increase to 15,000,000, including 12,400,000 ground
troops in 650 divisions, bolstered by an additional 1,000,000 allied soldiers. Against this, the entire U.S. Army in June 1947
consisted of 990,000 soldiers; within one year it would dip to
574,000 and 10 divisions. Roughly half of these troops were stationed overseas, but few were organized into combat-ready formations. In Western Europe, the point of greatest danger, there
was a single under-strength and ill-equipped infantry division
and a few battalions of lightly armed constabulary, prompting
one veteran to admit, "If the Russians had decided to start World
War III at that point in time, hell, we would have been wiped
out."[11]

Pincher predicted that Soviet armies would rapidly overrun
Western Europe in forty-five days, press on into the Middle East
to threaten the Suez Canal, and then invade China. The U.S. response, after ensuring the defense of its homeland, would be to
launch a strategic bombing campaign on industry, transportation, and communications from airbases surrounding the USSR
while simultaneously establishing a naval blockade. In Plan
Pincher, and in subsequent plans, the role of ground forces was
limited, inglorious, and definitely subordinate. In the face of the
Soviet onslaught they would withdraw from the European mainland and attempt the defense of Norway and Great Britain. Only
after the nation had mobilized, and long after the initiation of the
air and naval campaigns, would army expeditionary forces seize
air bases and, if necessary, attack Russia through the Dardanelles
into the Caucasus.[12]

However much these postwar plans reflected military realities and national security policy, they held limited appeal for most army intellectuals. These military thinkers sought to replace this air-and-atomic-weapons-based concept of war with an alternative scenario in which land forces played a significant, if not dominant, offensive role. This was a daunting challenge, and for the first years after World War II they were frustrated. To create a distinct army way of war for an atomic age, army intellectuals first had to revise their definition of modern warfare to incorporate both new weaponry and the reality of a permanent Cold War. Then they had to demonstrate how the army's way could better achieve the nation's political and military goals than could all-out nuclear attack. To make their case, officers searched the past for immutable military truths transcending the ephemeral technocratic notions of war promulgated by the air force and proponents of strategic nuclear warfare. In so doing, they revived long-held beliefs from their three traditional perspectives on preparing for war.

The army had made a conscientious effort to learn the lessons of World War II even while fighting it. Both overseas and in the continental United States, boards composed of the service's top leadership reviewed everything from personnel to weaponry to future strategy. A host of staff officers analyzed, codified, taught, and disseminated reports on tactics, weapons, enemy psychology, and myriad other topics. Selecting the correct lessons of the war spurred much debate: should they commemorate the army's greatest victory or provide guidance for the future? The great bulk of postwar writings tended toward the former.

The service's official histories exhaustively chronicled the maneuvers of corps and divisions, and the logistical and administrative agencies that supported them, as they fought across Africa, Europe, and the Pacific. They were models of narrative detail, but taken together they created the impression that World War II had set for all time the standard for modern warfare. Many senior of-

ficers, particularly in the first decade after the war, also invoked
the purported lessons of the war for both inspiration and justification. Typifying their attitude was General Jacob L. Devers,
who in 1948 defended the continued relevance of ground forces
with the claim: "World War II demonstrated the invincibility of
the United States Army's infantry-tank-artillery team; any future
war would prove the same combination an even better bet, no
matter what the odds."[13]

Perhaps not surprisingly, the early army scenarios for future
warfare closely resembled the last conflict against the Axis. Similarities abounded not only in the plans' geographic areas of operation but also in force structure, military methods, and even a
projected common narrative of early defeats, mobilization, and
victorious offensive. The service's internal strategic disagreements
also paralleled those of World War II. For example, one senior officer unfavorably compared a strategy of fighting the Soviets in
Europe with his own Pacific-influenced "island hopping campaign."[14]

Each of the three traditional schools interpreted the war as vindicating its beliefs; each sought to incorporate its lessons into a
distinct vision of future conflict. The Guardians could take mor-
bid comfort in how Pearl Harbor confirmed their century-long
warning of a surprise attack. Their postwar disciples soon revived
scenarios of metropolitan areas blasted into smoking ruins and
the rapid collapse of the nation; the only difference was that the
Soviet Union replaced Great Britain, and atomic warheads replaced battleships. Their solution closely resembled that of the
Fortification Board: the army should devote itself to defending
the continental United States, albeit with missiles and antiaircraft
guns instead of fortifications and cannon. Opponents derided the
neo-Guardian view as "the Gibraltar theory" or "Fortress America," but it resonated in some military communities.[15]

For the Heroes, the war proved *"the supremacy of man over the machine*" by showing that "men, not weapons, make war and peace."[16] General Walter Krueger testified, "I am keenly interested in a very powerful air force, but . . . let's not forget that we are going to fight the next war with guts and both ends of the bayonet just as in previous wars." The atomic bomb might kill millions, but the great lesson of the last war was that "the best weapon we have is the American soldier."[17] Colonel S. L. A. Marshall's influential 1947 work *Men against Fire* criticized Americans' "materialistic concept" of war and their misplaced faith that victory was "a purely mathematical problem of counting men and machines and what is required to supply them."[18] Relying as much on intuition as research, he argued that in World War II materiel had been less important than morale, leadership, and unit cohesion, and he concluded that such intangibles would still determine victory in the future.

World War II also confirmed many of the Managers' tenets, not least that modern warfare was a complex challenge and required highly trained professionals adept at concentrating personnel and materiel at the decisive point. Future war would need to be managed even more carefully, lest it degenerate into uncontrollable violence. The Managers' view of warfare recognized, in the words of Lieutenant General Albert C. Wedemeyer, that the "delineation between military and nonmilitary activities becomes less apparent with each additional conflict." He noted that the Army War College had adopted a new definition of strategy as the "art and science of employing all resources to accomplish national objectives."[19] Much of the Managers' agenda was codified by legislation culminating in the Army Organization Act of 1950. The newly created Department of the Army incorporated logistics, procurement, personnel, budgets, planning, and all other facets of administration into a single, complex corporation.

In the late 1940s both Managers and Heroes began to stand

postwar national security doctrine on its head, by shifting the emphasis from air power to land power. Instead of the army serving the air force, Chief of Staff Omar N. Bradley declared in 1949 that the bombing campaign should support the "eventual climactic ground attack" that would "destroy the enemy's armies in large-scale ground assaults."[20] With increasing force, army intellectuals insisted that under certain circumstances and with the proper weapons and organization, the United States and its NATO allies could actually defeat a Soviet land invasion. At the same time, they launched increasingly vitriolic attacks on what they perceived as a misplaced national strategy of nuclear retaliation. Some maintained that destroying cities and devastating industry could not ensure such strategic objectives as economic and political stability, the protection of allies, and the containment of Communism. After the USSR exploded its first atomic bomb in August 1949, military intellectuals argued it was only a matter of time before it had an arsenal sufficient to destroy American cities. Once it did, the USSR could force the United States to either fight a conventional war or acquiesce in Soviet expansion. The only solution, as far as army thinkers were concerned, was for the nation to field ground forces that were better trained, better equipped, and better able to deploy to wherever the enemy threatened.[21]

Among the most enthusiastic participants in the creation of this land-warfare vision were two Heroic communities of the army, armor and airborne. Both originated in World War II and both claimed the mantle of the Cavalry branch as the new warrior elite. Armor advocates believed they alone had the necessary mobility, shock, protection, and firepower to win on the modern battlefield. Moreover, only their mechanized forces (mostly tanks) could overcome the Soviets' advantage in manpower and materiel by acting much as horse cavalry had supposedly done in the past, smashing though the enemy front, sweeping deep into the rear, paralyzing the enemy command system, and then driving the defeated foe back in headlong retreat. Armor officers dismissed airborne, and indeed all non-mechanized infantry: "At the very best they are but light troops incapable of sustained action or of standing against heavily equipped mobile ground forces."[22]

Conversely, airborne advocates insisted that the "greatest change to be expected in the conduct of ground warfare will be the use of aircraft to fly troops and cargo anywhere in the world. Only through flight can future warfare be waged in accordance with the principles of surprise, mass, and economy of means."[23] They imagined entire armies moved and supplied by air around the globe, striking at Soviet weak points, seizing strategic bases, and disrupting enemy concentrations, so that, in Gavin's words, "the fight will be carried to the enemy on his own territory and a decision gained."[24] He portrayed airborne troops as a new "sky cavalry" and criticized heavy mechanized forces as anachronisms, incapable of anything but a grinding and ultimately futile war of attrition.

Both of these concepts of future war glossed over the gap between vision and reality. Airborne theorists grappled with the conundrum, repeatedly demonstrated in both World War II and peacetime exercises, that forces light enough to be air-transported were deficient in manpower, logistics, and firepower. Unless they were immediately reinforced by all the paraphernalia of heavy units—tanks, artillery, communications, truck-borne logistics, and so forth—airborne forces could be easily isolated and crushed by enemy tanks and artillery. Airborne advocates overlooked that their long-range air assaults required such complete control of enemy airspace that the war would probably be won before they were possible. Moreover, such operations depended on technology still on the drawing board: gigantic multipurpose cargo containers; helicopters that could accommodate a company of soldiers; chassis configured for everything from light tanks to bulldozers; light infantry weapons that could destroy a tank with one shot, and so on.

And while armor officers might boast of tanks' mobility, range, flexibility, and firepower, in reality their way of war required not only tanks but also supporting forces such as mechanized infantry, artillery, and engineers. These, in turn, required such a large logistical and transportation infrastructure that armored warfare was essentially restricted to North America and some parts of Western Europe. Armor's ambitions were similarly frustrated by the consensus that the existing American tanks were "distinctly inferior" to their Soviet opponents in both quality and numbers.[25]

As with past visions of future warfare, military thinkers once again failed to anticipate either the location of the conflict that broke out in June 1950 in Korea or its nature. Army strategists had been convinced, as were their political superiors, that the primary danger was a Warsaw Pact attack on Western Europe. They had paid little attention to the Far East and even less to peripheral areas. Of the three martial traditions, the Heroes came closest to foreseeing the next war's reliance on morale, leadership, and military skill. But even their vision of tank battles and paratroop assaults proved only marginally relevant. The Korean War soon became a struggle of attrition; the use of firepower in small battles for hills and ridges was more akin to World War I than to the rapid, decisive operations predicted by military theorists.

The war's opening weeks dramatically revealed the army's lack of intellectual and physical readiness. But beyond providing both contemporaries and later generations with yet another graphic example of American military unpreparedness, the war offered other important lessons. To General Matthew B. Ridgway, whose charismatic leadership was widely credited with averting disaster, "Korea taught us that all warfare from this time forth must be limited. It could no longer be a question of *whether* to fight a limited war, but of *how* to avoid fighting any other."[26] Neither America's atomic bomb nor its air force had deterred Communist aggression or prevented the North Koreans and Chinese from maneuvering and supplying their armies. According to General Mark Clark, Korea "clearly demonstrated that the army must bear initially the brunt of any armed action that Russia is likely to initiate."[27] For the Department of the Army, the war "affirmed in the eyes of the world the imperative necessity for the ground soldier in war."[28]

Much of the army's interpretation of the Korean War was shaped less by actual events than by service priorities. Rather than acknowledging that future land conflicts were likely to be long, costly, frustrating, and indecisive wars of attrition, military intellectuals concluded from Korea that it would be necessary to fight a quick war and secure an immediate decisive victory. Other inconvenient lessons were cloaked in counterfactual explanations. Infantry officers depreciated the crucial role played by fortifications and firepower and stubbornly championed offensive actions and mobility. The Armor community overlooked evidence that American troops were already overly dependent on their vehicles and hypothesized that, if properly used, mechanized forces could have secured victory through maneuver.[29] Nonsense, responded advocates of airborne warfare; heavy tanks had actually inhibited combat operations. Had the army only possessed air-transportable fighting vehicles, helicopters, and more paratroopers, it could have struck at the enemy flanks and rear areas. Perhaps the most insidious counterfactual was Major General Earle M. Weaver's 1957 claim that had the army committed a rapid reaction force in 1950 it would have avoided the "slow, costly defensive" struggle entirely and secured a quick victory.[30] Eight years later, Weaver would be the chairman of the Joint Chiefs of Staff when the fateful decision was made to commit ground forces to Vietnam.

Other efforts to draw lessons from Korea were even more controversial, particularly the explanations for the army's uneven combat performance. The disastrous early days of the war, symbolized most graphically when North Korean forces quickly overran Lieutenant Colonel Charles B. Smith's undermanned and poorly equipped command on 5 July 1950, demonstrated the pathetic state of the nation's ground forces. In the coming decades, the army leadership would take as a mantra "No More Task Force Smiths," to remind soldiers they must always be prepared to go into combat.[31] Ridgway's sour observation that the American soldier had "dropped far back on the military scale from the standards of our Civil War troops" reflected a widespread perception that American society had produced a generation of males lacking discipline, patriotism, and physical toughness.[32] But Brigadier General R. P. Shugg blamed the army's own internal problems. He pointed out that the General Staff had once again failed to anticipate the location, opponent, or nature of the next war, that officers were unprepared and overconfident, and that much of the senior leadership was mediocre.[33] Such self-reflection was rare. For many, the war was perhaps best summed up by an editorial in *Armor* journal: "Korea's most potent lesson lies in the fact that . . . it is not the kind of war to fight."[34]

The Korean War allowed the army to more than double, from fewer than 700,000 in June 1950 to 1,500,000 in June 1953, with appropriations increasing at roughly the same rate. Much of the short-term increase went to Korea, but the greatest long-term beneficiaries were the forces in Germany, whose expansion from 80,000 to 230,000 soldiers was fueled by fears of imminent Soviet invasion.[35] With this buildup, the army now believed it had the means to conduct major land operations against the Red Army with prospects other than humiliating defeat. In contrast to the unsatisfactory post-1950 stalemate in Korea and the equally unsatisfactory undeclared armistice in 1953, large-unit mechanized warfare in Europe presented a potent mixture of institutional self-interest and intellectual challenge that would captivate military thinkers for the next four decades.

The army's enthusiasm for the European mission is illustrated in the evolving visions of future warfare offered by J. Lawton Collins, chief of staff from 1949 to 1953. In 1948 Collins dismissed any prospect of a major ground campaign until very late in the war.[36] In an April 1950 lecture he argued that if war came, the United States would rely on the strategic bombardment of the Soviet Union. American ground forces would probably not return to Europe for two or three years.[37] But three years later, he claimed that the United States and NATO, fighting a mobile war with airborne and armor forces, could stop a Soviet invasion.[38] Collins' optimism reflected a new army concept of land warfare. But the former army chief of staff elected as president in 1952 did not share it.

President Eisenhower owed his election both to his military reputation and to public discontent with Korea and the Cold War. Eisenhower was optimistic about the United States' ultimate victory against Soviet Communism, but he believed this victory depended on preserving the nation's economic strength, democratic political institutions, and cultural values. The Manager concepts he had espoused as an army officer found expression in the New Look. Partly due to fiscal constraints—nuclear weapons were much cheaper than manpower-heavy land forces—Eisenhower built up the air force's strategic bombing elements. Secretary of State John Foster Dulles declared that the United States would follow a policy of "massive retaliation" based on the use, or threatened use, of nuclear weapons to counter Soviet expansion. Both the secretary and the president were deliberately vague on what would constitute sufficient provocation to justify an American attack. Determined to avoid a land war with the far superior Red Army, and as a practical check on further Korea-type military interventions, Eisenhower cut the army budget by nearly a third in fiscal year 1955, making it the smallest of the three services. Between 1954 and 1960, regular army strength declined from 1,400,000 to 870,000.

Eisenhower stated that even before taking office in 1953 he had become convinced that "since modern global war would be catastrophic beyond belief, America's military forces must be designed primarily to deter conflict."[39] The New Look and the threat of massive retaliation were intended to avoid a nuclear war, not to win it. In 1956 he told the NATO commander that a war would be a "holocaust" with "literally millions of dead" but without significant advantage to either side.[40] Accordingly, his commitment to massive retaliation was something of a bluff. He gambled that if the Russians believed that the United States would resort to an all-out nuclear war, they would avoid provocations that might lead to it. Soviet restraint would not only defuse international tensions, it would allow the United States to reduce military expenditures, enjoy domestic prosperity, and support its allies, thus paving the way for the eventual American victory.

Because bluffing the Soviets was at the heart of massive retaliation, Eisenhower required the armed forces to publicly support it. But throughout his presidency the army refused to play along. It rejected both his strategy and his call to present a united front. Instead, officers leaked information to the media, challenged the administration in their congressional testimony, and otherwise kept up a drumbeat of criticism. For Eisenhower, a consummate bridge player, the army must have seemed the most inept of partners, constantly trumping his aces and ignoring his leads.

Yet Eisenhower himself contributed to the confusion by pursuing such a vigorous, even confrontational foreign policy against the communist powers that some termed it "brinkmanship." By his drastic curtailment of ground forces, Eisenhower left the nation with little military resources short of strategic nuclear weapons, thereby amplifying the danger that a Soviet-American crisis would escalate into the very war he dreaded. And even more perilous, Eisenhower continued to tout massive retaliation long after the Soviet Union's nuclear arsenal was sufficient to destroy the United States. Thus, he increasingly risked the Soviets either launching a preemptive atomic strike or using their atomic deterrent to shield insurgencies, coups, and invasions.

Just as Eisenhower's views of postwar national security policy were the logical outgrowth of his prewar adherence to the Manager's way of war, so the army's 1950s critique of the New Look incorporated both Managerial and Heroic arguments. In Ridgway, who served as chief of staff between 1953 and 1955, these two martial traditions overlapped. As a Manager, he dismissed the New Look as a misguided strategy of attempting to "use the A-bomb to save money."[41] Supporters assumed that atomic weapons would ensure a quick, easy, and cheap victory over the communist powers; Ridgway emphatically disagreed. At best the war would be a long and bloody struggle resulting in unprecedented devastation and ultimately requiring years of occupation and reconstruction. Instead of relying on all-out attack on Soviet cities, he argued, the United States required "the capability for *selective* retaliation . . . to apply whatever degree of force a particular situation demanded."[42]

Ridgway also drew on Heroic themes when he criticized Eisenhower's policies. He was appalled by how easily discussion of massive retaliation shifted to advocacy of preventive war, a strategy he viewed as a sign of "complete and utter moral bankruptcy." Once having initiated such an immoral war of aggression, the United States would "have to rely on conquest for survival" and would soon crumble from the "inner decay" that had destroyed all civilizations based on conquest.[43] It was the height of folly to base the nation's defense on airplanes and nuclear warheads, for "man is and will remain the essential element in war. Men, not weapons, make war or peace; men, not machines, win and lose the battle. If a war is to be won, the root and source of the enemy power must be seized and controlled. It is men—men armed with efficient machines and weapons to be sure—but in the final analysis, men themselves who will these things."[44]

Ridgway's successor, Taylor, who served between 1955 and 1959, extended these arguments. Appealing to Managerial concepts, Taylor criticized the New Look as both irrational and ineffective. Borrowing a business analogy, he maintained that the nation's reliance on strategic nuclear weapons had reached the point of diminishing returns. Paradoxically, as its nuclear arsenal proliferated, America grew ever less secure. This was because massive retaliation gave the United States only two options: appeasement or all-out "general war." The first would lead to eventual defeat and the second to annihilation. Taylor disputed Eisenhower's contention that the Communist leaders feared atomic warfare as much as Americans did. Both the USSR and Red China were land powers. Even if their cities were bombed into rubble they would still control vast territories and populations.

Taylor approached the problem of national defense with a Manager's eye for organization and policy process, which he often articulated in language reminiscent of an advertising agency. In place of the New Look, Taylor advocated a "National Military Program of Flexible Response" centered on "versatile, highly mobile" ground forces with "an integrated atomic capability" to deter or punish "local aggression" without escalation into general war. Since only ground forces could occupy territory, destroy Soviet ground forces, and liberate populations from Communist rule, the army was the "decisive instrument in the attainment of a victory compatible with post-war national objectives."[45] Moreover, it "could restore warfare to its historic justification as a means to create a better world upon the successful conclusion of hostilities."[46]

While he prized Managerial rationality and organization, Taylor wove Heroic themes into his argument. He publicly extolled the primacy of the individual soldier and claimed that an essential lesson of history was that adaptability, leadership, and morale were more important than weaponry or numbers in determining victory.[47] During his tenure, the army issued *The Soldier and the Army,* a pamphlet that emphasized the service's commitment "constantly to improve the moral, physical, and intellectual quality of its men" and "create for them an environment of decent, clean living, and of intolerance of vice, dissipation, or flabbiness."[48]

The Heroic-Management arguments of the army's senior leaders illustrate a service consensus on modern warfare that directly challenged Eisenhower's priorities. The army's primary doctrinal manual, the 1954 *Field Service Regulations 100–5: Operations,* advocated limited war and criticized massive retaliation for its indiscriminate destruction. The 1960 edition warned that the failure of nuclear deterrence might "conceivably result in disaster to all participants and to other nations," and promised that the army could prevent such a catastrophe by limiting escalation.[49]

Military intellectuals shared these views. Colonel Wallace Hanes declared, "To use nuclear weapons indiscriminately is to repeat past blunders. The way in which they are used will determine whether the millions of enslaved peoples are to be our allies or the unwilling defenders of Moscow. They seek liberation—not obliteration."[50] Another officer reasoned, "Wholesale destruction and obliteration of the Soviet urban industrial complex—except as may be patently necessary for victory's sake—is undesirable . . . we have learned, to our cost, how expensive it is to refill and vitalize economic and military vacuums, and to reestablish conditions which further the prosperity and safety of this country."[51] General Lyman L. Lemnitzer warned, "The absolute destruction of the enemy . . . would tend to defeat the purpose of war; conceivably, there would be no one left on whom the victor could impose his will; there would be nothing left to control except a radioactive wilderness, uninhabitable by human beings." He offered as a counter-strategy "Limited War," which he defined as "any form of conflict other than that which involves an initial massive nuclear exchange" and in which national survival was not at stake.[52]

The vagueness of Lemnitzer's guidelines was probably deliberate, for the army desperately needed atomic firepower if it was to stand any chance at all against the Warsaw Pact. As early as 1951 the Office of the Chief of Army Field Forces had concluded, "Enemy combatant manpower is the real tactical hurdle . . . If by mass destruction of combat personnel the enemy can be forced to revise steamroller tactics and disperse units more thinly over a given area, conventional operations in conjunction with tactical air can defeat enemy land forces on any selected objectives. Under favorable circumstances, the Atomic Bomb is a weapon which can produce mass battle casualties."[53] A 1954 study determined that "the army, facing the probability of being out-numbered by the enemy ground forces, must have weapons systems for delivering mass destruction weapons against tactical targets." Atomics would "provide the shock effect now associated with massed armor and infantry actions and massed artillery fire. But ground combat forces will be required, first to maneuver the enemy into forming lucrative targets and, second, to exploit the effects of mass destruction before the enemy ha[s] time to recover."[54] That same year, a General Staff officer wrote that the army must learn to fight "enemy hordes" and win. "A modern army, highly mobile, fast striking, and equipped with a complete line of atomic ordnance will meet the requirement."[55]

By the mid-1950s the service's redefinition of modern warfare to mean limited atomic warfare permeated the professional education of officers. Students at the Army War College analyzed the effects of nuclear weapons and wrote papers on atomic warfare that remain classified today. In what may be typical of these stud-

ies, the War College's 1956 Project Binnacle, tasked with outlining the "concepts and doctrine for future warfare," set as a goal
for 1961 some 17,000 tactical weapons in the 3-to-5 kiloton
range and 3,400 in the 20-to-40 kiloton range.[56] By 1957 over
half the instruction at the Command and General Staff College
(CGSC) was on atomic warfare. Indeed, the premise of that
year's curriculum was that "since the threat of atomic warfare
will be present in nonatomic war, doctrine, organization, tactics, and techniques will stress concepts for atomic warfare."[57]
Between 1950 and 1954, the CGSC's *Military Review* published
32 articles on atomic warfare; between 1955 and 1959 it published 139.[58]

The army's faith in limited atomic warfare was predicated on
two debatable assumptions. First, "the factor that precludes the
use of weapons of mass destruction against the homelands of nations—the threat of annihilation for both sides regardless of who
initiates such attack—need not preclude the use of atomic tactical weapons in the battle area."[59] This point was driven home in a
1957 lecture by Major General William C. Westmoreland. "We
must not work under any illusion that atomic weapons will not
be used should it be to our advantage to do so . . . atomic weapons can be used with discrimination without resulting in a mutual thermonuclear exchange."[60] The second assumption was that
the service already had concepts, tactics, and principles suitable
for waging limited atomic land warfare. Gavin had pointed out,
barely two years after the end of World War II, that the concentration of troops and materiel necessary for the Normandy landings would be suicidal against an opponent armed with atomic
weapons. His solution was to field combat formations so small
and so dispersed as to present unsuitable targets for atomic weapons, yet they would have sufficient mobility to rapidly seize strategic points, and then, just as rapidly, disperse to avoid retaliatory
atomic strikes.[61]

In the mid-1950s, Gavin's ideas on mobility, dispersion, and concentration were coupled with atomic firepower and long-range airborne and armor attacks. Proponents argued that mobility and atomics would overcome the previously insurmountable Soviet supremacy in manpower and conventional weaponry. The "destiny of the army," declared one War College student paper, was to conduct "multiple pencil-like thrusts, aimed at deep penetrations, each following a path of devastation created by the successive application of nuclear weapons."[62] Another officer envisioned future warfare as a "very loose amorphous battlefield of great depth with no clearly defined front line . . . in which relatively small units are constantly moving, fighting independent engagements, rapidly concentrating for larger but short and very violent battles, then equally rapidly dispersing and moving on . . . Atomic firepower is the king of the battlefield. Devastation of savage magnitude is widespread, and entire units disappear in the flame and dust of the mushroom cloud that is becoming all too familiar."[63]

Three futuristic scenarios illustrate the army's perception of the atomic battlefield. In 1954 Ridgway hypothesized a war in which the USSR would promise, at the outset, not to use strategic nuclear bombardment unless first bombed by the United States. However, if the United States attempted strategic bombing, the Soviets would incinerate NATO cities. This threat would restrict atomic weapons to the battlefield. As the Red Army invaded West Germany, NATO would conduct a mobile defense east of the Rhine using a variety of measures, including tactical atomic strikes to hammer the Soviet mechanized spearheads. The air campaign would be limited to interdiction and securing air superiority over the battlefield, making the air force's strategic bomber force essentially redundant. Ridgway maintained the "army family of atomic weapons" was capable of "highly accurate delivery of atomic projectiles at the propitious moment without unduly en-

dangering front line troops." With the Soviet offensive shattered
"by Western land power, the West will be in a position to deal
with the European Russians. Closing with the cornered enemy
and completing his subjugation is army business."[64]

A year later, Brigadier General Paul Carraway prophesied a war
in Central Europe. American "atomic fires" disrupted the Red
Army's columns, followed within two months by a counterattack
to "decimate their combat forces, and place the NATO forces and
others allied to NATO in a position to terminate the war victori-
ously." Such a victory would require "the destruction of the enemy and seizure or control of vital land areas," a task that might
take the allies all the way to Smolensk. Like Ridgway, he believed
that in such a war "the army will naturally be the exploiting force
and will bear the brunt of the offensive operations visualized."[65]

One of the most detailed scenarios of future war appeared in
Lieutenant Colonel Robert B. Rigg's 1958 novel *War—1974*. As
much an apologia for army research and development programs
as a literary effort, Rigg's book was stuffed with detailed explanations and illustrations of prototype weapons destined to change
the conduct of battle. It began with a preemptive Soviet atomic
strike on Chicago. Fortunately, army air defense missiles pre-
served the rest of the nation's cities. The United States responded
with its own aerial nuclear strike that shattered six enemy industrial centers. Facing mutual destruction, the belligerents agreed to
restrict atomic weapons to the battlefield. In the ensuing global
offensive, the army employed an awesome array of technology—
helicopters, flying platforms, drones, space satellites, vertical take-
off jets, antimissile missiles, and so forth—to annihilate Soviet
and Chinese armies and overthrow Communist rule.[66]

At the same time that they so graphically portrayed battlefields
dominated by catastrophic weaponry, army officers testified to
the continued relevance of Heroic values. According to Ridgway,
"Despite the remarkable developments in military technology . . .

it is still a basic truth that the only absolute weapon is man. Upon his determination, his courage, his stamina, and his skill rests the issue of victory or defeat in war."[67] Taylor told a correspondent, "The army is convinced that in the next war the basic weapon will be—as it has been in all other wars—man. In the navy and air force, the function of men is to serve machines; in the army the function of machines is to put men into action."[68]

The army's commitment to the Heroic ethos is illustrated in the 1957 pamphlet *Progress 57,* which showed an infantryman with fixed bayonet superimposed on a mushroom cloud, suggesting he was charging out of (or into) the explosion. Underneath, large block capitals proclaimed that the individual soldier "will not be replaced by any weapon" but was "the Decisive Factor in War" who "Destroys the Enemy. Controls the enemy homeland and its people." Indeed, he was "our Greatest Restraining Force. The Communist will think long before attacking the American soldier who stands physically in his path."[69]

In retrospect, much of the army's critique of the New Look was both shortsighted and self-serving, just as reliant on debatable assumptions and outright bluff as Eisenhower's massive retaliation. The very arguments that Colonel Karl T. Gould used against the strategic bombardment of Soviet cities applied equally to the army's tactical armaments: "It is the height of folly to assume that any people receiving the effects of [atomic] weapons will rationalize our intentions in terms of K[iloton] equivalent."[70] Colonel Arthur S. "Ace" Collins viewed with incredulity the army's faith in assaults deep into Soviet rear areas. He noted, "Airborne operations by their very nature form a circular pattern on the ground. This circular pattern corresponds to the effects pattern of an atomic explosion. This is perhaps the only time in military history that a nation is placing a major emphasis on a type of operation when it is known that the enemy has the ideal counter weapon in its arsenal."[71] Brigadier General T. J. H.

Trapnell observed in 1957 that the army's doctrine for limited war focused exclusively on destroying the enemy's military forces and ignored political and civil affairs. Anticipating a problem that continues to plague American strategic thinking to the present, he warned that the results of "quick military conquest" would "be transitory and fleeting, unless the gains are consolidated by other than military forces."[72]

These theoretical problems paled beside those the army encountered when it tried to turn its new concept of warfare into practice. In 1958 Major General Lionel McGarr, the new commandant at CGSC, declared that henceforth in all tactical scenarios atomic war would be typical and nonatomic war would be atypical. The ensuing chaos in the curriculum, the polarization of students and faculty, and "Splithead" McGarr's alleged insanity soon became army lore. Other schools had similar experiences. One officer recalled that of the forty hours he spent on atomic tactics at the Infantry Advanced Course, "I think we developed little understanding of nuclear weapons; probably we were set back in our understanding of them."[73]

Throughout the early 1950s the army conducted large-scale maneuvers to test doctrine, equipment, and organizations in conditions simulating atomic limited war. The results were not encouraging. Umpires in the 1954 Exercise Flashburn criticized as "unrealistic" the central premise that an airborne division could parachute into enemy territory, seize an airhead, hold out for a week until reinforced, and then break out and destroy the enemy. They noted that congestion and delays "rendered the entire operations tactically unsound"; enemy armor repeatedly broke through the perimeter, while the "airfield remained an ideal atomic target throughout most of the exercise." Atomic strikes were "enthusiastically executed" by both teams, but "the execution of all strikes was poor" and "the availability of atomic weapons to divisions tended to create in the minds of some personnel a ready tactical solution to any difficult situation."[74] Exercise Indian Summer that same year revealed similar problems. Implementing a new doctrine emphasizing mobility, dispersion, and concentration created a chaotic battlefield, which, when coupled with "considerable" delays in simulated atomic strikes, led to troops on both sides being indiscriminately nuked.[75]

In 1955 the army tested its proposed atomic-age organization with Exercise Sagebrush, which involved over 100,000 soldiers and another 40,000 air force personnel. Each service hailed the maneuver as a success, but the exercise revealed serious conflicts between them. For example, air force staffers so delayed clearance for army aircraft that pilots took off without authorization. In retaliation, a senior army officer ordered his subordinates to ignore all air force directives. In his report he accused his service rivals of designing "unrealistic scenarios" to present a "false picture which follows very closely the Air Force line that any future war will be won in the first few hours by air action" and thus justify its mistaken policy of "annihilation bombing."[76]

Much of this finger pointing may have been intended to deflect attention from the internal problems that Sagebrush revealed. To prepare the maneuver area for Sagebrush, the army spent several months and millions of dollars, impossible in a real war. To most observers, the army's new tactical organizations for atomic-age warfare had less firepower, less ability to disperse or concentrate, and less mobility than the ones they replaced. When units tried to execute the high-speed mobile tactics the army had devised to overcome Soviet mass and firepower, they quickly bogged down in traffic jams. Compounding this problem were faulty communications and a cumbersome intelligence process that sometimes took two days to disseminate information to field commanders. Defending forces quickly surrounded and destroyed the one attempt at a large-scale airborne assault, leading the army's senior evaluator to conclude that such operations would never be attempted in the future.

The exercise also revealed some serious unintended consequences of the army's focus on atomic warfare. Commanders were obsessed with the lethality of atomic weapons and failed to either attack or defend with determination, displaying a disturbing reliance on atomic strikes to resolve even relatively minor tactical problems. Equally troublesome, Sagebrush suggested that because even small-scale atomic weapons inflicted such devastation, it was doubtful, according to Chief of Staff Taylor, that any NATO member would allow their use on its own territory.[77]

Taylor's conclusions had serious implications, and not just for the foundations of America's defense plans for Europe. Only a few months before Sagebrush he had declared with great passion, if little historical accuracy, that "an army without atomic weapons on the battlefield of the future will be more helpless than the French knights at Crecy before the English cannon."[78] But, like Sagebrush, the gap between vision and implementation remained wide. In 1953 the army had rushed into production a massive 280-mm artillery piece that fired an 800-pound atomic warhead. Unfortunately, the cannon—soon nicknamed "the Widowmaker" for the danger it posed to its own crews—was too unwieldy for the mobile warfare the army envisioned. Within a few years it was withdrawn from service. Meanwhile, the army's program for long-range tactical missiles proved so successful it was appropriated by the air force. Its short-range atomic weapons were another story: the infamous Davy Crockett, a light, portable mortar, had the singular defect of placing its own crew within the blast zone.[79]

The army had scarcely more success with other essential technologies. Years of effort and millions of dollars went into the development of a multipurpose air-transportable vehicle for airborne forces. In theory, this marvel would tow guns, haul freight, carry communications equipment, conduct long-range reconnaissance, and perform other essential tasks for paratroopers after landing. No longer dependent on their backs and legs, paratroopers could rapidly move off the landing zone, employ missiles and artillery, carry supplies to scattered commands, and otherwise fight the war of mobility, concentration, and dispersion that army doctrine called for. But the end result was the unsatisfactory "Mule" that was not only inadequate as a transportation, logistics, or engineering vehicle, or as a weapons platform, but was also too slow to escape from tanks. Despite these considerable limitations, it was still deployed in NATO war games in the late 1970s.

The army was equally stymied in creating a fleet of combat vehicles for the atomic battlefield that could withstand blasts and radiation, be transported by air, and travel hundreds of miles through areas devoid of refueling facilities. They also needed strong armor and powerful weapons to defeat the more numerous Soviet tanks and artillery. Ultimately, the design solution required a vehicle built from some as-yet-undiscovered substance, powered by an as-yet-undiscovered fuel source, and armed with an as-yet-uninvented weapon.[80] Over half a century later, the army still awaits delivery.

The army's most heralded effort to prepare for limited atomic warfare, and the most widely reviled, was the Pentomic Division experiment, which Taylor unilaterally imposed in 1956. Replacing the army's historic regiments with five small battle groups, Pentomic "was based on the concept that tactical operations on a dispersed or porous battlefield would be conducted by smaller, faster moving, harder hitting, high-quality units which would concentrate quickly to fight and disperse again quickly to avoid the atomic blast."[81] As described by one of the first battle group commanders, the Pentomic division was intended to be a "light, lean, and mean" force able to deliver devastating firepower, including its own tactical nuclear weapons.[82] It would also, in the words of *Progress 57,* counter the Red Army's masses by making full use of "the capacity of the American soldier for assuming greater responsibilities of leadership and initiative."[83] Taylor reactivated his World War II unit, the 101st Airborne, as the first Pentomic division and appointed his protégé, Westmoreland, to its command.

Taylor's attempt at military transformation encountered considerable resistance. From the beginning, many officers believed that Taylor's pet project "was sort of being rammed down our throats."[84] Another commented that Pentomic was "Taylor's attempt at least in a public relation's sense, and perhaps a substantial sense, to bring the army into the atomic age . . . From the beginning it seemed to be that the division was ill-started, ill-fated, and hopefully would be short-lived."[85] Gavin observed that Pentomic's problems reflected its creator. Taylor was "a drawing board soldier. He comes up to all specifications, except the capacity for creative thinking, thinking through new concepts."[86] Others ascribed a more political intention. The Pentomic reorganization allowed Taylor to claim he had increased the number of active divisions when he had actually cut combat manpower.[87]

Whatever his motives, Taylor failed to recognize that both conceptually and practically, Pentomic was deeply flawed. Gavin and others had been working on an organization for lightly armed, widely dispersed airborne forces to maneuver and fight together. Taylor appropriated their fragmentary concepts and imposed them on the entire army. Predictably, Pentomic inherited many of the problems inherent in airborne units, most notably a dependence on other organizations for logistics and firepower, and insufficient manpower, weaponry, and logistics for sustained combat operations. These problems were compounded by inadequate technology, particularly in communications equipment, fire control systems, artillery, and air transportable multipurpose vehicles, which collectively and perhaps individually made it all but impossible to wage the mobile, firepower-intensive warfare that justified Pentomic's organization.

Taylor did little to address these problems. He did not even revise the army's operational doctrine. The result was that divisions
touted as the solution for the battlefield of the future were trained
to refight World War II. Nor did he reconcile the army's existing
war scenarios to take advantage of the new organization's unique
capabilities and compensate for its logistical and materiel weaknesses, so that the "tactical plans for the defense of Europe or Korea . . . could not have sustained the pentomic divisions for more
than a few days of combat."[88]

In practice, Taylor's reorganization was better described as dis-
organization; it created units more Potemkin than Pentomic.
The 101st Airborne Division's commander boasted that his battle
groups could fight independently or combined and were light,
mobile, and flexible, uniquely suited for warfare in the atomic
age. Moreover, because it required only half the airlift of a normal
division, the 101st was a "true ready force" able to stop "creeping
aggression" throughout the globe.[89] But this boast was deflated by
his admission that much of his division's vaunted battlefield mobility was predicated on still unavailable air transport, weapons,
and equipment. Meanwhile, the division could not function, or
even supply itself, except as part of a larger corps organization.

With such problems plaguing even Taylor's pet division, the
rest of the army was in much worse shape. The 25th Infantry's experience may have been typical. Their orders for conver-
sion lacked "critical information such as organization structure,
number of personnel, equipment, and effective date." The 25th
resolved the problem of insufficient equipment by such artful
means as declaring its tanks to be assault guns and its trucks personnel carriers, but even this artifice left some units "crippled."[90]
Displaying true can-do spirit, the 25th turned to training, only to
discover that its officers lacked both the field experience and the
education to command Pentomic units. Although the division
pushed on gallantly, it is clear that the reorganization created a

great deal of trauma, led to a rapid decline in combat effectiveness, and was more often honored in the breach than the obser-
vance.[91]

Ironically, Taylor's most lasting legacy as chief of staff was not
advocating a new model army prepared to wage atomic war but
making superficial changes to uniforms, authorizing an official
army song, and, more dangerously, extolling controversial strategic concepts. Initially, Taylor focused on modernizing conventional land forces to defend Europe, making the army's "readiness
for the use of atomic weapons and our readiness for atomic warfare" his first priority.[92] But he also insisted that the army was
unique in its ability to stop communist aggression in the Third
World, and in 1956 he warned that the Eisenhower administration's "fixation on the big war" ignored a far greater danger of
Soviet-inspired subversion and "brushfire wars."[93] Three years
later, in *The Uncertain Trumpet*, he declared, "While our massive
retaliatory strategy may have prevented the Great War—World
War III—it has not maintained the Little Peace."[94] Communist-
backed guerrilla insurgencies were undercutting the United
States' allies and threatening to destroy its influence in the Third
World.

Taylor advocated a strategy of "flexible response" that "suggests
the need for a capability to react across the entire spectrum of
possible challenge, for coping with anything from general atomic
war to infiltrations and aggressions."[95] But although he had discerned some of the conceptual flaws in Eisenhower's massive retaliation, Taylor based many of his own arguments on equally
debatable assumptions. He mistakenly claimed that the Soviet
Union had a dangerous superiority in missiles and that the army's
antiballistic missile systems could provide effective continental
defense. He grossly underestimated the military difficulties of defeating guerrillas waging revolutionary warfare and failed to appreciate the depth of Third World nationalism and anti-imperial-

ism. Most ominously, Taylor publicly reiterated army orthodoxy
in claiming that the United States could wage a tactical atomic
war against the Soviets without inevitably escalating to strategic
nuclear exchange.[96]

If Taylor, like most of the army, remained committed to post-
Hiroshima modern warfare, his sporadic rhetoric on the dangers
of brush-fire wars and insurgencies resonated with a small group
of military intellectuals. These officers agreed with a 1950 CGSC
report that "partisan or guerrilla warfare has emerged from World
War II as one of the acceptable means for waging total war" and
that it was "sound and logical" to employ irregular forces to ha-
rass Soviet land operations.[97] Korea provided many officers with
ample evidence that, in the words of the Far Eastern Command,
"guerrilla warfare in future wars will be an integral and not a special operation of the war effort."[98] In 1954 the chief of army field
forces lectured CGSC students that guerrilla war was one of the
most important techniques of communist aggression and that the
army must devote more attention to its defeat.[99]

The army's focus on the European atomic battlefield greatly inhibited its response to revolutionary guerrilla war. Many military intellectuals assumed that the United States, not the Soviet
Union or Red China, would benefit from the increasingly ideological nature of irregular components. Projecting their own values onto other cultures, they expected peasants and industrial
workers to choose Western capitalism over Marxism. In his 1952
War College paper entitled "Unconventional Warfare," Lieutenant Colonel Gordon C. Gill declared that guerrillas and partisans
represented "the oppressed and freedom-loving individuals and
groups in foreign areas."[100] This may explain why, instead of developing the means to defeat communist guerrillas, officers instead emphasized "planning for the use of enemy-subjugated people against their [communist] oppressors."[101]

An institutional bias throughout the army held that irregular warfare could not achieve decisive results on its own and that guerrillas who lacked support from conventional forces were capable of no more than "sporadic raids of little better than nuisance value."[102] But the army's greatest error was in assuming that an army theoretically capable of defeating the Red Army on a European battlefield could certainly suppress Third World guerrillas. Less than 1 percent of the army's post–World War II manual on operational doctrine was devoted to counter-guerrilla activities, and in the mid-1950s students at the CGSC received not a single hour of instruction on the unique political-military strategy of communist revolutionary warfare.[103]

The army's institutional reaction to unconventional warfare was to emphasize tactical adjustments in reconnaissance, security, and training. Neither training nor doctrine adequately addressed pacification, nation building, or civic action. The army leadership contributed to this oversight, repeatedly emphasizing the importance of large-unit land warfare. In this context, the difference between Taylor's rhetoric and his actions is striking. He often pontificated on the danger posed by local aggression and brush-fire wars. But during his tenure as chief of staff, the army schools all but ignored the study of counter-insurgency.[104]

A selection of 1952 Army War College papers illustrates the concerns of some military intellectuals that the army's response to the challenge of revolutionary guerrilla warfare was woefully inadequate. One officer argued that industrial warfare had become too costly and destructive to achieve political goals; consequently, "unconventional warfare becomes a vital and possibly decisive instrument of national policy."[105] Another warned that the Soviet-American conflict was "total war" in which the Soviets had the initiative. "There are four means of pursuing war—political, economic, subversive, and military—and in total war no one of these means can be neglected . . . In the current war, the political and economic potentials have been crystallized, and the balance now lies in the subversive and military aspects."[106] Colonel Bruce Palmer emphasized that the army must correct its misperception that unconventional warfare required only minor tactical adjustments. "Guerrilla warfare" was not simply a style of fighting, it was "the sum of all military, political, psychological and economic operations carried on by irregular forces behind enemy lines."[107] He warned that irregulars might not be able to defeat conventional forces on the battlefield, but they could still win the war through political means.

One of the most forceful critiques was by Colonel Peter Schmick, who questioned whether his service's institutional culture might render it incapable of responding to the challenges of guerrilla war. Although in every conflict the United States had both encountered and employed irregular warfare, officers persisted in regarding it as a "peculiar phenomenon" and "promptly dismissed it from our thinking at the end of [each] war." Army doctrine failed to appreciate that "partisan warfare differs from orthodox warfare in that it springs from the people, not from their government." Schmick also criticized the Managerial focus on organization and materiel as a solution. Money, equipment, and training—especially training in "totally ineffective" conventional warfare—was less important than "convinc[ing] the peoples of the world that something better is in store for them if they fight with us."[108]

Army officers drew a number of lessons from the on-going conflict in Indochina. Colonel John V. Roddy concluded that "the future promises continued US participation in anti-guerrilla wars." Leftist revolutionaries waging a "People's War" had "a capability for winning against great apparent odds by exploiting the intangibles—morale, social unrest, cohesion, and leadership." He was also convinced that "Communist guerrillas are not defeated by tanks, airplanes, and military force per se, but by effective political and military leadership and a genuine motivation for victory." The United States must stop allying with colonial or corrupt regimes, and it should provide military and financial aid only "on the condition that the recipient government demonstrate that it has the basic strength to win support of the people and utilize our aid effectively."[109]

Lieutenant Colonel William F. Lewis warned the lesson of Indochina was that "a well-led and indoctrinated guerrilla force is more than a match in this sort of terrain for a better equipped US-type organization, less well-led and indoctrinated." American advisers had too often been guilty of "wishful thinking" and "emphasized the importance of manpower and materiel . . . Not too much was said about the factor of relative spirit." In revolutionary warfare, *substantial popular support is the decisive factor . . . Foreign units tend to be ineffective, despite superior force.*" Therefore, "the only fit adversary for a specially trained and politically inspired force is another such force . . . Foreign advisors should be strictly in the background . . . Foreign organization, equipment, and techniques must be boldly adjusted to the terrain and the people . . . rigid adherence to US-type standard organization and equipment for indigenous forces . . . appears impracticable." In the future, the nation's military effort in Indochina should be restricted to limited materiel aid and governed by "self-interest and circumspection."[110]

In practice, the army's efforts in Indochina bore out many of the warnings of military intellectuals, particularly those against wishful thinking or attempting to transpose American military institutions abroad. At their best, the military advisors and the special forces assigned to train foreign military organizations demonstrated the continued relevance of Heroic values, adapting to local conditions and providing inspired leadership. But they were seldom in charge of the advisory effort, and too often their reports were ignored by superiors who persisted in seeing irregular war as an organizational problem—one that could best be solved by turning indigenous forces into carbon copies of the U.S. Army. This inherent conflict between Heroes and Managers imparted a schizophrenic quality to the escalating army commitment to South Vietnam, well illustrated in the dispute between Lieutenant Colonel John Paul Vann and Major General Paul Harkins. Vann, a brilliant if deeply flawed Hero, ascribed the army's problems in Vietnam to moral factors such as corruption and abysmal leadership. But Harkins suppressed Vann's reports, and those of other field officers, and devoted his attention to developing massive training facilities, supervising the distribution of tons of sophisticated equipment, and creating an army designed to refight the Korean War.[111]

Harkins' successor, Westmoreland, was a highly capable Manager who organized the logistical infrastructure that allowed the army to fight a large-unit heavy-firepower high-tech war in an underdeveloped host nation. He established managerial production-quota indices of success, most notoriously the "body count." His style of leadership, in which he conducted whirlwind visits to the field resplendent in his starched fatigues, resembled nothing so much as a CEO taking a turn on the shop floor. Westmoreland's methods were embraced by generals such as William E. DePuy, who made a fetish out of firepower expended and kill ratios. It was only much later, and only after tens of thousands of casualties and the virtual destruction of the host nation, that the limits of this way of war became apparent.[112]

If irregular war highlighted the differences between Heroes and Managers, continental defense illuminated those between the Guardians and the rest of the army. What continental defense meant was seldom clear, since it was applied to issues as diverse as protection against Soviet warheads and anti-sabotage measures. And perhaps its vagueness was deliberate. Regardless of the specific nature of the threat, army journals, aided by the popular media, constantly warned of the nation's imminent danger, but at the same time promised that an integrated defense system using the latest technology—surface-to-air missiles, radar, early warning systems, and high-altitude interceptors—could guarantee protection. The proposed system was expensive—as much as $12 billion to build and an additional $2 billion a year to maintain—but Guardians insisted it was essential. When the air force refused to cooperate, the army, in the words of Taylor, undertook continental air defense "unilaterally," even though the early warning system, the interceptors, and the national command and control system remained under the rival service.[113]

Like earlier Guardians, their successors touted the effectiveness of their weapons systems, the strategic importance of their mission, and their technical expertise. The mid-1950s Nike and Hawk missile systems were hailed as the saviors of the nation. In a 1957 article, Lieutenant General S. R. Mickelsen, head of the army Air Defense Command, proclaimed, "Success after success with Nike has brought confident predictions that a completely effective air defense of our important cities, industrial complexes, and retaliatory bases can be achieved exclusively with surface-to-air missiles—and at less expense than a combination of different systems."[114] Recruiters bragged, "The vital statistics of the Nike-Hercules and the Hawk are even more devastating than those of Jayne Mansfield." Nike in particular was "a real boon to the overburdened taxpayer" because it could "eradicate entire fleets of enemy aircraft" with a single shot.[115]

Because they manned these state-of-the-art weapons, latter-day Guardians again asserted preeminence, echoing the nineteenth-century Corps of Engineers. They claimed that all those serving in air defense met the army's highest intelligence standards, had the best educational opportunities, and were engaged in "a mission which means the life or death of our beloved country."[116] Over 42,000 troops served on air defense missions in 1957, and Mickelsen boasted that they were "not the average soldier," for

each one required "specialized training [that] is a distinction in itself and a rarity among the troops who comprise the ground
forces."[117] Drawing a direct historical parallel, he noted that the
public had always relied on the army for continental defense. Just
as seacoast fortifications had justified their cost by deterring attack for over a century, so now army missiles were "the Nation's
Shield."[118] In their elitism, their scientific approach to warfare,
their simultaneous fear and embrace of technology, and their
conviction that their program would provide the nation with security, the neo-Guardians were worthy successors to Totten.

The air defense community shared another characteristic with
their coast defense predecessors—a persistent inability to reconcile technological limitations with their vision of ideal war. Until
the mid-1950s, army antiaircraft weapons were obsolescent and
inaccurate, early warning systems virtually nonexistent, and ammunition of dubious worth. In a 1955 exercise in the limited airspace of West Germany, air controllers could barely identify half
the aircraft operating in the defender's area, much less shoot them
down. By the end of the Eisenhower era, army accuracy against
aircraft had so greatly improved that it became routine for Nike
and Hawk batteries to destroy airplane targets with a single shot,
a skill that was, unfortunately, of diminishing importance since
the Soviets were rapidly converting to intercontinental ballistic
missiles. Against this new threat, the army had great faith in future weaponry, but no present means of defense.[119]

The army leadership had an ambivalent relationship with the
neo-Guardians. While lauding the technological sophistication
of the weaponry and boasting of their service's commitment to
protecting the homeland, they nevertheless feared continental
defense becoming its primary mission. Chief of Staff Collins
warned officers to "be careful not to wildly excite our people" to
such a "terrible frenzy" that they demanded "antiaircraft protection for every little podunk in the United States."[120] Taylor char-

acteristically praised the army's role in protecting the homeland, while declaring it "a mistake to attempt to erect a Chinese wall of static air defense around the United States at the expense of our offensive means of reaction."[121] Nevertheless, throughout the 1950s the nation's great cities, and some lesser municipalities with significant political clout, were uneasy hosts to dozens of missile batteries, some even located near the moldering remains of the old coastal fortifications.[122]

Just as the neo-Guardians of the air defense community adapted to new threats and new technologies, so all three martial schools attached their traditional complaints to new realities. For decades military intellectuals had bemoaned the American public's lack of knowledge about military affairs, its declining martial skills, and its resistance to professional advice. This litany continued in the 1950s, despite a draftee army, millions of veterans in the public and political sectors, and a five-star general as president. As Colonel George A. Lincoln warned a military audience in 1949, "the national security education of the great mass of our people is only superficial. Ten years ago that mass consisted of isolationists. A combination of recession and a peace offensive lullaby from Moscow might break the short-lived constancy of the U.S. in its security policy and plunge us into catastrophe."[123] Officers criticized American society for its materialism, lack of commitment, apathy, ignorance, and individualism. Typical of these attitudes was a 1952 Army War College essay that ascribed both Soviet success and American decline to "the secularization of Western culture [that] has produced too many muddle-headed 'liberals' who lack an understanding of the traditional Christian moral philosophy on which Western culture was founded."[124] There were, of course, exceptions. General Lucius L. Clay opined the United States would win the Cold War not through military means but because of democracy's inherent social and political strength.[125]

As had their predecessors, 1950s military intellectuals identified specific groups as particularly dangerous. Politicians remained a favorite target. One general termed them "casehardened
power-drunk cheats and rogues."[126] Another blamed the media
for "insidious propaganda" that aided the "Commies."[127] Academics, particularly prone to communist subversion, posed a
threat because their indoctrinated students might rise to high
places in government or business. But soldiers reserved some of
their deepest scorn for civilian "whiz kid" Department of Defense
employees—what one Infantry School commandant termed "the
beardless youths and the long-haired bastards"—who had the te-
merity to question, and sometimes dictate, army organization,
doctrine, and equipment.[128]

The army's response to what it perceived as a dangerously weak
national commitment was multifaceted. Managers responded to
both media and public criticism through relentless public relations. As Major General Floyd Parks told students at the War
College in 1953, as a large business, the army had to "sell the
message" it was a good employer and vital to the nation. In this
context, every officer must think of himself as a "public information servant."[129] Managers and Heroes cooperated in military
training bordering on ideological indoctrination. In the mid-
1950s the army imposed a mandatory "character guidance" program for soldiers with the goal of "combating atheistic materialism and strengthening adherence to the spiritual principles of
the free world."[130] Students in the 1960 CGSC leadership class
learned that for the United States to win the next war "a national
revival must take place which will return to our young people the
beliefs in God and country."[131]

The 1950s also witnessed a return of the traditional internal
critiques. Army officers blamed their superiors for failing to stand
up to politicians, particularly Eisenhower, and for bowing to
public pressure to cut defense spending. They agreed their leader-

ship had failed to articulate a clear vision. Responding to incessant demands by his seniors to "tell the army's story," Major John Cushman wrote, "I do not know what the army's mission is or how it plans to fulfill its mission . . . At a time when new weapons and new machines herald a revolution in warfare, we soldiers do not know where the army is going and how it is going to get there."[132] Heroes charged that managers and bureaucrats dominated the upper ranks while proven combat leaders were shunted off to dead-end assignments. They claimed the army coddled troops with post exchanges, iced beer, and USO shows when what it needed was "lean and hungry soldiers" who could meet the enemy hordes in combat.[133]

Managers declared quite the opposite. Command experience was overvalued in the promotion process, leading to senior officers incapable of performing the army's crucial staff and administrative assignments. As one War College student argued in a 1955 paper, "The American army has undergone a revolutionary change in the last 15 years, yet many of us are still unaware of all its implications," particularly "the tremendous advance of technology without a simultaneous development of the proper means for managing it." The days of direct command and charismatic warriors were long gone. "Now the army is a 'big business' and the opportunities for command leadership are very limited in the senior grades. There is an urgent need for 'executive leaders' who can control the more complex organization."[134]

In retrospect, in the 1950s the army performed a crucial role in alerting the public to the dangers posed by Eisenhower's faith that atomic weapons would allow the United States to purchase security on the cheap. Together with civilians such as Bernard Brodie and Henry Kissinger, officers undermined the philosophical tenets of massive retaliation and initiated an important debate over national security. But the army's influence was largely negative. Its intellectuals were far better at attacking Eisenhower's strategy then developing a viable alternative to ensure the nation's protection. At a time when national security decisions were being made by a complex and cumbersome defense establishment consisting of the president, the secretary of defense, the Joint Chiefs of Staff, and a plethora of other agencies, army intellectuals continued to maintain their parochial, service-centric perspective on the waging of war.

In the 1950s, modern warfare, in its new incarnation as atomic limited war, restored the army to an important if not central position in the nation's defense. But what began as an option short of all-out nuclear general war, whereby conventional military forces might achieve national objectives without escalation into mutual annihilation, soon morphed into a doctrine by which the army, virtually unassisted, could wage a victorious land war. And the same officers who delivered devastating critiques on the immorality of turning Soviet cities into radioactive shells embraced "limited atomic war" scenarios that would have obliterated most of Europe, even if they somehow failed to trigger nuclear Armageddon. Equally disturbingly, these terrifying visions of future conflict were not delivered as assumptions but as certainties. The army, boasted one general, could apply "discriminating power" so "swiftly and decisively" that victory was all but guaranteed.[135] Another claimed that the service possessed a "full scale of capabilities—ranging from the rifleman's butt stroke to the guided missile's nuclear blast. Consequently, it can select and apply a degree of force appropriate to a specific purpose and a specific objective."[136] Even the nineteenth-century Guardians had not been as confident as that.

By 1969, when the army was mired in a bloody, divisive, and corrupting conflict in Southeast Asia, such hubris was long gone. Responding to a War College student, Ridgway all but repudiated his former advocacy of limited atomic war, and even of war itself. Instead, the use of military force should only be committed

to "*vital national interests* . . . where all the other means offer little
or no hope of being effective. Recognize that the world has radically altered since the days of 'gunboat diplomacy,' or when . . . a
small military commitment might be rewarded with large national gains." Ridgway concluded with the sobering assessment
that "the era we have recently entered is not likely to offer much,
if any compensation for military intervention. The primary effort
should be to seek a political solution."[137] Like his former adversary, Eisenhower, Ridgway had come to embrace the old Guardian ideal that the purpose of the army was not to win wars but to
deter them.

7

FROM REFORMATION
TO REACTION

In military parlance, Vietnam nearly broke the army. So deep was
the bitterness, and so broad the army's internal problems, that in
the decade after 1972 the institution all but denied responsibility
for the defeat. As one War College student rhetorically demanded
in 1973: "Can a military subordinate be held accountable for a
tactical error which occurs in the framework of a faulty national
strategy?"[1] Convinced that others—politicians, the public, the
media—were to blame, the army had little interest in analyzing
the war's lessons.

After both world wars, boards staffed by some of the service's
most respected commanders had examined the recent past to
determine the future of war. No such institutional self-study
emerged from Vietnam. Instead, the army hired a private con-
tractor whose study, completed in 1979, had virtually no impact.
The mechanisms that had traditionally incorporated the most recent war's lessons into current practice—the professional schools,
journals, and official historians—accorded Vietnam less priority
than World War II or the yet-unfought war with the Warsaw
Pact. By 1981 the realities of Vietnam had been so thoroughly re-
pressed that the service's official mission statement lauded the

army's unique "capability to close with and destroy the organized and irregular forces of any enemy power or coalition of powers; to seize and control critical land areas and enemy populations."[2]

The dominant army interpretation of Vietnam was well established by the time most combat forces were withdrawn. Typical was Lieutenant Colonel Zeb B. Bradford's 1972 article refuting the charge that the army should have adapted its tactics to defeat its guerrilla opponents. Bradford insisted the service not only had employed appropriate tactics but had "developed a new and significant form of warfare."[3] Whereas in past wars the task of the infantry had been to close with and destroy the enemy, in Vietnam the infantry's task was merely to locate the enemy, who was then destroyed by the "massive application of firepower from aircraft and artillery."[4] Bradford claimed these tactics were not only appropriate for America's strategic objectives but had achieved battlefield success. Indeed, the army's tactics were so effective that Vietnam could teach more about conventional warfare than about counter-insurgency. From an amalgam of Heroic and Managerial arguments, Bradford concluded, "The great strength of US fighting forces historically has been precisely that they have exploited their peculiarly American qualities and attributes. Highly mechanized and technical warfare reinforces our tendencies and talents and serves as a vehicle for evolutionary advance—counter-insurgency goes against the grain. We are a rich, industrial, urban country. Highly technical forces are compatible with our characteristics and resources."[5]

Colonel Harry G. Summers' 1981 *On Strategy: The Vietnam War in Context* forcefully argued that army tactical excellence had been negated by strategic incompetence and public spinelessness.[6] Summers, a member of the War College faculty, postulated that the United States, by mistakenly focusing on nation building in South Vietnam, had neglected to attack the enemy's true center of gravity, North Vietnam. He criticized those senior military

leaders in Washington who had not provided honest assessments
to their political superiors and had instead agreed to an incre-
mental strategy of attrition that they knew was mistaken. But his
main targets were the political leaders who sent military forces to
fight without clear objectives, without sufficient resources, and
without mobilizing popular support. Despite winning on the
battlefield, the army had been unable to secure victory. Frustrated
by the war's length and cost, and misled by their political leaders,
the American people lost their collective "will" and demanded
withdrawal.

The influence of *On Strategy* was immense. Within two years
of its publication, it was assigned by all the services' war colleges
and was generally accepted, both inside and outside the army, as
the official interpretation of the Vietnam War. Within the officer
corps, Summers' thesis was often perverted into a stab-in-the-
back myth that persisted for decades. Officers took as a mantra
what one general would assert in 1997, "When our army left
Vietnam, they had not lost . . . They were victorious in every tactical engagement."[7] Since the army had won, the cause of defeat
must lie elsewhere. Many military officers truly believed that
"America lost the war, not because of failure on the battlefield,
but . . . because of the inability to develop and sustain the will of
the people in support of the cause."[8] The service's Vietnam myth
fostered a sense of grievance that would have serious implications
for relations between the military and their civilian commanders.
General Colin Powell later claimed that Vietnam veterans still in
the military had made a collective moral commitment. When
called upon, they "would not quietly acquiesce in halfhearted
warfare for half-baked reasons."[9] For officers of this generation,
who viewed themselves as spearheading the army's reformation,
Vietnam provided a collective identity, based paradoxically on
both martyrdom and entitlement, which silenced both internal
recriminations and honest assessment.

This distortion of the Vietnam experience was facilitated by a coalescence of external and internal factors. U.S. policymakers, disillusioned with nation building in far off places and recognizing that Vietnam had estranged the United States from its Western allies, shifted their attention back to Europe and NATO. In 1969, one of the bloodiest years of the Vietnam War, President Richard M. Nixon issued the Guam Doctrine, declaring that henceforth the United States would advise and support Third World nations threatened by communist aggression, subversion, and insurgency but would not necessarily commit ground forces. Congressional attacks on presidential prerogatives—symbolized by the War Powers Act of 1973—further lessened the likelihood of direct military intervention in areas that were not critical to the nation's security. With the economy in decline for much of the 1970s and a widespread feeling that the United States had lost direction, the limited interest in defense focused on slowing the escalating Soviet-American nuclear arms race. Yet for army officers, the situation in Europe seemed as precarious as the late 1940s. While the army exhausted itself in Vietnam, the Warsaw Pact nations had modernized their militaries, particularly the armor, mechanized infantry, artillery, and air defense forces required for offensive warfare. Moreover, the Soviets had developed a new operational doctrine that seemed destined to overwhelm NATO's defenses and overrun much of Western Europe.

For the army in the 1970s, reeling from the effects of Vietnam, the immediate future looked bleak indeed. The end of the draft resulted in an almost 50 percent cut in manpower. Mirroring problems in civil society, the new volunteer army struggled with racial tension, drug use, and indiscipline. A 1970 War College study found an army-wide "professional climate" reflecting the worst aspects of the Managerial way of war. The officer corps was rife with careerists who put their own interests ahead of both the mission and the service. Junior officers repeatedly described "an ambitious, transitory commander—marginally skilled in the complexities of his duties—engulfed in producing statistical results, fearful of personal failure, too busy to talk with or listen to his subordinates, and determined to submit acceptably optimistic reports."[10] The study confirmed that much of the army's problems in Vietnam had been internal and stemmed from the institution's failure to develop officers with the necessary confidence, moral courage, and professional skill to rise to the challenge of war.

The service's loss of confidence can be seen in the 1973 decision by Chief of Staff Creighton W. Abrams authorizing a War College strategic assessment to determine the future role—if any—of conventional land power. The study group concluded that both economic and political constraints made military interventions unlikely in areas that were not absolutely vital to national interests. There would be no more Vietnams, no more infantry-dominated land wars in the Third World. The only region where the army had both a legitimate and a politically acceptable role was in NATO's defense against the Soviet Union.

To meet the Soviet challenge and restore its own identity, the army believed it needed to regain its prowess at modern warfare. Dennis Hart Mahan had found direct tactical parallels between the Romans and the 1840s U.S. Army. But by the 1970s, land warfare was a complex phenomenon requiring a lifetime of study and practice. As Chief of Staff Edward C. Meyer explained, "The challenge in applying effective military power in combat is how to orchestrate maneuver forces composed of over 10,000 ground maneuver elements, several thousand additional fire support, combat support, and service units working behind those maneuver elements and additionally several thousand air support elements. Each of these roughly squad-sized elements is about the size of a football team, and the composite force maneuvers on and over physical areas immense in size and diverse in geography and climate."[11] Or, to put it more simply, "When you start talking about what happens when an individual fires a rifle and another guy fires an indirect mortar and another guy fires a direct fire anti-tank missile system and someone else is flying helicopters . . . it is very difficult to explain what takes place on the ground to somebody who has never been in that environment."[12]

For the three martial intellectual traditions, the post-Vietnam environment posed unique challenges. On the face of it, the Guardians were the most affected. By the mid-1970s their historic mission of continental defense had evaporated. The army was committed to overseas forward deployment, its political leadership accepted mutually assured nuclear destruction, and the new Soviet ICBMs rendered most of the army's antiballistic missile defenses obsolete. In the mid-1980s, President Ronald Reagan's Strategic Defense Initiative sparked a revival of interest in continental defense, but it was muted by the army's recognition that "Star Wars" was primarily an air force responsibility.

But the Guardian tradition continued to shape important aspects of post-Vietnam army thought. The first of these was in the realm of strategy, most notably in Secretary of Defense Caspar Weinberger's 1984 "doctrine," which imposed strict preconditions before deploying American combat forces. Powell, its most prominent advocate and its probable author, offered the doctrine as a "practical guide" to govern strategy. The essential question was, "Is the national interest at stake? If the answer is yes, go in, and in to win. Otherwise, stay out."[13] To this simplistic formula, the general added the following corollaries: military operations should be governed by "the fast, overwhelming and decisive application of maximum force in the minimum time," and no commitment should be undertaken without a clear "exit strategy."[14] These ideas resonated within the army so strongly that General Wesley K. Clark declared "the Powell Doctrine" no less than "the American way of war."[15] Its supporters claimed it guaranteed the nation's armed forces would never be used frivolously and, once committed, would secure victory. Less admirably, by allowing the military to decide after the fact whether the tests of sufficient resources, civilian support, and objectives had been met, it absolved them of any failure.

The Weinberger-Powell doctrine illustrates a second Guardian legacy, the propensity to view war as an engineering project in which the skilled application of the correct principles could achieve a predictable outcome. Like the earlier Guardians, their successors believed the army's primary mission was to deter war. Should conflict occur, they favored limited military operations that provided soldiers and policymakers with "the ability to define and adopt precise, attainable political goals and achieve them rapidly with unswerving and bold use of military force."[16] Some placed their faith in new technology, while others sought to establish rules and formulas to govern military operations. Some, like Powell, sought to establish precise criteria for the use of military force. But all shared a conviction that it was possible to wage a scientifically exact, one-sided war, making the enemy no more than the passive recipient of overwhelming military power.

Vietnam left the Heroes in disarray, not least because the martial spirit of their opponents exceeded that of the army in the later stages of the war. Despite the finger pointing and the blaming of draftees, Jane Fonda, politicians, the media, and lack of popular will, the Heroes could not avoid the conclusion that their warrior ethos had been tested and found wanting. General Joseph T. Palastra spoke for many veterans when he condemned "the bloated base camps, bloated headquarters staffs, luxurious living, in stark contrast to the life of the combat unit out in the field . . . as long as a policy is set that says we are going to make sure that all of headquarters have linen on their dining tables . . . and live with a minimum disruption to the normal American way of living during combat operations, then we deserve everything bad we get in the way of publicity. That is the way we fought that war in Vietnam."[17] To the Heroes it was clear that only a reformation in training, discipline, and ethics could restore the army's soldierly values.

Like the Guardians and the Heroes, the Managers had to recast their assumptions. Their analysis taught them that "we did not manage the war in Vietnam efficiently or effectively. In the main, our organizational problems stemmed from the omission of basic management theories and techniques."[18] Between the all-volunteer force and the doctrine of mutually assured destruction, their earlier industrial concept of war, predicated on mobilizing the nation's materiel and manpower resources, was no longer relevant. But other aspects of the Manager way of war still applied to the new priorities. With an officer-to-enlisted ratio twice that of World War II—almost one officer for every five soldiers by the mid-1990s—the post-Vietnam army was increasingly committed to bureaucracy, to planning and process, and to measuring and quantifying. As one officer noted, "The leader's close personal contact with his troops essentially ends at [battalion] command, and the executive managerial ability takes on added importance. The skillfulness with which managerial traits are exhibited will either limit or increase the officer's potential for future assignments of responsibility within the military organization."[19] The Managers interpreted war as an immense organizational problem: how to coordinate "assets" (weapons, people) and "force multipliers" (intelligence, training) to achieve "total battlefield dominance." Significantly, in the mid-1970s a new "Profession of Arms" course emerged at the Command and General Staff College (CGSC). Second only to tactics in course hours, it focused on force structure, training, personnel, communication and writing, and other managerial skills only tangentially related to the practice of war.[20]

Managerial influence was behind the "training revolution" initiated by General Paul M. Gorman in 1973. Gorman formed a

joint army-academic analysis group and instructed them to identify and list all the steps necessary to accomplish a particular task
or mission in the most efficient manner. They then distributed
these lists in the form of training manuals mandating exactly
how each task was to be performed. The final step in the process, an annual evaluation, required soldiers and units to demonstrate their mastery of these "skill sets." For all the army's claims
of innovation, the entire process resembled the Scientific Management ideas extolled by Frederick Winslow Taylor in 1911.
Ironically, Taylor had been inspired to create his system after
watching industrial laborers deliberately slowing their pace of
work—a tactic commonly known as "soldiering."[21]

The dominant figure in the army's reformation was General
William E. DePuy, who took charge of the newly formed
Training and Doctrine Command (TRADOC) in 1973. If, as
one officer recently noted, "the army's intellectual rebirth after
Vietnam focused almost exclusively on a big conventional war in
Europe—the scenario preferred by US military culture," then
DePuy was its midwife.[22] A Manager with a pronounced authoritarian streak, DePuy believed he was overseeing a "historic turning point in the evolution of army forces" that required not only
new tactics, weaponry, and training, but a paradigm shift in the
army's approach to preparing for war.[23] He was convinced that
doctrine could serve as the compass for army reformation. It
would guide not only how the service would fight but also its
choice of weapons systems and its training procedures. Doctrine
would forge the professional identity of the officer corps. And
DePuy himself would redirect doctrine toward its proper course,
to the large-unit high-intensity conventional warfare of the sort
he had experienced in World War II. Determined to impose this
vision, he assembled a small staff of systems analysts and set to
work rewriting the army's keystone doctrinal manual, *FM 100–5:
Operations*.

Almost through serendipity, the 1973 Arab-Israeli War pro-

vided DePuy with a template for the future. This surrogate conflict between the US-supplied Israelis and the Soviet-supplied
Arab states revealed just how poorly prepared the army was for
conventional land conflict. It was short, intense, violent, lethal,
and almost the polar opposite of Vietnam. Columns of tanks and
mechanized infantry, supported by artillery and aviation, clashed
in enormous battles, inflicting catastrophic casualties in the space
of hours. TRADOC's analysis confirmed that not only were Soviet weapons and equipment excellent, but the Soviets' combined-arms doctrine was superior to the army's. General Donn
Starry, one of DePuy's most influential supporters, termed the
Arab-Israeli war "a fortuitous event" that "laid out for everyone to
see" the very "lessons" the reformers required to justify shifting
the army toward mechanized warfare.[24]

DePuy applied these lessons to the scenario of a future Soviet-
American war in Central Europe. He assumed political leaders
would be so fearful of nuclear escalation that they would impose
strict controls on weaponry and rapidly move to end any conflict.
He also assumed this war would begin with little warning, and
that it would be fought by conventional land forces, aided by air
force tactical strikes and interdiction missions. The Soviets would
stack up tanks and armored personnel carriers in columns several
miles deep in Czechoslovakia and East Germany, brush aside the
weak NATO defense cordon, and drive through the Fulda Gap
toward Frankfurt and beyond, overrunning so much territory
that NATO would be unable to mobilize. With Soviet troops
in possession of Western Europe's cities and intermingled with
its populace, the United States could not retaliate with atomic
weapons without destroying the very entities it was trying to protect.

Further complicating the NATO defense problem was that
logical military solutions—a preemptive attack, a fighting retreat
to a geographical barrier, or a defense in depth to channel attack-

ers into killing zones far from their supporting artillery and air support—were politically impossible because they would compromise West Germany's territorial and political integrity. Nor could the army return to its 1950s solution of tactical atomic limited warfare. As one 1975 War College study noted, "By the time the conventional situation had deteriorated to the point where nuclear weapons had to be used to halt aggression, the Warsaw Pact forces would probably be relatively deep in Allied territory, and their bargaining power would be strong . . . Given a possible Soviet retaliation, the weapons of both sides would create catastrophic damage to Western Europe, twice the devastation one would expect from the enemy alone. The effort to save Western Europe would truly destroy it."[25] For DePuy this frustrating scenario—termed "The Battle of the Fulda Gap" within the army—served as the inspiration for doctrinal reform.

DePuy's views were manifested in the opening sentence of 1976 *FM 100–5:* "The Army's primary objective is to *win the land battle.*" Barely acknowledging the need to prepare for "war in any of a variety of places and situations," the manual declared that "Battle in Central Europe against forces of the Warsaw Pact is the most demanding mission the US Army could be assigned . . . this manual is designed mainly to deal with the realities of such operations."[26] The likelihood of "a short, intense war" meant the army "must, above all else, *prepare to win the first battle of the next war.*"[27] And, unlike previous *FM 100–5s* that valued the human element over technology, the 1976 version declared that "battlefield effectiveness" resulted from weapons wielded by skilled technicians.[28] To turn these concepts into practical skills, *FM 100–5* provided a formulaic method, usually termed "active defense," for smaller forces to mass the fire of their weapons systems and inflict devastating casualties on an attacker. The emphasis on attrition was clear from the first page. "The purpose of military operations, and the focus of this manual, is to describe how the US Army destroys enemy military forces and secures or defends important geographic objectives."[29]

Although it was a radical break in terms of its methods, conceptually DePuy's manual owed a substantial debt to earlier martial traditions, most notably those of the Guardians and the Managers. As the Guardians used the War of 1812, so DePuy took as his model the 1973 Arab-Israeli conflict and from it extrapolated the nature of future war. And, like the Guardians, he envisioned just one threat, one scenario, and one appropriate response. *FM 100–5* devoted an entire chapter to NATO defense; it made numerous comparisons between U.S. and Soviet weapons systems; and its references were almost exclusively to European scenarios.[30] *FM 100–5* emphasized technology and tried to impose mathematical rules and predictability. Much like an engineering text or a nineteenth-century tactical manual, it was filled with charts, graphs, diagrams, and statistics.

Like the Guardians, DePuy emphasized technical skill over subjective factors such as morale. Soldiers were important largely in their role as operators of machinery. In active defense, units maneuvered principally to improve their firepower; victory was defined as the physical destruction of materiel and personnel. Faced with an attacking enemy, commanders calculated relative strengths and weaknesses and engaged in combat based on precise "force ratios." A six-to-one disadvantage was acceptable in tank-to-tank combat, a three-to-one for infantry on the defense, and so on. They assigned their subordinates "target servicing" goals, such as one tank to destroy ten targets or one battalion to destroy two hundred in ten minutes. And, like the Guardians, *FM 100–5* strongly suggested that if its complicated formulas were followed, victory was inevitable.

In its holistic approach, *FM 100–5* was simultaneously Managerial. The manual not only directed how the army would fight but how it would evaluate its weaponry, training, force structure, and professional skills. It treated combat commanders as mid-level executives whose primary tasks were to master their organization's materiel and methods, plan military operations, and train and supervise an unintelligent and unmotivated labor force.

DePuy intended *FM 100–5* to stir discussion in the army, and he succeeded. By making doctrine the cornerstone of army reform, and thus the authority on not just fighting but training and procurement, DePuy all but ensured that any disagreement with one part weakened the entire edifice. The crucial area of weapons procurement serves as an example. Active defense was predominantly a method for "heavy" armored and mechanized forces to defeat equivalent Soviet heavy forces. The doctrine's success, as one officer noted, "rests on the proposition that the U.S. weapons have a qualitative value which to some extent balances the quantitative advantage of the Warsaw Pact."[31] But the Big Five weapons systems developed to fight this war—the M1 Abrams tank, UH-60 Blackhawk helicopter, AH-64 Apache helicopter, the Patriot air defense missile, and M2/3 Bradley fighting vehicle— were not all ready for deployment until the mid-1980s. Every one of these systems went dramatically over budget and experienced significant problems in development and testing. The Bradley's difficulties spawned congressional hearings, several books, and a farcical television special.[32] Thus during the entire period *FM 100–5 (1976)* was in force—indeed, up until just before the Soviet Union collapsed—the army lacked the necessary weapons systems to fully execute its doctrine.

There were other problems as well. By 1978, nine of the army's sixteen divisions were armor or mechanized and required a sophisticated transportation and logistical infrastructure for sustained combat. Such a support system existed only in Western Europe. If the army wanted to fight anywhere else, it would have to build an extensive network of base camps, administrative centers, communications nets, supply lines, and a host of other requirements. Moreover, it would need to restructure its divisions and add the necessary combat support organizations to sustain them. To illustrate the difficulties this might entail, in 1999 the army required several weeks, 500 air sorties, millions of dollars, and 5,350 support personnel simply to deploy the 24 Apache helicopters of Task Force Hawk from Germany to Albania. Critics, both then and later, charged that DePuy's doctrine created an army equipped for a war in Central Europe but ill-prepared for any other conflict.

Military reformers, particularly the advocates of "maneuver warfare," also challenged *FM 100–5*. A mélange of civilian defense theorists, military dissidents, politicians, and followers of the air force iconoclast John Boyd collectively claimed a unique ability to interpret history, assess technology, and promulgate strategy. In their view, active defense was symptomatic of a flawed army approach to war that was overly reliant on firepower, linear formations, and overwhelming resources. They championed an alternative approach based on rapid action, dislocation and disruption, mobility, exploitation, and quick and precise strikes at physical and psychological targets. Their army critics ridiculed their selective use of history—"if you study half a war, you will probably become half a warrior"—and their blithe confidence that concepts designed for individual combat between airplanes could be easily applied to campaign planning.[33] Whether their influence on national defense policy was as great as they claimed, military reformers did force the army to justify its doctrine to Congress, the defense analysis/security studies community, and the press.

This external critique paralleled a growing recognition within the army that *FM 100–5* rested on flawed concepts. Chief of Staff Meyer, who served from 1979 to 1983, pushed for a major revision of operational doctrine. In his view, DePuy's attempt to win a battle of materiel with the Soviets ignored the American forces' limited means. As he pungently quipped, "We couldn't fight an attrition war if we wanted to today. We'd be the first attritted!"[34] Even before the botched Iranian hostage rescue attempt, Meyer warned of the "shibboleth" of the "Fulda Gap Syndrome," of "focusing in too much on the . . . greatest scenario and not maintaining sufficient flexibility—of mind, of design, of capability—to react elsewhere."[35] He insisted the army must prepare to respond to a "spectrum of conflict" ranging "from terrorism to insurgency to highly intense conventional warfare." The nation's security required not only the heavy armored phalanxes in Central Europe but also light, globally deployable expeditionary forces ready for immediate combat, since "the critical phase of the conflict is likely to take place within the first few weeks as enemy forces attempt a quick, decisive victory."[36]

In 1981 Meyer authorized *FM 100–1: The Army,* and in the process challenged some of DePuy's most fundamental ideas. *FM 100–5 (1976)* defined the army's primary mission as winning the first battle through mechanized conflict in Europe. In contrast, *FM 100–1* described four distinct types of war, including unconventional war and revolutionary war. And it emphasized the military's responsibility to deter and control conflicts as well as win the first battle.[37] Deliberately or not, *FM 100–1* placed the army's mission statement at odds with its doctrine of how to conduct warfare.

Meyer's subversion of *FM 100–5* addressed his fear that the doctrine inhibited the army's recovery from Vietnam. Ironically, although DePuy was personally innovative, open to new ideas, and tolerant of dissent, both the manual and the way he disseminated his doctrine throughout the service was through top-down directive.[38] In training, active defense was often translated into a rigid adherence to force ratios and target servicing, as if combat was merely an arcade shooting game with real bullets. As the post-Vietnam survey at the War College had shown, the army's professional culture was already prone to micromanagement and to holding subordinates to a rigid zero-defects standard. DePuy's doctrine and training methods reinforced this, while at the same time demanding these same subordinates behave as Heroes, that they fight outnumbered and win, accept risks, anticipate, adjust, and react to a mobile, fluid, and violent battlefield.

In a letter to his fellow generals, Meyer indirectly addressed the long-term effects of DePuy's reforms: "Frankly, I am troubled when I observe apparently competent officers . . . who fail to scrutinize rather basic but critical assumptions underlying our plans, or who substitute program guidance in situations which clearly demand military judgment."[39] He was even more direct in a 1981 speech to the Army War College. A recent visit to a joint deployment task force had left him "shaken at the ineptitude of many of our military in contingency planning. Shaken in the fact that the senior leaders weren't teaching . . . [Shaken that we] had become so focused on specifics we weren't able to apply principles." Determined to prevent this slide, Meyer told the students that their curriculum would now "focus on broader issues and principles that will stand you in good stead regardless of whether or not the enemy attacks frontally in the Fulda Gap or whether the attack comes elsewhere as might be more likely."[40]

Meyer's concerns were supported by a growing body of evidence from Europe. Starry, originally one of the strongest advocates of *FM 100–5 (1976),* had drawn different lessons from the Arab-Israeli War, most notably the importance of Heroic intangibles such as leadership, discipline, and an offensive spirit. He soon discovered a number of fatal flaws in the doctrine while commanding V Corps in West Germany in 1976. One of the most serious was that the officers charged with its execution had no faith in it, and referred to themselves as "speed bumps on the way to the Rhine."[41]

Starry's field tests and simulations demonstrated that active defense resulted in uncoordinated combat, predictable tactics, and piecemeal destruction. Even if a battalion or division repelled the first attack, it could not counterattack, maneuver, or otherwise avert destruction by the following Soviet echelons. In a best-case scenario—with two days warning to deploy, blow bridges, and build barriers—V Corps might be able to hold for six days, but at a cost of half its personnel and equipment. In the words of Starry's successor, "The sum total of it is that we are not ready right now to fight sustained combat in Europe. We could do well the first day or two and then we would have shot our wad."[42] Starry concluded that such a complex and kinetic battlefield required a corps headquarters to coordinate the "central battle" against the first Soviet attack with the "deep battle" against the enemy's follow-up echelons. Indeed, the deep battle stretched so far back—over fifty miles—that fighting it required a joint army-air force doctrine.

Starry's return from Europe in 1977 to command TRADOC placed him in a unique position to revise *FM 100–5*. Fortunately, CGSC, which the authoritarian DePuy had virtually cut out of the doctrine-writing process, now contained a core of brilliant officers such as colonels Huba Wass de Czege and L. D. Holder. They embraced the challenge of revision. The difference in both tone and substance of the resulting *FM 100–5: Operations (1982)*, often termed "AirLand Battle," was so great that some took it for another doctrinal revolution. In a most unDePuyian manner, the new manual declared, "There is no simple formula for winning wars. Defeating enemy forces in battle will not always insure victory."[43] Throughout the text, DePuy's most sacred concepts were modified or discarded. "Force ratios" and firepower were important, but the outcome of battle also depended on "intangible factors" such as training, morale, and determination. And whereas the 1976 manual was predicated on defensive, attrition warfare, the 1982 version extolled "maneuver," allowing the commander to "use the advantages of surprise, psychological shock, position, and momentum which enable smaller forces to defeat larger ones."[44]

FM 100–5 (1982) introduced "deep battle" and "deep attack" to disrupt a Soviet second or follow-up attack with air force and army aviation (hence the term AirLand Battle). It incorporated a Managerial solution of decentralized command at the lower tactical levels with corps direction at the higher, and relied on "synchronization"—an "all pervading unity of effort throughout the force" to magnify the impact of individual efforts toward the collective objective. The size and complexity of AirLand Battle required a new "level" of war—the operational—which the Managerial authors defined as using "available military resources to attain strategic goals within a theater of war. More simply, it is the theory of larger unit operations." But the revised doctrine extolled Heroic values as well, declaring "improvisation, initiative, and aggressiveness—the traits that have historically distinguished the American soldier—must be particularly strong in our leaders."[45]

From its inception, army officers interpreted *FM 100–5 (1982)* as decisive, and perhaps the apogee of the post-Vietnam army's reformation, so much so that with its publication, "the doctrinal revolution was over."[46] Slightly revised in 1986, AirLand Battle was the doctrine executed, at least in theory, by the army in Grenada (Operation Urgent Fury) in 1983, in Panama (Operation Just Cause) in 1989, and the Gulf War (Operation Desert Storm) in 1991. But most of what seemed revolutionary in AirLand Battle were operational differences with DePuy's 1976 doctrine. Their common focus on a great land conflict in Central Europe made Active Defense and AirLand Battle far more similar than different. As Lieutenant Colonel Richard M. Swain noted in 1987, AirLand Battle "restored the army's confidence in its own doctrine for warfighting," but it also constrained the army's view to "continental war between two modern superpowers."[47]

From the mid-1970s until the end of the Cold War, the army's new version of modern warfare was taught or, perhaps more accurately, indoctrinated. Every officer who passed through the CGSC, and thus almost every officer who would wear a general's stars, memorized Soviet organization and doctrine, played variations of "The Battle of the Fulda Gap," and took military history courses that focused, in excruciating detail, on World War II corps and division operations in Europe. Subjects falling outside this unilateral approach to war were ignored or co-opted into it. Thus, contingency exercises based on the Middle East, Korea, or North Africa rapidly escalated into conventional warfare and soon required the deployment of an army corps to wage AirLand Battle. Even in the late 1980s, when it was clear that the Soviet Union was suffering from severe internal economic problems and its military was hard put to win even a limited war in Afghanistan, CGSC's focus remained fixed on NATO defense, Soviet military power, and large-scale conventional land warfare.[48] Just when its doctrine called for increasing flexibility and adaptability, the army's own concept of war was becoming more rigid and specialized.

The army's identification with its new definition of modern warfare can also be seen in the evolution of the elite School of Advanced Military Studies (SAMS) in 1983. The school owed its origin to TRADOC commander Lieutenant General William R. Richardson and to Wass de Czege, who both believed that CGSC was too focused on tactics and procedures and that its pedagogical methods were inherently flawed. As Meyer once remarked, CGSC provided students with a "handy-dandy checklist."[49] Through months of reiterative exercises, it taught officers the practical skills they needed for their next assignment. But this tradecraft came at some cost; in many courses a heavy workload and rote learning substituted for intellectual stimulation. A culture in which the students played games like "Buzzword Bingo" in the "Big Blue Bedroom" also hindered the development of the innovative staff officers needed to implement AirLand Battle.[50]

Its founders intended SAMS to serve as the equivalent of a "masters degree in warfighting."[51] It offered a rigorous education in the tactical and operational levels of warfare, staff procedures, planning, and problem solving. Indirectly, SAMS signified to the officer corps that the army rewarded intellectual brilliance as much as physical fitness. Through extensive study of division and corps battle and campaign planning, by immersion in military history and theory, and from their own research, SAMS students identified, explored, and sought to resolve the complex problems of land warfare. Upon graduation, they were assigned immediately to demanding but career-enhancing high-level planning staffs, giving them influence and exposure far beyond their military rank. SAMS graduates were expected to educate their fellow officers, and their superiors, on the need to direct war plans toward operational goals, and thus ensure that the cumulative result of battles and campaigns was strategic victory. In the 1980s, their intellectual ability was displayed in a growing corpus of research papers on specific problems related to operational art, AirLand Battle doctrine, equipment, force structure, and so on. After the 1991 Gulf War, the army hailed a cadre of SAMS students as the "Jedi Knights" who planned the victorious campaign.

Yet at its heart, SAMS was essentially an honors version of the CGSC curriculum. The papers that students wrote, the exercises they planned, the military theorists they read, indeed their entire education was directed at mastering modern warfare. Moreover, SAMS clung to this vision of warfare even in the face of evidence that the army was far more likely to encounter other ways of war. As one student admitted in 1998, in the fifteen years since the school's inception, American military forces were committed to eleven significant operations, but only Desert Storm resembled any conflict SAMS taught its students to fight.[52]

SAMS was only one example of how the army's fixation on its new interpretation of modern warfare led it to ignore other forms of conflict, including irregular warfare. Even the terms assigned to irregular warfare in the three decades after Vietnam reflect its low status: Internal Defense and Development (IDAD); Low-Intensity Conflict (LIC); and Military Operations Other Than War (MOOTW). Despite much rhetoric from senior officers about flexibility, power projection, and mobility, Lieutenant Colonel Donald B. Vought's 1977 comment that "an observer could be left with the impression that *the defense establishment does not recognize irregular or low-intensity conflict as a legitimate form of conflict*" still described much of the army.[53] And while the 1982 and 1986 versions of *FM 100–5* claimed to incorporate unconventional warfare into doctrine, the treatment was so superficial that the 1986 edition's specific references totaled barely a page.[54]

The army schools reinforced the service's neglect of alternatives to large-unit conventional conflict in Central Europe. Indeed, until the 1990s, it was possible for officers to pass through their entire professional education—branch school, CGSC, and the Army War College—and acquire only the most rudimentary appreciation of irregular warfare. In 1973 the War College dropped the required five-week course on unconventional warfare introduced in 1967 as a response to Vietnam. For the next two decades, this topic would be addressed only tangentially, as part of the military strategy course. During this same period, the core curriculum at the CGSC allocated unconventional warfare a fraction of the hours devoted to large-unit tactics. The class of 1982 received only 8 hours of instruction in low-intensity conflict out of a total of 482 in the core curriculum; the class of 1990 received 39 hours out of 672. Even these statistics are deceptive. In some years the irregular warfare component was tossed into courses on joint or special operations. In other years, the assigned contingency scenario soon escalated into full-scale conventional war.[55]

Another measure of continental warfare's dominance was the army's effort to create light forces. Reacting to a series of crises, including oil embargos and the Soviet invasion of Afghanistan, in 1980 President Jimmy Carter committed the United States to securing access to the Middle East oil fields. To support this doctrine, he authorized the creation of the Rapid Deployment Joint Task Force that, according to its supporters' enthusiastic predictions, would be able to deploy 200,000 troops to the Middle East. Chief of Staff Meyer, charged with turning Carter's initiative into a reality, envisioned the light force as a mix of rapidly deployable mechanized vehicles and infantry able to defeat enemies equipped with modern Soviet equipment. But the light force initiative soon evolved into something quite different. Meyer's successor, John A. Wickham, issued *White Paper, 1984: The Light Infantry Divisions,* which promised "offensively oriented" and "highly deployable, hard hitting" units of 10,000 soldiers "organized for a wide range of missions world-wide, particularly where close fighting terrain exists." Wickham believed that new technology and "soldier power"—a Heroic construct that combined morale and leadership—provided the divisions a "crucial edge" in combat.[56] As he recalled, "What I wanted to try to do was create more combat capability with this small army and to demonstrate more deterrence. To make the army more warrior oriented."[57]

Although light infantry divisions were often justified on the strength of their ability to intervene in small wars and insurgencies, throughout the 1980s the majority of their training, doctrine, and equipment were largely directed at fighting AirLand Battle in Central Europe. And since light infantry divisions were unable to withstand Soviet tanks—a humiliation repeatedly demonstrated in maneuvers—they were deployed to woods and towns, assigned to protect essential posts and depots, and otherwise free the mechanized units for the decisive battles. Critics castigated

Wickham's divisions as "Not Light Enough to Get There, Not Heavy Enough to Win," but they missed the essential point: the army's European fixation had swallowed up a force created for expeditionary service and small wars.[58]

Training, and particularly training at the National Training Center (NTC) at Fort Irwin, California, further cemented the service's unilateral vision of warfare. This multi-billion-dollar facility opened in 1982. It employed laser weapons to precisely calibrate damage (so that a rifle could not destroy a tank) and teams of observers to conduct immediate on-site seminars. Cameras and computers recorded the words and actions of individuals and units engaged in combat against a surrogate Soviet mechanized force (the Krasnovians). Armor, mechanized, and even light units rotated through the NTC, conducting tactical exercises (or missions) that simulated the violent and intensive combat environment expected in a war with the Soviets.

Widely credited with preparing the army for victory in Desert Storm, the NTC further focused the officer corps toward large-unit mechanized operations and the winning of battles. By the mid-1980s, rotation through the NTC largely controlled an officer's command tour and a tactical unit's training cycle. The training center captured the army's military imagination as well. One officer urged his colleagues to remember that "your trip to the NTC is more than a mere training event—it's World War III."[59] Others wrote graphic accounts of their NTC experiences resembling wartime memoirs.

Ironically, some evidence suggests that this preoccupation with pseudo-war at the NTC actually inhibited preparation for real war. Daniel P. Bolger, who went through both the NTC and the light infantry equivalent, the Joint Readiness Training Center (JRTC), noted that American units soon learned their equipment and doctrine were sufficient to defeat Krasnovian tanks but were largely ineffective against small bands of guerrillas who enjoyed the passive support of the population.[60] In another instance, a unit recently returned from Panama was so intent on preparing for its upcoming NTC rotation that it devoted no attention to analyzing its recent experience. A few months later, in the streets of Panama City as part of Operation Just Cause, it struggled with such unforeseen and untrained-for contingencies as developing intelligence networks, searches, and policing.[61] The NTC may have had other, less identifiable negative results. In particular, the fixation on winning day-long battles in a two-week NTC rotation may well have distracted an entire generation of combat officers from learning, or even thinking about, how to turn short-term tactical victories into long-term strategic results.[62]

The significance the army attached to the NTC as a preparation for war may have been won by default. Results from other tests were far more ambivalent. One example was the annual Reforger maneuvers, a "strategic mobility exercise" involving as many as 100,000 military personnel, which began in 1969 "to practice action required to reinforce Europe and fight as part of the NATO team using host nation support."[63] A typical Reforger transported one or two U.S. combat units and some supporting personnel—perhaps 15,000 in all—to participate in a simulated NATO (Blue) defense against a Soviet (Orange) attack on the very terrain the army anticipated fighting the real war. Reforger after-action reports touted their realism. The 1974 Reforger V's report glowingly described "battles . . . characterized by deep penetrations, violent attacks, and extensive night operations" and ended with the ringing declaration, "We have reassured our allies and advised our potential enemies that the armed forces of NATO are strong, professional, and ready."[64]

In practice, Reforger's public relations and diplomatic goals were at odds with its military objectives. Holder complained in 1986 that most were "sedentary, constricted exercises that bear no resemblance to the conditions of active campaigning."[65] To mol-

lify the locals, demonstrate American sensitivity to German sensi-
bilities, and foster NATO solidarity, Reforgers followed strict and
implausible rules. Massive armored columns crept along main
highways like ducks in a shooting gallery; combat vehicles deli-
cately threaded their way through narrow village streets; "maneuver damage control officers" handed out cash for smashed cars or
trampled crops; and farmers suffering through bad seasons cor-
dially invited tank crews to drive over their fields. Beyond their
surrealistic execution, Reforgers, particularly those conducted in
the 1970s and early 1980s, revealed serious weaknesses. Too often, the Orange forces simply rolled through the outmanned
NATO defenders. In 1976 troops from the elite 101st Airborne
Division lasted barely a day before they ran out of room to retreat, losing many of their obsolescent antitank vehicles in the
process.[66]

But these tactical setbacks for Reforgers distracted from far
graver problems. Particularly vexing were the army's efforts to
incorporate the use of nuclear, biological, or chemical (NBC)
weapons. Secure in the safety of their own homelands, Soviet and
American doctrines both included NBC. And army evaluators
concluded that based on the evidence of Reforger exercises in the
late 1970s, active defense was impractical without NBC weapons. But Western European public, political, and military opinion believed such weapons would do more damage than a Soviet
invasion, and they opposed any inclusion of NBC into the exercises. They were certainly justified in this view, since simulations
showed atomic warfare would cause nearly 2,000,000 West German and perhaps 20,000,000 European casualties.

The attempt to balance NATO's abhorrence of NBC weapons
with U.S. doctrine sometimes led to ludicrous results. In the
1977 exercise one side launched numerous NBC strikes, but
these strikes were either ignored by the putative targets or "simply
disappeared into the system."[67] The implications of this fiasco—

that the army could not even track NBC strikes in peacetime—
were glossed over in the final report. Like so much of the post-
Vietnam army's efforts to master modern warfare, Reforger
achieved its greatest realism only when the scenario it had been
designed to defeat—a Warsaw Pact invasion of Europe—was no
longer a possibility.

In the late 1980s the rumble of discontent among military intellectuals over army preparations for war grew louder. Much of
this grumbling came from Heroes, who complained the service
had "become stultified by tiers of staff oriented on management,
logistics, and weapons engineering."[68] The army embraced slogans and fads, often adopting corporate techniques such as total
quality management at the very time the business community
was rejecting them. Indicative of this was the adoption of the
term "warfighter," a word redolent in imagery but devoid of substance. Lieutenant Colonel John N. Abrams' definition merged
Heroic and Managerial ideals. On the one hand, "Warfighters are
those leaders who by their very presence and skill assure strategic
confidence that victory on the battlefield and during campaigns is
imminent without sacrificing large numbers of the nation's citizenry." On the other, "A warfighter is a leader, or a staff officer,
who is required routinely to deliver individual arms or combined
arms effects in coordinated effort during a specific phase of a
campaign plan, or at a specified moment of truth in a battle . . .
Logistics officers are as much warfighters as the infantryman on
point, for they marshal the means to the battlefield." Abrams was
worried that the army was not developing "warfighting" skills and
that, as critics argued, the officer corps was "filled with milocrats,
cowboys, and few warfighters."[69]

Other officers echoed Abrams' concerns. Noting that the great
majority of his colleagues had either limited combat experience
or none, Major Robert Maginnis found it "rather presumptuous"
for the army's 1985 survey to claim that 80 percent of the officer

corps "exemplifies the warrior spirit . . . all the physical, mental, moral and psychological qualities essential for an officer to successfully lead the army in its mission of protecting the nation." He believed the opposite was true. "The modern army has cultivated legions of bureaucrats, systems men, and managers. These men have inherited a legacy of self-doubt that runs from the tragedy of Vietnam to the failed Iranian rescue mission to the lackluster success in Grenada."[70]

According to a controversial 1985 report, most officers believed the service was riddled with careerism and that the promotion system rewarded ticket-punching functionaries, not professional competence. An internal, and unpublished, survey of 14,000 revealed a consensus that "the bold, original, creative officer cannot survive in today's army" and that the senior military leaders behaved more as corporate managers than as commanders.[71] Heroic dissatisfaction permeated Bolger's 1989 article contrasting the "two armies." The so-called display army in Europe was the source of the army's doctrine, its procurement programs, and its vision of war. The second, the fighting army, was engaged throughout the world in a variety of expeditionary contingencies ranging from peacekeeping to small wars. It had to "hobble along with borrowed display army doctrine, organizations, and weaponry."[72]

Fortunately, the limits of the expeditionary army were never tested. The army, as its bountiful distribution of medals demonstrated, interpreted the interventions in Grenada and Panama as great victories. But neither conflict fit its declared concept of warfare. One officer's description of combat operations in Grenada—"tossing AirLand Battle aside, army forces used overwhelming firepower to advance against even minor opposition"—graphically illustrates the disconnect between doctrine and practice.[73] Major James M. Simmons, a SAMS student, found that in the same operation, "numerous errors in operational planning which could have produced fatal flaws were overcome by the sheer application of overwhelming US combat power" against a "second-rate, poorly equipped, and disorganized opponent."[74]

Operation Just Cause, which also deviated from AirLand Battle doctrine, revealed extensive problems in the transition from combat operations to reconstruction. The army's failure to anticipate looting, rioting, and criminal violence, and the propensity of some soldiers to rely on firepower to resolve Panamanian civil unrest, were of particular concern. But for the most part, these problems were overlooked in the flood of self-congratulation. One official history trumpeted that the operation "represented a bold new era in American military force projection: speed, mass, and precision . . . and early anticipation of postcombat mandates."[75] Lieutenant General Frederic J. Brown boasted it was "a textbook study of ALB [AirLand Battle] execution," thus somehow equating victory over a rag-tag militia with defeating the Red Army in the Fulda Gap.[76] The most triumphant verdict came from Just Cause's commander, Lieutenant General Carl Stiner: "There were no lessons learned in this operation . . . But we did validate a lot of things."[77]

If any more validation was needed, the Gulf War of 1991 provided it. Indeed, judging from the service's rhetoric, Operation Desert Storm, in one blow, shattered the ghost of Vietnam and proved that the army had charted the right course. These themes appeared early and often, and were illustrated by *Certain Victory,* a history written in much the style of a biblical redemption narrative, replete with prophets and miracles. In the foreword, army Chief of Staff Gordon R. Sullivan set forth what became the semi-official interpretation: "The victory vindicates the tireless and often unheralded work of a generation of army leaders who forged a new army from the dispirited institution that emerged from Vietnam."[78] Lieutenant Colonel Douglas A. Macgregor proclaimed the Gulf War a "watershed even[t] in military history," one which could provide the template for future warfare.[79] DePuy agreed. Desert Storm had shown that "there is emerging a distinctive American style of warfare, a style that is essentially joint, drawing on the unique capabilities of each service via centralized planning and decentralized execution. This jointness, plus an amalgam of surprise, discriminate use of overwhelming force, high operating tempo, and exploitation of advanced technology, has led to a whole new order of military effectiveness. This is the 'revolution in military affairs.'"[80]

To their great credit, some military intellectuals immediately challenged this redemption narrative. And to the great credit of the army, it tolerated such dissent. Very quickly, a counterargument emerged: the Gulf War was not the first war of the new millennium but the final conflict of the last. In 1991 Lieutenant Colonel Robert Leonard boldly asserted, "The U.S. Army that led the coalition forces to success was not a good army. It was simply a better army than its opponent."[81] That same year, Bolger warned the army against hubris. Desert Storm, he wrote, was a relic from the past, a restaging of World War II, and no predictor of the challenges of the future, or even the present.[82] Another officer blamed the war with infecting army commanders with a "victory disease," manifested in "arrogance, complacency, and the habit of using established patterns to solve military problems."[83]

The critiques of junior officers were echoed by more established authorities. Challenging *Certain Victory*'s teleology, a 1997 CGSC history of the Third Army in the Gulf War asserted, "The popular view of the Persian Gulf War, at least in the army, is that it was a war of maneuver. It was nothing of the sort, at least not if 'maneuver' is defined as the psychological undermining of an enemy by movement alone. Viewed from the theater level, Desert Storm was a war of attrition based upon air power."[84] The most disturbing and prescient observation came from General Fred Franks. "If students of military history and operations want to

learn the major lesson the Gulf War teaches, they should look at
the war's end state . . . it seemed we gave a lot more thought (at
least in the theater) to how to get in and get started than how to
conclude it. The intellectual focus seemed to be in inverse pro-
portion. The closer we got to the end, the less we focused."[85]

A turbulent decade separated the end of the first war with Iraq
from the beginning of the second. The primary justification for
the post–World War II military buildup had disappeared with
the collapse of the Soviet Union. Why should the United States,
as the sole military superpower, still spend more on defense than
the next five nations combined? Between 1989 and 1996 army
manpower shrank from 770,000 to 500,000. Nearly 30,000 officers were voluntarily or involuntarily separated from the service.
Yet this drastic reduction in force structure was not matched by a
reduction in commitments. If anything, the operational tempo of
the 1990s exceeded that of the previous decade.[86]

The Somalia intervention of 1993–1994, a particularly harsh
experience, revealed significant flaws in the army's preparation for
a post–Cold War world. Major Tim W. Quillin criticized senior commanders for emphasizing "force protection" over the
accomplishment of the mission. Their lack of leadership had contributed to a "siege mentality" that yielded the initiative to Somali warlords and nullified American military superiority.[87] Major Mark E. Duffield was struck by how rapidly the situation had
spun beyond the commanders' control, or even comprehension.
Soldiers committed for humanitarian reasons were soon involved
in "the absurdity of outright combat against the very people
meant to be saved." He believed Somalia provided a graphic lesson. Planners must guard against "hyper-rationality where stagnant, even fragile, assumptions once proven are never again
revalidated." In Somalia, "an untrained, ill-equipped, and undisciplined enemy quickly adapted their tactics, invalidated key US
planning assumptions, and evolved into a lethal force . . . [that]

achieved their tactical, operational and strategic goals at US expense."[88] Major Roger Sangvic saw in Somalia proof that the very concepts underlying the army's preparation for future warfare—"battlefield dominance, precision engagement, and precision maneuver"—were ineffective against the opponents it was most likely to encounter.[89]

There was no lack of rigorous self-examination, or of brutal honesty, within the army intellectual community. And yet, despite the dramatic changes in international relations, in resources, and in missions, and despite the army's own post–Cold War experiences, there was little commensurate shift toward a new vision of warfare. General Carl E. Vuono's tenure between 1987 and 1991 encompassed the Gulf War and the breakup of the USSR. Throughout this period, he stuck with his conviction that "modern warfare remains decisively focused on ground combat."[90] As would his successors, he declared, "As good as we are today, we must aggressively shape the future . . . we must move ahead to confront the challenges and seize the opportunities in a brave new world."[91]

But what future was the army to shape? Vuono was unclear, alternately, and sometimes simultaneously, warning against the Russians, the Chinese, the Iraqis, nuclear proliferation, low-intensity conflict, and a host of other threats. All or any of these meant the United States "must have the capacity to project land combat forces in the responsible exercise of power worldwide; we must be able to defend our interests wherever and whenever they are threatened."[92] Vuono's solution was simple. The nation should retain the heavy and light forces it had developed to fight the Cold War, and the army should devote itself to the organizational "imperatives"—doctrine, force mixture, recruiting, and, above all, training—at which it already excelled.

In the decade after the Gulf War, neither the army leadership nor the institutions charged with preparing for the next war could refocus from the Cold War's epic Soviet-American clash. What had been billed in the 1970s and early 1980s as a doctrinal revolution congealed into intellectual inertia and institutional complacency. As Richardson, one of the great innovators of the 1980s, commented on the 1990s, "I think the army can be criticized for not thinking enough about the next war, and instead thinking about the past war, about the Desert Storm type war. The reason it is not thinking about the next war is that it does not have the people to do the thinking."[93]

All the army chiefs of staff in the post–Cold War era faced the challenges of reduced budgets and manpower, widespread expectations of a peace dividend, an often erratic political leadership, and a rapidly changing global environment bristling with materializing threats. All were competent and dedicated officers, and all proclaimed their commitment to reform, or what was termed "army transformation." But as officers who had witnessed firsthand the painful recovery from Vietnam and redemption in the Gulf War, it was difficult for them to question the concepts and practices they believed responsible for, to cite the service's slogan, "the best trained, best led, and best equipped army in the world."

Unfortunately, much of the evidence refuted this boast. A 1995 study of 24,000 officers showed many believing "the state of ethical conduct is abysmal . . . Telling the truth ends careers quicker than making stupid mistakes or getting caught doing something wrong." Subordinates accused their superiors of "the 'zero defects' and ticket-punching mentality of the 1960s and 1970s that nearly destroyed the officer corps."[94] Between 1996 and 2000 the percentage of captains who resigned their commissions almost doubled, and the number of officers who turned down battalion or brigade command skyrocketed.

Chief of Staff Sullivan, who served between 1991 and 1995, made a strong effort to transform the army to meet the challenges of the post–Cold War environment. Once in office, he initiated the Modern Louisiana Maneuvers, taking as a precedent the 1941 field exercises in which the army had tried out the organizations, equipment, and leadership soon used in World War II. His goal was to promote an army-wide dialogue about methods, purpose, and concepts for the next century, all without sacrificing its capability for large-unit conventional operations. The maneuvers would serve as a "vehicle to assess progress as well as focus and facilitate change in a warfighting context through exercises, simulations, and intellectual interface."[95]

Sullivan's efforts to change army doctrine sparked but did not catch fire. Even the maneuver's supporters insisted the army was already "an intimidating land force that only needs operational fine tuning."[96] Like most army transformation initiatives in the 1990s, the maneuvers proved little more than a series of disconnected technical and managerial experiments. The army tried organizational restructuring (the so-called Force XXI), it tried digitization, and it tried to simplify command arrangements. But when Sullivan retired, the army still had made no substantial effort to adapt to the chaotic nonstate warfare it had encountered in Somalia and would encounter again in the Balkans and postinvasion Iraq.

Sullivan's successors, Chiefs of Staff Dennis J. Reimer (1995–1999) and Eric K. Shinseki (1999–2001), were less ambitious and less committed to change. Both were intelligent and dedicated officers, and Shinseki showed considerable courage in opposing the military adventurism of his political superiors. But neither had been conspicuous in the post-Vietnam reformation; both had been implementers rather than originators. In army parlance they were "operators," skilled executives steeped in the institutional culture who could be trusted to run the organization competently and pass it on to their successors. Yet each faced significant problems taxing to a far more imaginative and daring leader. The shrunken manpower base and restive officer corps they inherited were stretched thin by overseas deployments and by the frenetic pace of operations. Compounding these man-power shortages, both the public and politicians were eager to cancel expensive and apparently unnecessary weaponry and modernization projects while cashing in on the anticipated post–Cold War peace dividend.

Perhaps the greatest challenge the army faced was ideological. Defense reformers announced a "revolution in military affairs" (RMA) that, together with new concepts such as "network-centric operations," had created a "new American way of war."[97] Extrapolating from their interpretation of the Gulf War and the promise of still-developing technologies, RMA proponents claimed that this opportunity, if but seized, would grant the U.S. armed forces a quantum leap and assure global supremacy into the foreseeable future. Unfortunately, the RMA benefited the other services, particularly the air force, far more than the army. Advocates envisioned precision-guided munitions, stealth aircraft, sensors, and a host of other technologies designed to detect and destroy enemy forces from a safe distance. They assigned the army the mundane tasks of locating targets, base security, and providing garrisons for postwar stability operations.

Neither Reimer nor Shinseki fully rose to these multiple challenges. Reimer's 1996 *Vision 2010* purported to be a "template" to "channel the vitality and innovation" of soldiers in order to "manage change and advance into the 21st century with the most capable army in the world." It introduced a barrage of concepts or buzzwords—mass effects, dominant maneuver, precision engagement, shaping the battlespace, full dimensional protection, and asymmetric leverage—that supposedly guaranteed future victory. But on closer examination, these concepts were more ideals than practical goals. "Information-age technologies" were to provide the means for "decisive operations, resulting in the successful accomplishment of all missions." "Precision engagement" and "shaping the battlespace" would "allow the force to overcome the enemy's center of gravity and result in the total takedown of an opponent." And "dominant maneuver" was predicated on "creating an image in the mind of an adversary of an unstoppable force of unequaled competence."[98]

Reimer's successor, Shinseki, proved even more enamored of what proved to be quite mistaken assumptions about army capabilities. In his forward to the 2001 *FM 1: The Army*, the "capstone doctrinal manual" for the future, Shinseki posited "rules of thumb applicable at every level of war." But once again, these were not so much rules as a wish list: "we win on the offensive"; "we want to initiate combat on our terms"; "we want to build momentum quickly"; "we want to win—decisively." Even more confusing, Shinseki declared as the cardinal doctrine, "The army provides human interaction—the basis for our warfighting doctrine, our crisis management philosophy, and our engagement strategy."[99]

Given this muddled prescription, it is not surprising that the army's 2001 *Vision* was characterized more by sloganeering than substance. Although Shinseki maintained that "the army is trained and equipped for the overwhelming and synchronized application of land combat power," he also promised the service would soon "transform itself into a full spectrum force . . . capable of dominating at every point on the spectrum of operations."[100] Whether he realized it or not, Shinseki's *Vision* was as shortsighted as his much maligned catchphrase, "An Army of One." The message of the *Vision* was a "war of one" in which the enemy was simply a passive recipient, a human and materiel target upon which the army would impose "full spectrum dominance" rapidly, decisively, and without risk.

The senior leadership's inability to provide a coherent, practical vision of future warfare contributed to a decade of doctrinal floundering. Much of the impasse stemmed from the legacy of

DePuy, who had made doctrine, especially the *FM 100–5: Operations* manual, a crucial component of an officer's professional identity. Problematic even in the 1980s, when the army was focused on AirLand Battle and an officer's "warfighting" skills could be assessed at the National Training Center, it proved insoluble in the post–Cold War world. In order to be a "full-spectrum force" capable of global deployment, the army required, in Vuono's words, "an evolving warfighting doctrine that focuses overwhelming combat power against any enemy, on any battlefield."[101] But Vuono's statement contained a host of assumptions—that the army could, or should, create a single doctrine applicable to every operational contingency; that overwhelming combat power was an end to itself; that future opponents would risk a battlefield decision—all of which were shared by the service's senior leadership in the 1990s.

The 1993 version of *FM 100–5*, with the pretentious title of *AirLand Battle Future,* was a compromise. It held to such Cold War concepts as rapid, decisive battlefield operations by large combat forces that would result in a short, decisive war. Much of it was based on the promise of new, and still unavailable, technology. The army's experience in Haiti and Somalia soon revealed AirLand Battle Future as impractical. By 1995 officers were hard at work on a new version of *FM 100–5.* For over five years this project dragged on, plagued by rotating directors, institutional resistance, and bitter disputes. A decade after the Gulf War, the army could not produce a doctrine that could, as DePuy's had done, provide a vision of war and a template for change.[102]

The army's professional education system was also stuck in a holding pattern for most of the 1990s. Despite the merit of its faculty and students, CGSC spent the decade after Desert Storm marking time, content to teach concepts and methods of warfare best suited for the plains of Europe. The class of 1993 was typical; students were exposed to 80 hours on combat operations

based on AirLand Battle, 116 hours of corps and division operations, and 112 hours of Prairie Warrior exercises to practice their
large-unit command and staff skills. But in the same year, when
18 soldiers died in a street fight in Mogadishu, the core curriculum at CGSC devoted only 45 hours to unconventional warfare.[103]

A year after the humiliating withdrawal from Somalia, students honed their planning skills on a scenario predicated on a
reconstituted Soviet Union launching vast mechanized armies
against NATO. The CGSC class of 1997 had 162 hours devoted to Advanced Warfighting that focused on the "21st century's strike force and its digitized battle staff."[104] The former low-
intensity conflict course, now entitled Military Operations Other
Than War, devoted much of its time to studying joint doctrine
and unit training plans.

The college's stubborn adherence to large-unit operations extended throughout the curriculum. The military history course—
the Evolution of Modern Warfare—narrowly defined "modern"
as European-style nation-state conflict and bestowed the bulk of
its attention on the epic battles of World War II. The college's
complacency with curriculum was extended to students. During
the entire decade, virtually no one failed CGSC. Indeed, in 1993,
99.5 percent of the students in the corps and division combat operations course were graded as "above average," and over half received an A. And yet 34 of these students had to take a remedial
course to understand the basic material.[105] Whatever else the college was in the 1990s, it was not the center of a vibrant dialogue
on how the army would wage war in the future.

Nor were other army intellectual centers able to provide a new
concept of war. As SAMS' own students noted, its 1998 curriculum was essentially that of 1983.[106] The Army War College's
curriculum focused on national strategy, interagency relations,
and corporate management (termed "strategic leadership"). Even

courses with titles such as War, National Policy, and Strategy devoted more attention to international relations and the political process than to military theory or warfare. And what did pass for instruction on warfare was problematic. The class of 2000 learned more about the obsolescent navalism of Alfred Thayer Mahan and the airpower fantasies of Guilio Douhet than it did about unconventional warfare.

The Advanced Warfighting Studies Program, a history-based course introduced in 1986, and made mandatory for combat arms officers shortly afterward, narrowly focused on World War II–style campaigns. As was true at CGSC, officers at the War College were given a wide choice of electives on subjects such as unconventional conflict, expeditionary operations, and future warfare, which were taught by expert faculty. Where else in the United States could a student take a course on African failed states from a veteran of the Liberian civil war and have as a classmate a Ugandan general? But these courses remained optional. Despite the efforts of their faculty, the army's educational institutions were slow to recognize the changing conditions of twenty-first-century warfare.[107]

The reluctance of those agencies charged with shaping the army's concept of war—doctrine, the senior leadership, the school system—to confront the present was all the more serious because no new Wagner or Gavin stepped forward to challenge their conservatism. A few prescient critics noted that the service's overcommitment to "rapid, decisive operations" made it difficult to conduct any other form of warfare. They pointed out that only the most foolish opponent would attempt to meet the sole remaining superpower's armed forces on the battlefield. Instead, enemies would pursue "alternative or asymmetrical methods of warfare designed to exploit U.S. weaknesses and disrupt or paralyze the decision-making apparatus."[108] They warned that the army's transformation plan was so predicated on a short, decisive war that the resulting tactical units might "be nearly impotent in the emerging attrition warfare."[109] But there they stopped. Beyond repeating the army mantra that the future battlefield would be characterized by "complexity, ambiguity, uncertainty, and speed," and thus require even more intelligent and adaptive officers, they could not reach any consensus on the problem of future war.[110]

Many who claimed to speak for the next generation of war-fighters were actually conservatives. General Robert H. Scales appreciated the enormous changes precision munitions had effected, but his vision of future warfare remained that of Gulf War–style conflicts waged against conventional opponents.[111] General Clark maintained his position that the conduct of operations in the Balkans foreshadowed "modern war—limited, carefully constrained in geography, scope, weaponry, and effects."[112] But few army officers could accept Clark's thesis, for they believed it was based almost entirely on the use of air power and so specific to the Balkans as to be inapplicable anywhere else. Macgregor's much-discussed 1997 book *Breaking the Phalanx* was a Manager's organizational plan for combat forces. And had it been followed, it might have resulted in tactical units that were more flexible and better able to communicate, maneuver, and shoot. But the vision of land warfare Macgregor extolled was a return to World War II or Desert Storm.[113]

The most grandiose sibyl of all was Lieutenant Colonel Ralph Peters. A prolific and influential writer, his limited ability to predict the future was first displayed in a novel about a Soviet-American war published shortly after the USSR dissolved. Throughout the 1990s, Peters produced a literary flood most notable for its dogmatism and inconsistency. In one instance, he claimed to have overthrown Clausewitz and discovered a "new strategic trinity" of the "state, its population, and information" that would be "the crucial determinant in our time." Fortunately for Americans, "we are already masters of information warfare, and fail to realize it."[114] But Peters' own definition— *"Information warfare is the use of information by a military, by any other government agency, or by any other actor, to gain an advantage over an opponent in peace or war"*—was so all-encompassing as to be virtually useless.[115] Unfortunately, too many officers took Peters' incoherent, scattershot rants for provocative "outside-the-box" thinking.

As the army entered the twenty-first century, it faced an almost insurmountable problem. It had to overcome its own past, and its own mythology about that past, if it was to prepare for the future. Under senior officers determined to exorcise the ghost of Vietnam, it had undergone a reformation in the 1970s and 1980s. But this reformation had proved more a revival than a revolution, retaining the three traditional army ways of war even as it created a new vision of modern warfare based on a great land conflict in Central Europe. The opportunity to defeat the Soviets at the Fulda Gap never came, leaving the army to find proof of its reformation in Panama and the Persian Gulf. The broken army's thirty-year climb back from the depths of Vietnam was impressive. But it was achieved at considerable cost, and it had many unanticipated, and unpleasant, long-term consequences. Most seriously, it fostered an intellectual rigidity, a propensity to mistake slogans for strategic thinking, and the dogmatic belief in itself as the "best trained, best armed, best led" force that had ever existed. Too few officers asked the central question—best trained, best armed, and best led for what war? As retired Colonel Douglas V. Johnson noted, in the wake of the Gulf War, "Hubris set in."[116] The results would be all too apparent in Iraq.

EPILOGUE

A military institution's concept of war is a composite of its interpretation of the past, its perception of present threats, and its prediction of future hostilities. It encompasses tactics, operational methods, strategy, and all other factors that influence the preparation for, and conduct of, warfare. During active hostilities, this vision must be focused on the here-and-now, on recovering from the last battle and preparing for the next one. Only after the guns fall silent, in the echo of battle, can military intellectuals refer to the lessons of centuries and contemplate a variety of futures. They can anticipate the effects of weapons still on the drawing board, of new tactical schemes, of radical organizational reforms. They can speculate on probable enemies and possible battlefields. They may debate for years the relative merits of annihilation versus attrition, offensive versus defensive, firepower versus maneuver. And they can, in theory, develop and cultivate the methods that will allow them to emerge victorious from the next conflict.

The U.S. Army has spent most of its existence at peace, if time spent fighting official wars is the standard. Yet both historians and officers have persistently identified the American philosophy, or way, of war by focusing on the relatively few years of active hostilities. From this perspective, peacetime military thought is important only for what later proved right or wrong on the battlefield.

In this book I have taken a different approach. I argue that the army's way of war has been shaped as much or more by its peacetime intellectual debate as by its wartime service. For almost a century its fortification boards defined the service's understanding of the foreign threat and developed the strategy and methods to deter invasion. In the post–Civil War era, military intellectuals defined "modern warfare" and thus justified the service's transition from a frontier constabulary-harbor defense force to a global military power. During the interwar period, the debate over the lessons of World War I both constrained and inspired the service's preparation for World War II. Without the officer intellectuals who created a concept of land warfare for the atomic era, the army might have reverted to a home defense force. And without the post-Vietnam reformers, the service would have lacked a unifying vision of future battle to save it from internal division and external apathy. In short, the army's peacetime thinkers, as much as its wartime commanders, have defined the service's martial identity, identified its mission, determined professional standards, and created its distinct way of war.

These military intellectuals have tended to separate into three distinct, and often antagonistic schools of thought, which I have called the Guardians, Heroes, and Managers. Together, these martial traditions form the peacetime army's intellectual construct of warfare. Like a braid, each strand will, for a time, be visible on the surface and at other times will disappear, only to emerge farther down the braid. At times the strands are so closely knit as to be indistinguishable; at other times they practically pull apart.

It is a common criticism, even a cliché, that peacetime soldiers prepare to refight the last war. Yet few ask the obvious question: what version of the last war are they preparing to fight? This is an important qualification, since all three of the army's martial traditions claim a unique ability to understand the nature of war and to predict its future, yet all three have consistently proven unable to do so. The recent complaint of a senior officer in Iraq—that the enemy the army encountered was not the enemy it had prepared for—is but the latest in a long litany.

Civilians erroneously assume that individual officers, and certainly generals, speak for the entire service when they articulate the army's mission and strategy. This trust is misplaced, particularly today. The officer corps may share a unifying ethic and ideology, but it has never shared a unifying philosophy of warfare. It is equally fallacious to conclude that criticism from uniformed mavericks represents "outside-the-box" thinking or that these critics are really agents of change. In fact, they often represent the more conservative elements. This was true of the 1890s cavalrymen who eschewed rifles for the saber charge, the 1920s advocates of "open warfare," and the 1990s proponents of "network-centric operations" who sought to reprise the Gulf War. It is certainly true of many self-proclaimed reformers today.

Indeed, interpreting both past and current military thought as a struggle between progressives and conservatives obscures how much the dead hand of the past shapes the parameters of discussion and dictates the positions that proponents assume. Today, as in the past, most officers who write on war almost invariably represent factions rooted in one of the three martial traditions. Their arguments both for and against a particular policy, weapons system, strategy, or doctrine are filled with assumptions drawn from these three schools of thought. Recognizing the strength of this intellectual legacy, or legacies, allows both soldiers and civilians to better understand the underlying suppositions that inform peacetime budget and policy initiatives, influence its doctrine and training, guide its procurement of armaments, and thus ultimately shape the army's conduct of warfare.

The army's vision of war has seldom involved public participation, except on the services' own terms. Instead, military intellectuals have either dismissed the citizenry altogether or ascribed
to them a largely negative influence. Army intellectuals have
portrayed themselves as enlightened and informed professionals
struggling against venal, ignorant politicians and an apathetic,
selfish public. The army's lack of empathy for the nation's own
citizens, its distrust of the political system, and its insistence that
defense be the nation's overriding priority have greatly influenced
its way of war. With few exceptions, peacetime officers have underestimated the latent power of patriotic civilians and democratic institutions. As a result, they have tended to envision future
conflicts in which the public is little more than a frightened mob,
the political system is ineffectual, and the regular army has been
granted carte blanche to fight the war it imagines. And in assessing the lessons of past conflicts, it has tended to focus on its own
contributions and to ignore those of industry, the home front,
political leaders, and citizen-soldiers. At its most insidious, this
bias has contributed to an institutional fable that the regular
army's success on the battlefield has often been undermined by a
lack of sufficient "will" on the home front.

One of the army's most cherished myths is that its greatest peacetime successes—the Root reforms, the post-Vietnam renaissance—were entirely self-generated, carried through in the
face of public apathy or opposition. Yet rarely have these transformation initiatives—from the 1820s harbor fortifications to the
1990s AirLand Battle Future—actually prepared the service for
the war it would have to fight. The absence of direct causation—
the ability to demonstrate that a specific reform actually had
the effect its planners intended—should make both officers and
civilians more skeptical of the tendency of some military intellectuals to present guesses as certainties. This unwarranted certainty about what former Secretary of Defense Donald Rumsfeld
termed "known knowns" has been matched by an equally danger-

ous dismissal of "known unknowns." Despite decades of personal experience to the contrary, army officers have consistently underestimated the difficulty of unconventional warfare, military occupation, and pacification. The price of this hubris has been high, in both the past and the present.

The army's inability to recognize the weaknesses of its intellectual traditions is manifest in its selective use of historical examples. All three schools appeal to a mythical past, sometimes contrasting golden eras such as the Civil War or World War II with the allegedly dark periods that followed them. At times, this historicism approaches the ludicrous. During the late 1990s, it was almost mandatory that any briefing by a senior officer would show a slide juxtaposing German tanks with the Maginot Line as warning of the dire fate that awaited should the nation not fund the army's transformation program. The choice, the slide intimated, was between overwhelming victory and humiliating defeat—history proved it. That the blitzkrieg-Maginot analogy was of almost no relevance to the United States even in the 1930s, much less today, appeared to escape an entire generation of officers. In this case, as all too often, historical cherry-picking does the very thing that the study of history should guard against. Rather than encourage informed analysis and criticism, the army's interpretation of the past serves to enforce complacency and the "comfortable vision of war."

The Global War on Terror is, according to its supporters, a war totally unlike any other—a war that calls for new concepts, new methods, even a new vocabulary. Army vision statements speak less of war than of a variety of "challenges" such as terrorists, "nonstate entities," rogue nations, and "breakthrough technologies" in the hands of opponents, which might prove crucial in a particular "operational domain." Yet despite the inflated rhetoric, in many ways GWOT has highlighted long-term problems in each of the three army ways of war.

The pre-GWOT army was enamored of the Guardians' propensity to reduce the chaos of war into rules, principles, and predictable outcomes. Many in the army were convinced they could dictate to politicians the rules that governed military deployment, a naive conviction that Colin Powell helped perpetuate. Their references to war were filled with pseudoscientific terms like "battlefield calculus," "seamless synchronization," and "massed effects." Even the service's slogan—"Soldiers on Point for the Nation . . . Persuasive in Peace, Invincible in War"—conveyed the impression of waging war with such precision that the enemy was virtually helpless. After the 9/11 attacks, some rushed to revive apocalyptic Guardian scenarios of the nation's cities in ruin and to demand an all-encompassing "homeland security" plan akin to the national defense scheme proposed by Totten in the 1820s. More disturbing, the Guardian tradition of military deterrence was distorted into a doctrine of preemptive war. Today, a half-decade after the invasion and occupation of Iraq, some still claim that only by killing "terrorists" in Baghdad can the nation avoid similar battles in New York City. This conflation of protecting the United States with aggressive or preemptive action against potential enemies goes far beyond what the originators of the Guardian tradition would have ever imagined.

Even before GWOT, the Managers were too immersed in the day-to-day tactics of administration and too little concerned with long-range strategic planning. For all the rhetoric of "breaking the phalanx," "working the interagency process," or "coordinating the instruments of national power," senior officers clung to a Cold War vision of battle. They referred to their service's "inviolate contract" with the American people, but they limited its obligations to fighting conventional wars against other nations' armies. Viewing themselves as executives of a highly successful corporation—the best army in the world—they fixated on issues as picayune as the color of berets. The service's leadership proved unprepared for the twin challenges of Iraq and Rumsfeld. Too often they were so busy reacting to the immediate crises that they did not exercise their responsibility to lead the army.

Chief of Staff Eric Shinseki did provide realistic assessments for the occupation of Iraq and challenged, albeit too quietly, the sanguine pipedreams of Rumsfeld and his theater commander. His successor, General Peter Schoomaker, did a commendable job maintaining his overstretched forces, and he initiated a significant intellectual shift throughout the service from the Fulda Gap to counterinsurgency. Unfortunately, the army has also had a number of senior officers who were essentially caretakers, adequate executives in peacetime who have proven unable to adapt to wartime challenges. One of these was Lieutenant General Ricardo S. Sanchez, who presided over what army officers refer to as "the lost year" in Iraq that witnessed the Abu Ghraib scandal and the outbreak of civil war.

The Heroes have also had a mixed record. Today, their values appear in the service's dominant philosophy, or at least in its rhetoric. The army issues each soldier metal identification cards stamped with the "Soldier's Creed," the "Warrior Ethos," and "Army Values," and virtually every mission statement emphasizes that the foundation of "warfighting" is the individual soldier. But the flaws of the Heroic tradition were nowhere more apparent than in the person of General Tommy Franks, commander of U.S. Central Command and architect of the invasions of Iraq and Afghanistan. He epitomized the propensity for simplistic solutions to complex problems, as well as the inclination toward self-promotion. Openly scornful of Managers, Pentagon "bean counters," and his civilian superiors, Franks opined that victory in Iraq depended on individual character, patriotism, and military genius. He intimidated his staff and excoriated critics, but acquiesced when Rumsfeld redrew his operational plans, revised the deployment schedule, and slashed troop strength. While claiming credit for great victories in Iraq and Afghanistan, he denied any blame for their postconquest descent into violent disorder.

Fortunately, Franks is not typical, and in many ways Iraq has spurred a renaissance of the Heroic tradition within the army. At a fundamental level, officers and soldiers now recognize that winning battles is less important than winning the peace, that no plan can result in a predetermined outcome, and that "the enemy gets a vote." The ability of soldiers, from privates to generals, to innovate and adapt to constantly shifting battle conditions has been impressive. However much they question the wisdom of the Iraq War, or doubt its success, returning veterans are immensely proud of their service and their comrades. The cohesion of the army's forces, their willingness to sacrifice, and the quality of leadership have surprised even the service itself. As one soldier, returning from his second tour, said, "I cannot believe how good we have become." Veterans speak of small "flat" staffs functioning more like teams than military hierarchies, of a command climate that fosters individual responsibility, and of tactical organizations so receptive that a private's idea may become a general's policy almost overnight.

These Heroic traits are also thriving in the army's intellectual community. Ultimately, Heroic practicality—crudely expressed as "what you don't know can kill you"—has done what years of top-down directives to "transform" could not. The service's school system has undergone enormous change in the course of responding to the challenge of the Iraq War. Thanks to reformers such as Brigadier General Volney J. Warner, Leavenworth's curriculum is moving rapidly away from its previous emphasis on rote learning and planning for conventional large-unit warfare. The Army War College's Strategic Studies Institute (SSI) has published a flood of provocative and often harshly critical essays on Afghanistan, Iraq, and GWOT. Although SSI has often incurred the wrath of powerful military and political chiefs—including Rumsfeld—the army leadership protects and encourages these military intellectuals. The War College itself is shifting from an exclusive focus on conventional warfare and strategic decision-making at the highest levels to emphasizing irregular conflict, cultural awareness, the necessity of working with civilian federal agencies and private organizations, and nonmilitary solutions to complex contingencies.

The more innovative and flexible approach of soldiers has shaken the army out of its self-referential peacetime mentality. Charged with developing a new manual for dealing with modern insurgencies, General David H. Petraeus assembled a top-notch staff, headed by Conrad Crane, a Stanford-educated historian, that incorporated advice from academics, federal agencies, nongovernmental organizations, journalists, medical specialists, and even an Australian officer-anthropologist. A crop of relatively junior officer intellectuals have emerged—John A. Nagl, Peter Mansoor, Daniel Bolger—who are already drawing lessons, concepts, and methods from the recent past to guide the service in the future, rather than letting the three traditions straitjacket the army's vision of war. Most importantly, Iraq has revitalized the old frontier-imperial Heroic belief that securing the peace is as important as winning the campaign. Paradoxically, although many officers refer to Iraq as "breaking the army," it may also have served to bond it into a more cohesive, more flexible, and more appropriate instrument for executing the nation's military policies.

If a GWOT-inspired Heroic renaissance is to truly have an impact on the army, it must be accepted and assimilated by the other two traditions. This is not at all certain. It is likely that Guardians will reject the preemptive adventurism of the Bush administration, along with grandiose objectives such as imposing democracy through military force. Adhering to their belief in scientific and rational warfare, they may also reject much of their service's recent experience with unconventional operations. They will probably reaffirm the Powell Doctrine that the nation's military forces should be deployed only to secure vital interests, that they should be sent in overwhelming strength, that they should have limited objectives, and that there should be a clear "exit strategy." Guardians may continue to seek in new technologies and new doctrines the means to engineer war with precision and predictability. And they will probably maintain that the ultimate goal of the nation's armed forces is to dominate so as to deter war all together. All these goals are understandable, possibly laudable. But the Guardians must defend against a revival of the pre-GWOT hubris which led to their insistence that the army could impose its vision of war on any opponent, at any time, in any place. And they must guard against their tendency to discover in one weapons system and one doctrine the solution to all strategic problems.

Managers may find in Iraq support for both a thorough reorganization of the service and a new concept of modern warfare. They will see in the rapid drive to Baghdad and the destruction of Iraqi conventional forces evidence that, properly transformed, the army can dominate future battlefields. Citing this and other carefully chosen historic examples, they may argue that the army needs to refocus on large-unit, high-tech conventional operations, and raise the specter of an expansionist China or a resurgent Russia. And, like the post-Vietnam generation, they will seek to fix a broken army by holistic reform, interweaving doctrine, training, officer education, promotion, procurement, and force structure into a coherent program.

However, Managers may also recognize that Iraq offers evidence of a need to return to their intellectual roots, to acknowledge that modern warfare requires not only well-organized military forces but also mobilization of the nation's economic, diplomatic, political, and popular resources as well. Like Eisenhower, they may realize that winning the "long war" entails as much attention to preserving American values, individual human rights, and economic diversity as it does building up the nation's military strength. If so, they may become more willing to end branch and service parochialism and more accepting of outside advice and assistance. They might even be willing to spend real intellectual and financial capital on the "interagency process" instead of trying to shuffle off the difficulties of peacemaking and nation building to grossly understaffed and underfunded federal bureaucracies.

Whether the army emerges from the Global War on Terror prepared for future challenges, or whether a postwar malaise will require decades of rebuilding, will depend to a large measure on how Heroes, Managers, and Guardians choose to interpret the conflict. They can all justly claim the army was given inadequate resources for an impossible mission. And they have more than sufficient targets to blame. So the question is not whether, from this foundation of collective grievance, military intellectuals can revive and reaffirm their three traditional martial schools. Whether they can create a new army way of war depends to a great extent on what they choose to hear in the echo of battle.

Abbreviations

ACJ	*Armored Cavalry Journal*
AHR	*American Historical Review*
AID	*Army Information Digest*
AFB	US Air Force Base
AFF	US Army Field Forces
AFHRA	Air Force Historical Research Agency, Maxwell Air Force Base, Montgomery, AL
AG	Adjutant General
AJ	*Antiaircraft Journal*
ASPMA	*American State Papers Documents, Legislative and Executive of the Congress of the United States. Military Affairs,* 7 vols. (Washington, DC: Gales and Seaton, 1832–1861)
ASPNA	*American State Papers Documents, Legislative and Executive of the Congress of the United States. Naval Affairs,* 4 vols. (Washington, DC: Gales and Seaton, 1834–1861)
AWC	Army War College
AWCCA	Army War College Curriculum Archives, MHI
AWCIR	Army War College Instructional Records, RG 165, NARA 2
AWCSP	Army War College Student Paper, MHI
CAFF	Chief of Army Field Forces
CAJ	*Coast Artillery Journal*
CARL	Combined Arms Research Library, Fort Leavenworth, KS

CFJ	*Combat Forces Journal*
CG	Commanding General
CGSC	Command and General Staff College/School
CJ	*Journal of the U.S. Cavalry Association/Cavalry Journal*
CMH	US Army Center of Military History, Fort McNair, DC
CONARC	Continental Army Command
C/S	Chief of Staff
DDEL	Dwight D. Eisenhower Presidential Library, Abilene, KS
E	Entry
EUCOM	European Command
F	File or Folder
FSR	*Field Service Regulations*
GPO	Government Printing Office
HIA	Hoover Institution Archives, Stanford University, Palo Alto, CA
IJ	*Journal of the U.S. Infantry Association/Infantry Journal*
JCS	Joint Chiefs of Staff
JMH	*Journal of Military History*
JMSI	*Journal of the Military Service Institution*
JUSA	*Journal of the U.S. Artillery Association*
MA	*Military Affairs*
MDLC	Manuscripts Division, Library of Congress, Washington, DC
MHI	US Army Military History Institute, Carlisle, PA
MMAS	Masters of Military Art and Science, CGSC
MR	*Military Review*
NASP	Benjamin Franklin Cooling, ed., *The New American State Papers,* 19 vols. (Wilmington, DE: Scholarly Resources, 1979)
OCAGF	Office of the Chief of Army Ground Forces
RG	Record Group, National Archives 2, College Park, MD
RWD	*Annual Report of the War Department*
SAMSM	School of Advanced Military Studies Monograph, CARL
SecWar	Secretary of War
SOOHP	Senior Officers Oral History Project, MHI

SRP	Student Research Paper
TRADOC	US Army Training and Doctrine Command
USAREUR	US Army Europe
USMA	United States Military Academy
WPD	War Plans Division

NOTES

Prologue

1. Donald Rumsfeld, speech of 27 September 2001, http://
www.defenselink.mil/speeches/s20010927-secdef.html, accessed 23 January
2002.

2. Wesley K. Clark, *Waging Modern War: Bosnia, Kosovo, and the Future of Combat,* rev. ed. (New York: Public Affairs, 2002), xxxviii.

3. Throughout this book the term "military intellectual" will be used
to denote army officers who write or speak on war, regardless of the merits
of their views. Lloyd J. Matthews, "Anti-Intellectualism and the Army Profession," in *The Future of the Army Profession,* 2nd ed., ed. Don M. Snider
and Lloyd J. Matthews (Boston: McGraw Hill, 2005), 61–92.

4. Department of Defense, Office of Force Transformation, "Operational Sense and Respond Logistics: Coevolution of an Adaptive Enterprise Community," 6 May 2004, http://www.oft.osd.mil/initiatives/srl/
S&RL_Concept_Short.doc, accessed 8 December 2006.

5. James L. Abrahamson, *America Arms for a New Century: The Making of a Great Military Power* (New York: Free Press, 1981); Fred
Greene, "The Military View of American National Policy, 1904–1940,"
AHR 46 (January 1961): 354–77; Ronald G. Machoian, *William Harding Carter and the American Army* (Norman: University of Oklahoma Press,
2006); Russell F. Weigley, *Towards an American Army: Military Thought*

from Washington to Marshall (New York: Columbia University Press, 1962). On U.S. military history, see Allan R. Millett and Peter Maslowski, *For the Common Defense: A Military History of the United States of America,* rev. ed. (New York: Free Press, 1994); Richard W. Stewart, ed., *American Military History,* 2 vols. (Washington, DC: Center of Military History, 2005); Russell F. Weigley, *History of the U.S. Army* (Bloomington: Indiana University Press, 1984).

6. Antulio J. Echevarria II, *Toward an American Way of War* (Carlisle, PA: Strategic Studies Institute, 2003). For treatments of national ways of war, see Robert M. Citino, *The German Way of War: From the Thirty Years' War to the Third Reich* (Lawrence: University Press of Kansas, 2005); Victor Davis Hanson, *The Western Way of War: Infantry Battle in Classical Greece,* 2nd ed. (Berkeley: University of California Press, 2000); David French, *The British Way of Warfare, 1688–2000* (London: Unwin-Hyman, 1990); Richard M. Harrison, *The Russian Way of War: Operational Art, 1904–1940* (Lawrence: University Press of Kansas, 2001); Basil H. Liddell Hart, *The British Way of Warfare* (New York: Macmillan, 1937); Russell F. Weigley, *The American Way of War: A History of United States Military Strategy and Policy* (1973; rept., Bloomington: Indiana University Press, 1977).

7. John R. Galvin, "Uncomfortable Wars: Toward a New Paradigm," *Parameters* 16 (Winter 1986): 2.

8. Department of the Army, *Army Vision 2010* (1999), 10.

9. George S. Patton, "Success in War," *CJ* 40 (January 1931): 26.

10. George S. Patton, "The Effect of Weapons on War," *IJ* 37 (November 1930): 488.

11. Tommy Franks with Malcolm McConnell, *American Soldier* (New York: Regan Books, 2004), 531. Franks was quite correct in his assessment of his managerial abilities. Some might conclude the results of Afghanistan and Iraq leave his claim to being a "warfighter" open to debate.

1. Fortress America

1. John C. Calhoun to John W. Taylor, 12 December 1820, *The Papers of John C. Calhoun,* vol. 5, *1820–1821,* ed. W. Edwin Hemphill (Columbia: University of South Carolina Press, 1971), 481. C. Vann Woodward, "The Age of Reinterpretation," *AHR* 46 (October 1960), 2–8.

2. Edward M. Coffman, *The Old Army: A Portrait of the American Army in Peacetime, 1784–1898* (New York: Oxford University Press, 1986); Peter Maslowski, "To the Edge of Greatness: The United States, 1783–1865," in *The Making of Strategy: Rulers, States, and War,* ed. Williamson Murray, MacGregor Knox, and Alvin Bernstein (New York: Cambridge University Press, 1994), 205–41; William B. Skelton, *An American Profession of Arms: The Army Officer Corps, 1784–1861* (Lawrence: University Press of Kansas, 1992), 87–105.

3. James McHenry to President, 8 April 1797, *NASPMA,* 1: 5–11. "Military Academy, and Reorganization of the Army," 13 January 1800, *ASPMA* 1: 133–39.

4. "Washington's Farewell Address," 17 September 1796, *Compilation of the Messages and Papers of the Presidents (1989–1923),* 19 vols., ed. James D. Richardson (New York: Bureau of National Literature, 1897–1922), 1: 221–23.

5. James Monroe to House of Representatives, 30 January 1824, *NASPNA,* 1:107–8.

6. The Fortification Board was also known as the Board of Engineers for Fortifications and the Board of Engineers. Robert S. Browning III, *Two if by Sea: The Development of American Coastal Defense Policy* (Westport, CT: Greenwood Press, 1983); David A. Clary, *Fortress America: The Corps of Engineers, Hampton Roads, and United States Coastal Defense* (Charlottesville: University Press of Virginia, 1990); Jamie W. Moore, *The Fortifications Board 1816–1828 and the Definition of National Security* (Charleston: Citadel, 1981); Mary Margaret Thomas, "Science, Military Style: Fortifications, Science, and the U.S. Army Corps of Engineers" (Ph.D. diss., University of Minnesota, 2002); Samuel J. Watson, "Professionalism, Social Attitudes, and Civil-Military Accountability in the United States Army Officer Corps, 1815–1846" (Ph.D. diss., Rice University, 1996).

7. Joseph G. Totten was appointed to the board in 1816, briefly reassigned from 1817–1818, rejoined it in 1819, and in 1831 became the sole permanent member of the board.

8. "Fortifications," 12 February 1821, *ASPMA,* 3: 307–8; "Revised Report of the Board of Engineers on the Defence of the Seaboard," 24 March 1826, *ASPMA,* 3: 297.

9. "Revised Report," 283.

10. "Fortifications," 308.

11. "Revised Report," 284–85.

12. Constitution of the United States, Article 1, Section 8, Clause 15.

13. "Revised Report," 285.

14. Ibid. "Fortifications," 310. Samuel J. Watson, "Knowledge, Interest, and the Limits of Military Professionalism: The Discourse on American Coastal Defense, 1815–1860," *War in History* 5 (1998): 280–307.

15. C. P. Stacey, "An American Plan for a Canadian Campaign" *AHR* 46 (January 1941): 348–58; C. P. Stacey, "The Myth of the Unguarded Frontier," *AHR* 56 (October 1950): 1–18.

16. James L. Morrison, *"The Best School in the World": West Point, the Pre-Civil War Years, 1833–1866* (Kent, OH: Kent State University Press, 1986).

17. John C. Calhoun to John W. Taylor, 12 December 1820, *Papers,* 480–90. William B. Skelton, "The Commanding General and the Problem of Command in the United States Army, 1821–1841," *MA* 34 (December 1970): 117–21. The army postgraduate schools were essentially for training and not the theoretical study of war. An artillery school was founded in 1824 and an infantry school in 1826, but both were moribund by 1829 and ceased existence by 1831. The Corps of Engineers established a postgraduate school at West Point in the 1840s.

18. Ethan Allen Hitchcock, *Fifty Years in Camp and Field* (1909; rept., Freeport, NY: Books for Libraries Press, 1971), 322. Skelton, *American Profession,* 340–45.

19. "Extract from Annual Message of the President," 5 December 1826, *NASPNA* 1: 117.

20. Marius (pseud.), "On the Necessity and Advantages of an Army and the Utility of War," *Military and Naval Magazine of the United States* 2 (December 1833): 212.

21. John F. Marszalek, *Commander of All Lincoln's Armies: A Life of General Henry W. Halleck* (Cambridge: Belknap Press of Harvard University Press, 2004), 42–46; Thomas E. Greiss, "Dennis Hart Mahan: West Point Professor and Advocate of Military Professionalism, 1830–1871" (Ph.D. diss., Duke University, 1968).

22. Henry W. Halleck, *Elements of Military Arts and Science; or, Course of Instruction in Strategy, Fortification, Tactics of Battles, etc.; Embracing*

the Duties of Staff, Infantry, Cavalry, Artillery, and Engineers (1846; rept. Westport, CT: Greenwood Press, 1971), 145.

23. Ibid., 63.

24. Dennis Hart Mahan, *Advanced-Guard, Out-Post, and Detachment Service of Troops, with the Essential Principles of Strategy, and Grand Tactics for the Use of Officers of the Militia and Volunteers,* new ed. (New York: John Wiley, 1861), 8–9.

25. Ibid., 31.

26. Ibid., 36–37.

27. Ibid., 37–47.

28. "Compendium of the Report of the Chief Engineer," 3 December 1855, 34th Cong, 1st Sess, S. Ex. Docs, vol. 2, p. 24.

29. Edward B. Hunt, *Modern Warfare: Its Science and Art* (New Haven: T. J. Stafford, 1860), 923–27. "Report of the Secretary of War," 1 December 1856, 34th Cong, 3rd Sess, H. Ex. Docs, vol. 1, pt. 2, pp. 3–28.

30. Richard Delafield, *Report of the Art of War in Europe in 1854, 1855, and 1856, by Major Richard Delafield . . .* (Washington, DC: George W. Bowman, 1860), 2–3, 5. Matthew Moten, *The Delafield Commission and the American Military Profession* (College Station: Texas A&M University Press, 2000).

31. "Report of the Secretary of War," 30 November 1843, 28th Cong, 1st Sess, S. Docs, vol. 1, p. 57.

32. Browning, *Two if by Sea,* 42, 44–46; Watson, "Knowledge, Interest," 290.

33. Lewis Cass, "On the Means and Measures Necessary for the Military and Naval Defences of the Country," 7 April 1836, *ASPMA,* 5: 369.

34. Edmund P. Gaines, "A System of National Defence," 6 March 1840, *NASPMA,* 2: 97–98.

35. [Joel R. Poinsett] to R. M. J. Hunter, 12 May 1840, *NASPMA,* 2: 143. Joseph G. Totten to Charles Gratiot, 29 March 1836, *ASPMA,* 5: 377–91.

36. "Memoir of American Fortification Submitted to the Hon. John B. Floyd, Secretary of War, by James St. C. Morton, first Lieutenant Engineers," 31 October 1859, in "Report of the Secretary of War," 1 December 1859, 36th Cong, 1st Sess, S. Ex. Docs, vol. 2, pt. 2, p. 486.

37. Ibid., 528.

38. Ibid., 496–97. Browning, *Two if by Sea,* 49–53.

39. Hunt, *Modern Warfare,* 910–11.

40. Ibid., 912–13.

41. Browning, *Two if by Sea,* 115–23; Clary, *Fortress America,* 108–12.

42. Henry L. Abbot, "The School of Sub-Marine Mining at Willet's Point," *JMSI* 1 (1880): 207.

43. George W. Van Deusen, "What are the More Needed for Our Future Protection, More War-Ships or Better Coast Defenses," *JMSI* 15 (September 1894): 986.

44. Henry L. Abbot, *Defence of the Sea-Coast of the United States* (New York: D. Van Nostrand, 1888), 17.

45. Ibid., 5–6. Clary, *Fortress America,* 108–26; Browning, *Two if By Sea,* 133–46.

46. H. M. Lazelle, "Important Improvements in the Art of War during the Past Twenty Years and Their Probable Effect on Future Military Operations," *JMSI* 3 (1882): 309.

47. "Report of the Lieutenant General of the Army," 1 November 1884, 48th Cong, 2nd Sess, H. Ex. Docs, vol. 2, no. 1, pt. 2, pp. 48–49. Browning, *Two if By Sea,* 142–46; Kenneth E. Hamburger, "The Technology, Doctrine, and Politics of U.S. Coast Defenses, 1880–1945" (Ph.D. diss., Duke University, 1986).

48. Arthur L. Wagner, "The Military Necessities of the United States and the Best Provisions for Meeting Them," *JMSI* 5 (September 1884): 248.

49. George F. Price, "The Necessity for Closer Relations between the Army and the People, and the Best Method to Accomplish the Result," *JMSI* 6 (December 1885): 322–23.

50. Quoted in Clary, *Fortress America,* 112. Philip St. John Cooke, "Our Army and Navy," *JMSI* 8 (December 1887): 426–30.

51. Tasker H. Bliss, "The Strategical Value of the Inland Canal Navigation of the United States," 1884, Box 1, Tasker H. Bliss Papers, MDLC.

52. Abbot, *Defence of the Sea-Coast,* 15. Italics in original.

53. *Report of the Board on Fortifications or Other Defenses, Appointed under Act of March 3, 1885* (Washington, DC: GPO, 1886), 6. Edward Ranson, "The Endicott Board of 1885–86 and the Coast Defenses," *MA* 31

(Summer 1967): 74–84; Jamie W. Moore, "National Security in the American Army's Definition of Mission, 1865–1914," *MA* 46 (October 1982): 127–31.

54. John M. Schofield to SecWar, 27 November 1894, Box 1, Bliss Papers.

55. "Report of the Major-General Commanding the Army," 4 November 1895, 54th Cong, 1st Sess, H. Ex. Docs, vol. 3, no. 2, p. 67.

56. "Report of the Major-General Commanding the Army," 21 October 1897, 55th Cong, 2nd Sess, H. Ex. Docs, vol. 2, no. 2, pp. 64–65. Nelson A. Miles, "Our Coast Defenses," *Forum* (January 1898): 513–19.

57. "Notes and Diaries," p. 72, Box 1, William E. Lassiter Papers, USMA.

58. A. D. Schenck, "Organization of the Line of the Army," *US* 13 (February 1895): 107–27.

59. Samuel E. Allen, "The System to be Observed in Directing and Controlling the Fire of Sea-Coast Guns," *Essays in the Development of Artillery, U.S. Artillery School: Class of 1892* (Fort Monroe, VA: Artillery School Press, 1892), 61.

60. Abbot, *Defence,* 20.

61. Ibid., 155.

62. Charles P. Summerall, "Coast Defenses," 1 April 1896, Box 27, Charles P. Summerall Papers, MDLC.

63. Abbot, *Defence,* 155–58.

64. "Notes and Diaries," p. 20, Lassiter Papers. Charles P. Summerall, "The Training of Recruits for the Artillery Service," [1896], Box 27, Summerall Papers.

65. "On the Edge: Personal Recollections of an American Officer" (1934), vol. 1, p. 165, Cornelius de Witt Willcox Papers, USMA.

66. Nelson A. Miles to SecWar, 9 January 1900, Box 7, Nelson A. Miles Papers, MHI.

67. "Revised Report," 284.

68. "Compendium of the Report of the Chief Engineer," in "Report of the Secretary of War," 3 December 1855, 34th Cong, 1st Sess, Sen. Ex. Docs, vol. 2, pp. 23–25.

69. Wagner, "The Military and Naval Policy of the United States," *JMSI* 7 (December 1886): 245–46. Italics in original.

70. "Report of the Major-General Commanding the Army," 23 October 1890, 51st Cong, 2nd Sess, H. Ex. Docs, vol. 2, no. 1, pt. 2, p. 44.

71. John M. Schofield to SecWar, 27 November 1894.

72. Ibid. Tasker H. Bliss to John M. Schofield, 26 November 1894, Box 1, Bliss Papers.

2. Modern Warfare

1. Samuel P. Huntington, *The Soldier and the State: The Theory and Politics of Civil-Military Relations* (New York: Vintage Books, 1957), 229. Edward M. Coffman, "The Long Shadow of *The Soldier and the State*," *JMH* 55 (January 1991): 69–82; Robert E. Wiebe, *The Search for Order, 1877–1920* (New York: Hill and Wang, 1967).

2. A. D. Schenck, "Organization of the Line of the Army," *US* 13 (February 1895): 116.

3. Shelford Bidwell, *Modern Warfare: A Study of Men, Weapons and Theories* (London: Allen Lane, 1973); Manfred F. Boemeke, Roger Chickering, and Stig Förster, eds., *Anticipating Total War: The German and American Experiences, 1871–1914* (Cambridge: Cambridge University Press, 1999); Antulio J. Echevarria II, *After Clausewitz: German Military Thinkers before the Great War* (Lawrence: University Press of Kansas, 2000).

4. Marius (pseud.), "On the Necessity and Advantages of an Army and the Utility of War," *Military and Naval Magazine of the United States* 2 (December 1833): 212.

5. Edward B. Hunt, *Modern Warfare: Its Science and Art* (New Haven: T. J. Stafford, 1860).

6. Edward Hagerman, *The American Civil War and the Origins of Modern Warfare: Ideas, Organization, and Field Command* (Bloomington: Indiana University Press, 1988); Joseph G. Dawson III, "The First of the Modern Wars?" in *The American Civil War*, ed. Susan-Mary Grant and Brian Holden Reid (New York: Longman, 2000), 121–41; Stig Förster and Jörg Nagler, eds., *On the Road to Total War: The American Civil War and the German Wars of Unification, 1861–1871* (New York: Cambridge University Press, 1997).

7. *Instructions for the Government of Armies of the United States in the Field* (Washington: GPO, 1898).

8. Dennis H. Mahan, *Advanced-Guard, Out-Post . . . for the Use of Militia and Volunteers,* new ed. (New York: John Wiley, 1863), 165–70, 214–16. Dennis H. Mahan, *Advanced-Guard, Out-Post . . . for the Use of Officers of Militia and Volunteers* (New York: John Wiley, 1853).

9. Robert G. Carter, *The Art and Science of War Versus the Art of Fighting* (Washington, DC: National Publishing Co., 1922), 4. "Lectures by Prof Mahan on Art of War Strategy and Grand Tactics, Commenced May 21st 1862," James Eveleth Wilson notebook (1862), James Sprigg Wilson Collection, USMA. I am indebted to Dr. Conrad Crane for permitting me to read his copy of these notes.

10. Ulysses S. Grant, *Personal Memoirs of U.S. Grant* (New York: C. L. Webster, 1885).

11. William T. Sherman, *Memoirs of General W. T. Sherman* (1886; rept., New York: Literary Classics of the United States, 1990), 887–98. Mark R. Grandstaff, "Preserving the Habits and Usages of War: William Tecumseh Sherman, Professional Reform, and the U.S. Army Officer Corps, 1861–1881," *JMH* 62 (July 1998): 521–45.

12. *RWD* 1884, 50–51. Philip H. Sheridan, *Personal Memoirs of Philip Henry Sheridan,* with additions by Michael V. Sheridan (New York: D. Appleton, 1902), 487–88.

13. John M. Schofield, *Introductory Remarks upon the Study of the Science of War* (New York: Nostrand, 1877). Russell F. Weigley, "The Military Thought of John M, Schofield," *MA* 23 (Summer 1959): 77–84.

14. John M. Schofield, "Inaugural Address," *JMSI* 1 (1880): 1.

15. Ibid., 8.

16. John M. Schofield, *Forty-Six Years in the Army* (New York: Century, 1897), 527.

17. Nelson A. Miles, *Serving the Republic: Memoirs of the Civil and Military Life of Nelson A. Miles* (New York: Harper and Brothers, 1911), 311. Nelson A. Miles, *Personal Recollections and Observations of General Nelson A. Miles* (Chicago: Werner, 1896); Robert Wooster, *Nelson Miles and the Twilight of the Frontier Army* (Lincoln: University of Nebraska Press, 1993).

18. Nelson A. Miles, "The Political Situation in Europe and the East," *Forum* (April 1898): 159–65.

19. T. Bentley Mott, *Twenty Years as a Military Attaché* (New York: Oxford University Press, 1937), 49.

20. David John Fitzpatrick, "Emory Upton: The Misunderstood Reformer" (Ph.D. diss., University of Michigan, 1996), 156. Perry D. Jamieson, *Crossing the Deadly Ground: United States Army Tactics, 1865–1899* (Tuscaloosa: University of Alabama Press, 1994).

21. Emory Upton, *The Armies of Asia and Europe* (1878; rept., Westport, CT: Greenwood Press, 1968), esp. 317–70. Stephen E. Ambrose, *Upton and the Army* (Baton Rouge: Louisiana State University Press, 1964); Richard C. Brown, "General Emory Upton—the Army's Mahan," *MA* 7 (1953): 125–31; David J. Fitzpatrick, "Emory Upton and the Citizen Soldier," *JMH* 65 (April 2001): 355–89.

22. Emory Upton, *The Military Policy of the United States* (Washington, DC: GPO, 1904).

23. Arthur L. Wagner, "The Military and Naval Policy of the United States," *JMSI* 7 (December 1886): 371. T. R. Brereton, *Educating the U.S. Army: Arthur L. Wagner and Reform, 1875–1905* (Lincoln: University of Nebraska Press, 2000).

24. Arthur L. Wagner, *The Campaign of Königrätz: A Study of the Austro-Prussian Conflict in the Light of the American Civil War* (1889; rept., Westport, CT: Greenwood Press, 1972), 5–6.

25. Arthur L. Wagner, "The Military Necessities of the United States and the Best Provisions for Meeting Them," *JMSI* 5 (September 1884): 238.

26. Arthur L. Wagner, *Strategy* (Kansas City: Hudson-Kimberly, 1903), 48. Carol Reardon, *Scholars and Soldiers: The U.S. Army and the Uses of Military History, 1865–1920* (Lawrence: University Press of Kansas, 1990), 4, 19–22.

27. Arthur L. Wagner, *Organization and Tactics* (New York: B. Westermann, 1895); Arthur L. Wagner, *The Service of Security and Information* (Washington, DC: James J. Chapman, 1893); Arthur L. Wagner, *Elements of Military Science* (Kansas City: Hudson-Kimberly, 1898).

28. John Bigelow, "The Sabre and Bayonet Question," *JMSI* 3 (1882): 95.

29. John Bigelow, *The Principles of Strategy. Illustrated Mainly from American Campaigns,* 2nd ed. (1894; rept., New York: Greenwood Press, 1968); Reardon, *Scholars and Soldiers,* 95–97.

30. Bigelow, *Principles,* 265.

31. Francis V. Greene to William T. Sherman, 17 December 1877, Box 2, Manuscripts and Archives Division, New York Public Library, New York, New York. Francis V. Greene, *Report on the Russian Army and Its Campaigns in Turkey in 1877–1878* (New York: D. Appleton, 1879).

32. Francis V. Greene to William T. Sherman, 10 October 1877, Box 2, Greene Papers.

33. John P. Wisser, "Glances at the Wars of To-Morrow," *US* 3 (February 1890): 118.

34. Wagner, "Military Necessities," 239–43; "Report of the Board of Award, Prize Essay," *JMSI* 4 (September 1884): 231–36; H. R. Brinkerhoff, "A Plea for the Increase of the Army," *US* 14 (December 1895): 489–98; Harry C. Egbert, "Is an Increase of the Regular Army Necessary?" *US* 16 (November 1896): 377–96.

35. John M. Schofield to SecWar, 27 November 1894, Box 1, Tasker H. Bliss Papers, MDLC.

36. Stephen M. Foote, "Based on Present Conditions and Past Experience, How Should Our Volunteer Armies be Raised, Organized, Trained, and Mobilized for Future Wars," *JMSI* 22 (January 1898): 1–49.

37. *RWD* 1880, 5.

38. William R. Hamilton, "If Attacked, Could the United States Carry on an Offensive War?" *US* 14 (November 1895): 395–405. Bigelow, *Principles of Strategy,* 37–39.

39. George P. Scriven, "The Nicaragua Canal in Its Military Aspects," *JMSI* 15 (January 1894): 11.

40. Article 30, *Instructions.*

41. Henry M. Lazelle, "Important Improvements in the Art of War during the Past Twenty Years and Their Probable Effect upon Future Military Operations," *JMSI* 3 (1882): 307.

42. W. A. Campbell, "The Magazine Rifle: Its Development and Use," *US* 12 (November 1894): 403.

43. Clinton B. Sears, "The Legitimate in War," *US* 2 (March 1880): 350–65.

44. John M. Schofield, "Notes on 'The Legitimate in War,'" *JMSI* 2 (1881): 1–10.

45. Frank H. Edmunds, *Principles of the Art and Science of War and Their Application in Modern Warfare, With Remarks on the Handling of Troops on the Field of Battle as Presently Practiced* (Fort Leavenworth, KS: Regimental Printing Office, 20th U.S. Infantry, 1883), 214.

46. E. S. Avis, "Practical Work for Infantry," *JMSI* 11 (May 1890): 423. Lyman W. V. Kennon, "Considerations Regarding the 'Battle Tactics' of Infantry," *JMSI* 7 (March 1886): 1–45; John P. Wisser, "The Influence of Small-Calibre Magazine Rifles and Smokeless Powder on Tactics," *US* 6 (February 1891): 109–26.

47. Wisser, "Glances at the Wars of To-Morrow," 117–27.

48. *RWD* 1879, 13.

49. Donald B. McLean, ed., *The 1873 'Trapdoor' Springfield Rifle and Carbine* (Forest Grove, OR: Noremont Armament, 1969), 41.

50. Greene, *Report on the Russian Army,* 422.

51. Philip M. Shockley, *The Krag-Jorgensen Rifle in Service* (Aledo, IL: World Wide Gun Report, 1960); Lazelle, "Important Improvements," 333.

52. *RWD* 1884, 48.

53. Sherman, *Memoirs,* 886.

54. *RWD* 1884, 50–51.

55. Edward Field, "No Footsteps but Some Glances Backward," *JMSI* 6 (September 1885): 238–50.

56. Wesley Merritt, "Cavalry," *JMSI* 1 (1880): 52.

57. Tasker H. Bliss, "The Siege of Plevna," *JMSI* 2 (1881): 50.

58. "Notes for Book on Military Tactics" (c. 1882–86), Frank H. Edmunds Papers, USMA.

59. Schofield, "Inaugural Address," 11–13.

60. Schofield, *Forty-Six Years,* 234.

61. Junius B. Wheeler, *A Course of Instruction in the Elements and Art*

and Science of War for the Use of the Cadets of the United States Military Academy (New York: D. Van Nostrand, 1878), 319.

62. Charles P. Summerall, "Modern Infantry Tactics" [c. 1892], Box 27, Charles P. Summerall Papers, MDLC. Brinkerhoff, "A Plea for the Increase of the Army," 489–98.

63. Lazelle, "Important Improvements," 373.

64. Edmunds, *Principles of the Art,* 221–26.

65. Schenck, "Organization of the Line," 115–16.

66. James Chester, "Battle Entrenchments and the Psychology of War," *JMSI* 7 (October 1886): 309.

67. Schofield, *Forty-Six Years,* 457.

68. Wisser, "Glances," 118.

69. E. V. Sumner, "American Practice and Foreign Theory," *CJ* 3 (June 1890): 141–50; Moses Harris, "The Union Cavalry," *CJ* 4 (March 1891): 3–26; Wagner, "Discussions," 151.

70. William T. Sherman, marginalia in Francis V. Greene, "Important Improvements," 25–27, Greene Papers; *RWD* 1884, 50–51.

71. Merritt, "Cavalry," 51–52.

72. E. P. Andrus, "The Saber," *CJ* (December 1892): 378. Wesley Merritt, "Notes on Cavalry," *JMSI* 33 (November–December 1903): 325–28; J. B. Batchelor, "The Modern Cavalry Destroyer Again," *CJ* 4 (December 1892): 373–78.

73. Charles D. Rhodes, "The Duties of the Cavalry in Modern Wars," *CJ* 6 (June 1893): 179.

74. Harris, "Union Cavalry"; James H. Reeves, "Cavalry Raids," *CJ* 10 (September 1897): 232–47.

75. J. Y. Mason Blunt, "The Shock Action of Cavalry," *CJ* 4 (March 1891): 345.

3. Unconventional Warriors

1. Quoted in William B. Skelton, *An American Profession of Arms: The Army Officer Corps, 1784–1861* (Lawrence: University Press of Kansas, 1992), 240. Edmund P. Gaines, "A System of National Defence," 6 March 1840, *NASPMA,* 2: 91–113.

2. John Grenier, *The First Way of War: American War Making on the Frontier, 1607–1814* (New York: Cambridge University Press, 2005). Andrew J. Birtle, *U.S. Army Counterinsurgency and Contingency Operations Doctrine, 1860–1941* (Washington, DC: Center of Military History, 1998).

3. Edward B. Hunt, *Modern Warfare: Its Science and Art* (New Haven: T. J. Stafford, 1860), 912.

4. Emory Upton to Francis V. Greene, 3 October 1879, Box 2, Francis V. Greene Papers, Manuscripts and Archives Division, New York Public Library, New York, NY.

5. Dennis H. Mahan *Advanced-Guard, Out-Post . . . Militia and Volunteers,* new ed. (New York: John Wiley, 1863), 189–90.

6. "Report of the Secretary of War," 6 December 1858, 35th Cong, 2nd Sess, S. Ex. Docs, vol. 3, no. 1, pt. 3, p. 4. Durwood Ball, *Army Regulars on the Western Frontier, 1848–1861* (Norman: University of Oklahoma Press, 2001); Francis Paul Prucha, *The Sword of the Republic: The United States Army on the Frontier, 1783–1846* (1969; rept. Bloomington: Indiana University Press, 1977); Robert M. Utley, *Frontier Regulars: The United States Army and the Indian, 1866–1891* (New York: Macmillan, 1973); Robert Wooster, *The Military and United States Indian Policy, 1865–1903* (New Haven: Yale University Press, 1988).

7. Robert L. Bullard, "Military Pacification," *JMSI* 46 (January–February 1910): 4.

8. Arthur L. Wagner, *The Service of Security and Information* (Washington, DC: James J. Chapman, 1893); John Bigelow, *The Principles of Strategy. Illustrated Mainly from American Campaigns,* 2nd ed. (1894; rept. New York: Greenwood Press, 1968), 225–32, 265.

9. Nelson A. Miles, *Personal Recollections and Observations of General Nelson A. Miles* (Chicago: Werner, 1896), 537–44.

10. Edward Field, "No Footsteps but Some Glances Backward," *JMSI* 6 (September 1885): 249.

11. "A" (pseud.), "Notes on the Army of the U. States of America," *Military and Naval Magazine of the United States* 1 (April 1833): 101.

12. Joseph H. Dorst to [Alexander] Rodgers, 19 February 1890, Box 3, Joseph H. Dorst Papers, USMA.

13. John Gibbon, "Our Indian Question," *JMSI* 2 (1881): 117.

14. "Annual Report of the Secretary of War Showing the Condition of that Department in 1837," 2 December 1837, *ASPMA* 7: 571–72.

15. Gibbon, "Our Indian Question," 117–18.

16. Ethan Allen Hitchcock, *Fifty Years in Camp and Field* (1909; rept. New York: Books for Libraries Press, 1971), 128.

17. Nelson A. Miles, "Our Indian Question," *JMSI* 2 (1881): 279. Hugh Lenox Scott, *Some Memories of a Soldier* (New York: Century, 1928), 58–59, 108, 124, 131–32; Sherry Lynn Smith, *The View from Officers' Row: Army Perceptions of Western Indians* (Tucson: University of Arizona Press, 1990).

18. Albert G. Brackett, "Our Cavalry: Its Duties, Hardships, and Necessities at Our Frontier Posts," *JMSI* 4 (December 1883): 384. James M. Silver, *Edmund Pendleton Gaines: Frontier General* (Baton Rouge: Louisiana State University Press, 1949).

19. W. P. Clark, "Sign Language of the North American Indians and Some of the Peculiar Customs," *JMSI* 2 (1881): 68.

20. Gibbon, "Our Indian Question," 102.

21. Hitchcock, *Fifty Years,* 120.

22. Scott, *Some Memories,* 145.

23. Henry W. Halleck, *International Law; or Rules Regulating the Intercourse of States in Peace and War* (New York: D. Van Nostrand, 1861), 460, 465–67, 796.

24. Mark Grimsley, *The Hard Hand of War: Union Military Policy toward Southern Civilians, 1861–1865* (New York: Cambridge University Press, 1995); Robert R. Mackey, *The Uncivil War: Irregular Warfare in the Upper South, 1861–1865* (Norman: University of Oklahoma Press, 2004).

25. O. O. Howard, "Is Cruelty Inseparable from War?" *Independent* 54 (15 May 1902): 1162.

26. *Instructions for the Government of Armies of the United States in the Field* (1863; rept. Washington, DC: GPO, 1898).

27. Emory Upton to Francis V. Greene, 3 October 1879, Greene Papers.

28. Henry M. Lazelle, "The Strength and Weakness of England in India," *JMSI* 8 (September 1887): 247–58; Samuel M. Mills, "A Trip to India, China, and Japan," *JMSI* 11 (January 1890): 57–73; Emory Upton,

The Armies of Asia and Europe (1878; rept. Westport, CT: Greenwood Press, 1968).

29. "Report of the Lieutenant General of the Army," 1 November 1884, 48th Cong, 2nd Sess, H. Ex. Docs, vol. 2, no. 1, pt. 2, p. 45. Jerry M. Cooper, *The Army and Civil Disorder: Federal Military Intervention in Labor Disputes, 1877–1900* (Westport, CT: Greenwood Press, 1980); Joseph G. Dawson III, "The U.S. Army in the South: Reconstruction as Nation Building," in *Armed Diplomacy: Two Centuries of American Campaigning* (Fort Leavenworth, KS: Combat Studies Institute Press, 2004), 39–64.

30. Arthur L. Wagner, "The Military Necessities of the United States and the Best Provisions for Meeting Them," *JMSI* 5 (September 1884): 256–57. Elwell S. Otis, "The Army in Connection with the Labor Riots of 1877," *JMSI* 5 (September 1884): 292–323; E. L. Molineaux, "Riots in Cities and Their Suppression," *JMSI* 4 (December 1883): 335–60; Russell Thayer, "Movement of Troops in Cities in Cases of Riot or Insurrection," *US* 1 (January 1879): 92–99.

31. "Report of the Major-General Commanding the Army," 1 October 1894, 53rd Cong, 3rd Sess., H. Ex. Docs, vol. 4, no. 1, pt. 2, pp. 57–59.

32. George F. Price, "The Necessity for Closer Relations Between the Army and the People, and the Best Method to Accomplish the Result," *JMSI* 6 (December 1885): 323.

33. "Report of the Lieutenant General of the Army," 1 November 1884, 45.

34. John J. O'Connell, "The Great Strike of 1894," *US* 15 (April 1896): 300–303.

35. Hitchcock, *Fifty Years,* 411.

36. Joseph H. Dorst to AG, 30 June 1885, Box 3, Dorst Papers.

37. George W. Van Deusen, "Which Are More Needed for Our Future Protection, More War-Ships or Better Coast Defenses," *JMSI* 15 (September 1894): 990.

38. William R. Hamilton, "If Attacked, Could the United States Carry on an Offensive War," *US* 14 (November 1895): 395–405.

39. George P. Scriven, "The Nicaragua Canal in its Military Aspects," *JMSI* 15 (January 1894): 10.

40. Schofield, *Forty-Six Years,* 527.

41. James Parker, "Some Random Notes on the Fighting in the Philippines," *JMSI* 27 (March 1900): 340. Brian McAllister Linn, *The Philippine War, 1899–1902* (Lawrence: University Press of Kansas, 2000).

42. Arthur MacArthur to Theodore Schwan, 23 November 1899, in *RWD* 1900 vol. 1, pt. 7, p. 59.

43. Charles J. Crane, "Fighting Tactics of Filipinos," *JMSI* 30 (July 1902): 496.

44. John Leland Jordan to Mother, 28 April 1900, John Leland Jordan Papers, MHI.

45. Frederick Palmer, *With My Own Eyes: A Personal Study of Battle Years* (Indianapolis: Bobbs-Merrill, 1932), 147–54.

46. J. Franklin Bell to "My dear Colonel [William] Bisbee," 30 March 1900, LS 69, Letters Sent Book 1, E 2206, RG 395.

47. Archibald R. Colquhoun, *The Mastery of the Pacific* (New York: Macmillan, 1904), 98.

48. Henry T. Allen to [John A. Johnston?], 21 January 1902, Box 7, Henry T. Allen Papers, MDLC.

49. Robert L. Bullard, "The Army in Cuba," *JMSI* 441 (September–October 1907): 157. Allan R. Millett, *The General: Robert L. Bullard and Officership in the United States Army, 1881–1925* (Westport, CT: Greenwood Press, 1975).

50. Bullard, "Military Pacification," 1–24.

51. Augustus P. Blocksom, "A Retrospect and Prospect of War," *JMSI* 35 (September–October 1904): 215–26.

52. Rod Paschall, "Low-Intensity Conflict Doctrine: Who Needs It?" *Parameters* 14 (Autumn 1985): 33–45.

53. "Sand-30" (pseud.), "Trench, Parapet, or the Open," *JMSI* 31 (July 1902): 480. James Chester, "Musings of a Superannuated Soldier," *JMSI* 47 (November–December 1910): 387.

54. Bullard, "The Army in Cuba," 157.

55. Leonard Wood to James G. Harbord, 9 June 1909, Box 44, Leonard Wood Papers, MDLC.

56. James G. Harbord to Leonard Wood, 6 May 1909, Box 44, Wood Papers.

57. Montgomery M. Macomb to C/S, sub: Policy to be followed in returning troops from foreign service, 12 April 1915, AWC 9047–1, RG 165.

58. Leonard Wood to AG, 1 July 1907, Box 40, Wood Papers.

59. "Collation of Reports of the Various Staff Officers with the Army of Cuban Pacification, 1906," Appendix 6, Serial #11, E 299, RG 165; Allan R. Millett, *The Politics of Intervention: The Military Occupation of Cuba, 1906–1909* (Columbus: Ohio State University Press, 1966).

60. "Diary of a Special Mission to Mexico," p. 6, Rhodes Papers, MDLC.

61. HQ, US Expeditionary Forces, Vera Cruz, "Memorandum in Reference of the Methods to Be Employed in the Capture and Occupation of Latin American Cities," 10 August 1914, WCD 8699, E 296, RG 165.

62. Frank McCoy, "Patrolling the Rio Grande," *Military Historian and Economist* 2 (January 1917): 93.

63. U.S. War Department, *Field Service Regulations, 1923* (Washington, DC: GPO, 1924), iii.

64. Leon B. Komer to Fenton S. Jacobs, sub: Revision of manuscript for Cavalry Combat, 12 May 1937, Box 4, Fenton Stratton Jacobs Papers, HIA.

65. Hawaiian Department Brown Plan, Revision 1929—Unit Plan, Box 4, Entry 6051, RG 395. Steven T. Ross, *American War Plans, 1890–1945* (Portland, OR: Frank Cass, 2002), 126–28.

66. Briant H. Wells to C/S, sub: Revision of Special Plan Green, 3 March 1922, Green 573, Box 266, E 282, RG 165.

67. Appendix No. 5: Civil Affairs and Legislation, Special Plan—Green, 1923, AGO 381 (2–23–23), Box 33, E 37B, RG 407.

68. Harry A. Smith to C/S, sub: Plan 2, Special Plan Green, 18 January 1927, 2005–51, Box 266, E 282, RG 165. War Game, Special Plan Green, 27 March–6 June 1924, Green 1683, Box 266, E 282, RG 165.

69. "Some Unfinished Business," 22 July 1930, Diary, Box 5, William E. Lassiter Papers, USMA.

4. Providing for War?

1. *RSW* 1899, 45. Edward M. Coffman, *The Regulars: The American Army, 1898–1941* (Cambridge: Harvard University Press, 2004), 142–201;

Ronald G. Machoian, *William Harding Carter and the American Army* (Norman: University of Oklahoma Press, 2006).

2. Richard J. McCallum, "The Bugle's Ageless Call: U.S. Army Transformation Process Has Precedent 100 Years Ago," 2001, http://www.Army.mil/cmh/documents/1901/Bugle-Call.htm, accessed 20 December 2006; Eric K. Shinseki (lecture, AUSA, 12 October 1999), http://www.bus.ualberta.ca/rfield/Speeches/Eric%20Shinseki%201999.htm, accessed 9 December 2006.

3. Philip H. Worchester, "Preparedness of Fort Commands," *JUSA* 48 (July–August 1917): 1.

4. J. Franklin Bell, "Communication to the Secretary of War from the Chief of Staff Regarding Military Policy," 20 April 1910, Series 168, E 299, RG 165.

5. Army War College, "A Proper Military Policy for the United States," *JMSI* 59 (July–August 1916): 28.

6. *Report of the National Coast-Defense Board* . . . (Washington, DC: GPO, 1906); Emmanuel R. Lewis, *Seacoast Fortifications of the United States: An Introductory History* (1970; rept. Annapolis, MD: Leeward Publications, 1979), 89–100.

7. Thomas M. Anderson, "The Battle of Dorking: Some Reflections on Our Military Problems," *Pacific Monthly* (May 1908): 508–12.

8. Hugh Johnson, "The Lamb Rampant," *Everybody's Magazine* 18 (March 1908): 291–301.

9. *RWD* 1909, 202.

10. David A. Clary, *Fortress America: The Corps of Engineers, Hampton Roads, and United States Coastal Defense* (Charlottesville: University Press of Virginia, 1990), 154–55; Wilmot E. Ellis, "The Military Necessities of the United States and the Best Provisions for Meeting Them," *JMSI* 43 (July–August 1908): 1–24.

11. "Report on the Defenses of the Philippine Islands," 1915, AWC 4853–54, RG 165; Hugh L. Scott to AG, sub: Corregidor Garrison, 24 February 1915, AGO 2212633, Entry 25, RG 94.

12. James Regan, "Introductory Remarks upon the New Tactics," *JMSI* 35 (September–October 1904): 194. David A. Armstrong, *Bullets and Bureaucrats: The Machine Gun and the United States Army, 1861–1916* (Westport, CT: Greenwood Press, 1982); Henry B. Hersey, "The Menace of

Aërial Warfare," *Century* 77 (February 1909): 627–30; H. C. McArthur, "Auto-Trucks for the Army," *JMSI* 48 (March–April 1911): 248–57.

13. Ed., "Aeroplanes in War," *CJ* 21 (November 1910): 536–39.

14. "Report of Captain William V. Judson," U.S. War Department, Office of the Chief of Staff, Second (Military Information Division), *Reports of Military Observers Attached to the Armies in Manchuria during the Russo-Japanese War,* 5 sections (Washington, DC: GPO, 1906), 5: 216–17.

15. William Mitchell, "National Organization in War," 1915, Box 45, William Mitchell Papers, MDLC.

16. Edwin Landon, "The Needs of the Coast Artillery," *JUSA* 25 (March–April 1906): 147. S. G. Shartle, "Plans for Defense of Coast Artillery Districts," *JUSA* 32 (July–August 1909): 1–17.

17. George H. Shelton, "The Organization of the Land Forces of the United States," *IJ* 9 (July–August 1912): 31.

18. Charles A. P. Hatfield, "Use of Cavalry in Warfare under Existing Conditions," *JMSI* 43 (November–December 1908): 350. George H. Morgan, "Mounted Rifles," *CJ* 13 (January 1903): 380–84; Charles D. Rhodes to Editor, *IJ* 6 (July 1909): 121–22; Kirby Walker, "Cavalry Experiences from 1898 to 1901," *CJ* 13 (July 1902): 41–44.

19. "Revolver Versus Saber—Report of the Cavalry Board," *CJ* 17 (July 1906): 47.

20. James Parker, "Mounted and Dismounted Action," *JMSI* 39 (November–December 1906): 381–87. Edward. J. McClernand, "Mounted Troops," *JMSI* 34 (March–April 1904): 227–41.

21. "Report of a Cavalry Board on Observation and Study of European Cavalry," 15 February 1913; "Remarks on the Role of Cavalry by Col. James Parker," 1912, both in Box 3, James Parker Papers, USMA.

22. *RWD* 1901, 202.

23. William H. Monroe, "Military Efficiency," *JUSA* 33 (January–February 1910): 20–23; Carol Reardon, *Scholars and Soldiers: The U.S. Army and the Uses of Military History, 1865–1920* (Lawrence: University Press of Kansas, 1990), 21–23, 103–5, 118–19.

24. Herbert H. Sargent, *The Campaign of Santiago de Cuba,* 3 vols. (1907; rept. Freeport, NY: Books for Libraries Press, 1970), 3: 113–14.

25. W. H. Hart, "The Responsibility for Unpreparedness," *JMSI* 57 (September–October 1915): 201. William C. Bartlett, "A Prose Poem to War," *JMSI* 46 (May–June 1910): 479–86; Carl Reichmann, "In Pace Para Bellum," *IJ* 2 (January 1906): 3–19.

26. Louis C. Duncan, "The Evolution of a Military Arm," *JMSI* 54 (July–August 1916): 73. Augustus P. Blocksom, "A Retrospect and Prospect of War," *JMSI* 35 (September–October 1904): 215–26.

27. Charles D. Rhodes, "The Experiences of Our Army since the Outbreak . . . to Improve Its Fighting Efficiency," *JMSI* 36 (March–April 1905): 197–223. John Bigelow, *Reminisces of the Santiago Campaign* (New York: Harper and Brothers, 1898); Todd R. Brereton, "First Lessons in Modern War: Arthur Wagner, the 1898 Santiago Campaign, and the U.S. Army Lesson-Learning," *JMH* 64 (January 2000): 79–96.

28. Quoted in Graham A. Cosmas, "San Juan and El Caney, 1–2 July 1898," in *America's First Battles, 1776–1965,* ed. Charles E. Heller and William A. Stofft (Lawrence: University Press of Kansas, 1986), 145.

29. Charles J. Morton, "Philippine Campaigning," *CJ* 39 (January 1930): 20.

30. J. E. Kuhn, "From Port Arthur to Mukden with Nogi," *IJ* 2 (April 1906): 47. Tiemann N. Hord, "Recent Methods and Lessons in Regard to Field Artillery Taught by the Russo-Japanese War," *JUSA* 30 (November–December 1908): 251–62.

31. Howard L. Landers, "Initial Strategy on our North Atlantic Frontier: A Study in the Preparation of War Plans to Meet Certain Conditions," *JUSA* 47 (May–June 1917), 272. Anon., "Attacks Upon Fortified Harbors," *JUSA* 27 (January–February 1907): 121–25; John P. Wisser, "War Lessons for the Coast Artillery," *JUSA* 22 (November–December 1904): 262–71.

32. B. A. Poore, "Orange vs. Blue Session," 1914–1915 Lectures, vol. 57, Box 5, AWCIR.

33. Dana T. Merrill, "Infantry Attack," *IJ* 6:5 (March 1910): 633–54; Henry J. Reilly, "The Russo-Japanese War," *JMSI* 52 (January–February 1913): 40–61; John T. Greenwood, "The American Military Observers of the Russo-Japanese War (1904–1905)" (Ph.D. diss., Kansas State University, 1971).

34. Mark A. Stoler, *Allies and Adversaries: The Joint Chiefs of Staff, the*

Grand Alliance, and U.S. Strategy in W.W. II (Chapel Hill: University of North Carolina Press, 2000), 1.

35. W. W. Hughes, "The Training of an Infantry Soldier," 11 July 1914, AWC 7541–6, RG 165. Henry C. Davis, "Joint Exercises," *JUSA* 28 (November–December 1907): 286–90; George O. Squier "Team-Work in War," *CJ* 17 (July 1906): 5–10; G. N. Whistler "Remarks upon the Report of Captain Haan, Artillery Corps, on Fire Control and Fire Direction," *JUSA* 18 (November–December 1902): 292–98.

36. Monroe, "Military Efficiency," 21. Robert L. Bullard, "Cardinal Vices of the American Soldier," *JMSI* 36 (January–February 1905): 104–14; Frank Geere, "Our Military Individualism: The Relation of American Character to It, and the Importance of Its Effective Development," *JMSI* 39 (September–October 1906): 208–18; Frank P. Tebbetts, "War and Emotionalism," *CJ* 25 (October 1914): 221–25.

37. William O. Odom, *After the Trenches: The Transformation of U.S. Army Doctrine, 1918–1939* (College Station: Texas A&M Press, 1999), 3.

38. U.S. War Department, *Field Service Regulations, United States Army, 1905* (Washington, DC: GPO, 1905), 103. U.S. War Department, *Field Service Regulations, United States Army, 1913* (Washington, DC: GPO, 1913), 158.

39. U.S. War Department, *Infantry Drill Regulations, 1911* (Washington, DC: GPO, 1911), 95.

40. Ibid., 127.

41. Ibid., 112, 117.

42. U.S. War Department, *Cavalry Service Regulations* (Washington, DC: GPO, 1914), 220.

43. Ibid., 221, 242.

44. William Mitchell, "Our Faulty Military Policy," 1915, Box 45, Mitchell Papers.

45. "Problem: For Chief of Staff, Northern Division," 3 February 1904; "Problem: For Chief of Staff, Atlantic Division," 1 February 1904; Tasker H. Bliss to Secretary of Joint Board, 10 June 1904, all in Serial 12, JB 325, Roll 9, Microfilm 1421, NARA 2.

46. "Blue and Red Problem," 1909–10, AWCCA.

47. "Orange and Blue Problem, Part 2," vol. 10, AWC 1909–10, AWCCA.

48. "Fortification of the Panama Canal," 1910, Box 49, Wood Papers.

49. *RWD* 1912, 71. William G. Haan, "Coast Defense," *JUSA* 30 (September–October 1908): 135–58.

50. Army War College, "A Proper Military Policy," 30–31.

51. "One Soldier's Journey," pp. 94–95, George van Horn Moseley Papers, Box 1, HIA.

52. William A. Mitchell, "A Military Policy Suited to the United States," *JMSI* 46 (January–February 1910): 27.

53. *RWD* 1905, 397–98.

54. John H. Parker, "The Military Education of the Youth . . . for National Defense," *JMSI* (March–April 1912): 155–56.

55. William Wallace, "Our Military Decline," *IJ* 9 (March–April 1913): 633.

56. LeRoy Eltinge, *Psychology of War* (Fort Leavenworth, KS: Army Service Schools Press, 1911), 36–37.

57. Ibid., 42.

58. Reichmann, "In Pace Para Bellum," 12.

59. Hart, "Responsibility for Unpreparedness," 199–200. James S. Pettit, "How Far Does Democracy Affect the Organization and Discipline of Our Armies and How Can Its Influence Be Most Effectually Utilized," *JMSI* 38 (January–February 1906): 1–38.

60. Joseph M. Califf, *Notes on Military Science and the Art of War,* 4th ed. (Washington, DC: James J. Chapman, 1906), 62.

61. Ellis, "Military Necessities," 23.

62. John P. Finnegan, *Against the Specter of a Dragon: The Campaign for American Military Preparedness, 1914–1917* (Westport, CT: Greenwood Press, 1974); Jack C. Lane, *Armed Progressive: General Leonard Wood* (San Rafael, CA: Presidio Press, 1978).

63. "Memoir," Francis J. Kernan Papers, USMA.

64. J. G. Harbord to Leonard Wood, 29 October 1911, Box 52, Wood Papers.

65. Leonard Wood to Robert Bacon, 28 June 1915, Box 80, Wood Papers.

66. *RWD* 1910, vol. 3, p. 201. *RWD* 1906, 12; *RWD* 1908, 78–90.

67. *RWD* 1911, 8.

68. [Leonard Wood] to AG, sub: Annual Report, [30 June 1916], Box 221, Wood Papers.

69. 18 April 1915, "Notes and Diaries," Box 2, William E. Lassiter Papers, USMA.

70. Confidential Memo, [20 May 1914], Box 220, Wood Papers.

71. Army War College, "A Proper Military Policy," 31–32.

72. Landers, "Initial Strategy," 279–80.

73. Henry Jervey, *Warfare of the Future* (New York: P. F. Collier & Son, 1917), 19.

74. "Memoir," Kernan Papers. Mark E. Grotelueschen, *The AEF Way of War: The American Army and Ground Combat* (New York: Cambridge University Press, 2006).

5. Dissenting Visions

1. 20 October 1929, Diary, Box 5, William E. Lassiter Papers, USMA.

2. "Recollections of an Army Career," p. 3, Bradford G. Chynoweth Papers, MHI.

3. AG to All Chiefs of Bureaus and Services of War Department, sub: Approved policies governing the functions of the Army, Navy, and Marine Corps, 24 January 1920, AGO 381O, RG 407. Stanley C. Vestal, "The A.B.C. of the Peace Question" (lecture, Association of the Army of the US, 23 February 1923), LH 1/622/2, Basil Liddell Hart Papers, Kings College, London, UK.

4. George C. Dunham; Max B. Garber; Warren T. Hannum; C. F. Thompson, "The Causes and Prevention of War," 6 February 1926, Doct. 315A-36, G-2 Course, AWCCA. Fitzhugh Lee Minnigerode, "The Next War," *IJ* 24 (January 1924): 53–56; M. B. Stewart, "Lessons of the War," *IJ* 21 (October 1922): 371–75.

5. "Army Reorganization," *IJ* 17 (July 1920): 71–76; William Bryden, "Possibilities in the Act of June 4, 1920," *IJ* 17 (September 1920): 254–60.

6. *RWD* 1920, 1–4. *RWD* 1919, 57–59.

7. John J. Pershing to SecWar, 16 June 1920, endorsement on U.S. Army, A.E.F., *Report of the Superior Board on Organization and Tactics,* 27 April 1919, copy at MHI.

8. Robert L. Welshimer, "The Importance of Coast Artillery in our National Defense," *CAJ* 59 (July 1923): 56.

9. "The National Defense" [1938], John Henry Parker Papers, USMA. National Committee Members Biographies, Box 32; Thomas Hammond File, Box 28; Johnson Hagood File, Box 289, all in America First Committee Archives, HIA.

10. Transcript of radio broadcast, 14 December 1938, in "One Soldier's Journey," vol. 3, p. 40, George Van Horn Moseley Papers, Box 2, HIA. Johnson Hagood, *We Can Defend America* (Garden City, NY: Doubleday, Doran, 1937).

11. LeRoy Eltinge to C/S, sub: Plan for defense against air attack, 19 February 1925, AGO 381 (2-18-25), Box 16, E 37B, RG 407. On the Blue Plan, see Fox Conner to Assistant C/S, WPD, sub: Corps Area Defense Plans, 13 February 1926, AGO 381 (2-19-25), Box 16; LeRoy Eltinge to AG, sub: Basic Plan, Eastern Frontier Command (Special Plan Blue), 31 March 1925, AGO 381 (9-15-24), Box 19; both in E 37B, RG 407.

12. *Report of the Superior Board,* 46.

13. Johnson Hagood, "The United States in the Next War," *JUSA* 53 (July 1920): 3.

14. U.S. War Department, *Field Service Regulations, U.S. Army, 1923* (Washington, DC: GPO, 1923), iii.

15. H. C. Barnes, "The Mission of the Coast Artillery Corps," *CAJ* 57 (December 1922): 484.

16. "A Survey Showing the Necessity and Status of the Coast Artillery Corps" [1930?], Box 4, Campbell B. Hodges Papers, USMA.

17. Frank W. Coe, "The Chief of Coast Artillery and the Corps," *JUSA* 52 (March 1920): 200. William T. Carter, "The Influence of Aviation upon Coast Defense," *CAJ* 64 (May 1926): 464–75; J. T. McNarney, "The Influence of Air Power on Coast Defense," *CAJ* 63 (October 1925): 329–43; R. J. Gibson, "A Study of the Best Method of Cooperation between the Navy, the Air Corps and the Coast Artillery in Coast Defense," SRP #89, 1930, CARL.

18. Ed., "The Future of Our Harbor Defenses," *CAJ* 63 (February 1924): 140. H. J. Hatch and J. F. Stiley, "Coast Defense—Logical and Visionary," *CAJ* 63 (January 1924): 1–21.

19. Ed., "Defense against Air Raids," *CAJ* 62 (March 1925): 227.

20. Charles E. Kilbourne, "Coast Artillery," *CAJ* 65 (July 1926): 4.

21. Ed., "Future of Our Harbor Defenses," 141.

22. "Annual Report of the Chief of Coast Artillery," *CAJ* 64 (January 1926): 47–54.

23. P. P. Bishop, "The Effect of the Development of Aviation upon the Missions and Responsibilities of the C.A.C.," *CAJ* 74 (February 1931): 94. Arnold M. Krogstad to Chief of Air Service, sub: Training for Year, 1924, 14 November 1924, PF-HD/353.9, RG 18; Office of the Chief of Field Artillery to AG, sub: Anti-aircraft Defense, 26 March 1925, AGO 381 (1-6-25), Box 17, E 37B, RG 407.

24. Thomas R. Phillips, "Some Phases of the Effect of Aircraft on the Future Mission, Organization, Equipment, and Tactics of the Coast Artillery," *CAJ* 58 (March 1923): 216. E. J. Cullen, "Fixed Versus Mobile for Coast Artillery," *CAJ* 54 (February 1921): 143–52; Ed., "Gunners All," *CAJ* 54 (January 1921): 76–79; F. E. McCammon, "Future Seacoast Artillery," *CAJ* 54 (February 1921): 132–42.

25. Homer R. Oldfield, "The Passing of Permanently Emplaced Artillery," *JUSA* 52 (April 1920): 324. E. M. Benitez, "The Fundamental Principles of the Art of War Applied to the Problem of Coast Defense," *CAJ* 64 (March 1926): 257–61; J. C. Thom, "Naval Guns versus Shore Defenses," *CAJ* 64 (March 1926): 263–79.

26. "A Positive System for Coast Defense (Army)," *JUSA* 53 (December 1920): 558–72.

27. Johnson Hagood, "The Mission of the Coast Artillery," *CAJ* 62 (February 1925): 91–99.

28. F. J. Culles, "The Functions of Coast Fortifications in the Positive System of Coast Defense," *CAJ* 61 (September 1924): 212.

29. Grand Joint Army and Navy Exercises No. 3, (1925), John L. Hines Papers, Box 41, MDLC; John L. Hines and R. E. Coontz, Report of the Chief Umpires, Joint Army and Navy Exercises, April 1925, Joint Problem No. 3, 13 May 1926, WPD 1678-57, RG 165.

30. Frank Wesley Craven and James Lea Cate, *The Army Air Forces in World War II*, vol. 1, *Plans and Operations January 1939 to August 1942* (Chicago: University of Chicago Press, 1948), 17.

31. James Prentice, "The Effects of Air Service on the Tactics of Coast Defense," *JUSA* 52 (February 1920): 99. Glenn P. Anderson, "Defense against Aircraft," *JUSA* 55 (September 1921): 257–62; George H. Peabody, "What Damage Could Any Nation or Combination of Nations Do to the U.S. from the Air if War Were Suddenly Declared," 3 May 1929, 248.211-30B, AFHRA; Phillip S. Meilinger, "The Historiography of Airpower: Theory and Doctrine," *JMH* 64 (April 2000): 467–502.

32. William Mitchell, *Winged Defense: The Development and Possibilities of Modern Air Power—Economic and Military* (1925; rept. Port Washington, NY: Kennikat Press, 1971).

33. William Mitchell, "Our Faulty Military Policy," 1915, Box 45, William Mitchell Papers, MDLC.

34. William Mitchell, "When the Air Raiders Come," *Colliers* 77 (1 May 1926): 8–9, 35.

35. Hugh A. Drum to C/S, sub: analysis of Col. Mitchell's conclusions . . ., 24 September 1925 (9-21-25), Entry 580, RG 407.

36. AG to Chief of Coast Artillery, sub: Anti-aircraft defense, 2 May 1925, AGO 381 (1-6-25), Box 17, E 37B, RG 407.

37. Charles P. Summerall to AG, 9 May 1925, sub: Anti-aircraft defense, 9 May 1925; Mason Patrick to AG, sub: Anti-aircraft defense, 27 March 1925; Office of Chief of Field Artillery to AG, sub: Anti-aircraft Defense, 26 March 1925, all in AGO 381 (1-6-25), Box 17, E 37B, RG 407.

38. *FSR* 1923, 77. William O. Odom, *After the Trenches: The Transformation of U.S. Army Doctrine, 1918–1939* (College Station: Texas A&M Press, 1999).

39. Advertisement for Paul S. Bond, *Tactics,* in Paul S. Bond and Enoch B. Carey, *Wars of the American Nation* (Annapolis, MD: New Military Library, 1923).

40. "Address by Major General Charles P. Summerall at Fort Benning," 14 November 1924, Briant Harris Wells Papers, MHI.

41. Wilson B. Burtt, "The Fighting Unit," *IJ* 29 (September 1926): 238.

42. William R. Reed, "The Nine Principles of War," *IJ* 32 (March 1928): 299. *FSR 1923,* iii, 77–78; Edward S. Johnston, "Principles and Methods," *IJ* 33 (December 1928): 563–68; Thomas R. Phillips, "Word Magic of the Military Mystics," *CAJ* 82 (September–October 1939): 419. Although not acknowledged, the author of the Principles of War was British theorist J. F. C. Fuller.

43. W. K. Naylor, "The Principles of War (Part I)" (lecture, AWC, 5 January 1922), AWCCA.

44. E. S. Hughes, "Principles of War?" *IJ* 34 (April 1929): 358.

45. Bernard Lentz, "Men Make War; Men Must Fight It," *CAJ* 76 (May–June 1933): 188–90.

46. Walter R. Wheeler, "Some Thoughts on Military Leadership" (1940?), p. 72, Box 16, Williston B. Palmer Papers, USMA. E. L. Munson, "Morale and Leadership" (lecture, General Staff School, 11 and 13 January 1921), Box 30, Charles P. Summerall Papers, MDLC.

47. Robert McCleave, "Infantry: Its Role, Capabilities, Limitations in Relation to Other Arms," *IJ* 17 (November 1920): 42–43. Emphasis in original.

48. Frank Parker, "The Psychology of the Battlefield and Management of the Crowd Mind" (lecture, General Staff School, 23 January 1923), Box 30, Summerall Papers.

49. Hanson E. Ely, "Battlefield Psychology. Leadership-Morale" (lecture, AWC, 27 March, 1934), MHI. Emphasis in original.

50. *Report of the Superior Board,* 4.

51. *FSR 1923,* 11. Odom, *After the Trenches,* 41–44.

52. Edward F. McGlachlin, "The Art of Command (Part 2)" (lecture, AWC, 12 December 1921), AWCCA. Francis Bonham, "A Study of Combat Morale," SRP #14, 1931, CARL; John H. Burns, "Psychology and Leadership," SRP #110, 1933, CARL.

53. Rodney H. Smith, "Notes on Command," *CAJ* 58 (February 1923): 144–50.

54. Pete T. Heffner, "Leadership: An Analysis of the Leadership of Robert E. Lee," SRP #47, 1935, CARL. Louis B. Hershey, "Fear as a Factor in Leadership Problems," SRP #76, 1933, CARL; Robert S. Miller, "What Is the More Important Factor, Leadership or Tactical Skill?" SRP #71, 1935, CARL.

55. Jennings C. Wise, "The Soldier's Life in Battle," *IJ* 16 (May 1920): 930.

56. James G. Harbord, "The Greatest Fighting Machine," *IJ* 24 (September 1926): 242–44.

57. *Report of the Superior Board,* 44.

58. William E. Lassiter, "Report of the Defense of the Philippine Islands," 21 August 1928, WPD 3251, RG 165; *FSR 1923,* 21; Mason M. Patrick, "The Army Air Service" (lecture, AWC, 9 November 1925), 248.211-61L, AFHRA.

59. S.O.F. [Stephen O. Fuqua] to General Summerall, 10 October 1925, Box 30, Summerall Papers.

60. Minnigerode, "Next War," 55.

61. "Address by Maj. Gen. Charles P. Summerall at the Annual Convention before the Military Order of the World War," 24 September 1925, Box 27, Summerall Papers.

62. Clayton L. Bissell, "Is Air Attack against the Continental United States Practical?" SRP #118, 1933, CARL.

63. Edward F. Hart, "Mechanization of Combat Units: Its Desirability and Tactical Effect," SRP #51, 1932, CARL.

64. Joseph M. Scammell to Basil Liddell Hart, 20 November 1932, LH 1/622/3, Liddell Hart Papers; David E. Johnson, *Fast Tanks and Heavy Bombers: Innovation in the U.S. Army, 1917–1945* (Ithaca: Cornell University Press, 1998); Jeffrey W. French, "Intellectual Discourse during the Interwar Years" (Masters thesis, Texas A&M University, 2000), 55–60.

65. Adna R. Chaffee, "The Status of the Mechanized Combat Organization and the Desired Trend in the Future" (lecture, AWC, 19 September 1929), AWCCA; William Clarke, "Discuss Mechanization in Future Wars," SRP #38, 1931, CARL; Leland S. Hobbs, "The Tactical and Strategical Effects of the Development of the Fast Tank," SRP #59, 1933, CARL; Robert S. Cameron, "Americanizing the Tank: U.S. Army Administration and Mechanized Development within the Army, 1917–1943" (Ph.D. diss., Temple University, 1994).

66. J. L Bradley, "Reorganization of Infantry," *IJ* 37 (August 1930): 136.

67. "Notes Taken During the Conference at the President's Rapidan Camp, May 9, 1931," Box 4, Campbell B. Hodges Papers, USMA.

68. Stephen O. Fuqua, "The Trend of Development of Infantry" (lecture, AWC, 18 September 1930), AWCCA.

69. Captain [no first name] Kloepfer, "Cavalry in Mounted Attack against Infantry," SRP #106, 1930, CARL.

70. LeRoy Eltinge, "Review of Our Cavalry Situation," *CJ* 29 (April 1920): 14–22.

71. Cavalry School, Department of General Instruction, *The Palestine Campaign* (1922–23), 276, Box 2, Fenton Stratton Jacobs Papers, HIA. Cavalry School, Department of General Instruction, *History of the Cavalry during the World War,* 2 vols. (1922–23), Jacobs Papers.

72. R. J. Fleming, "Mission of the Cavalry School with Comments on Modern Cavalry and Cavalry Training," *CJ* 38 (January 1929): 52.

73. Cavalry School, *Cavalry Combat* (Fort Riley, KS: Cavalry School, 1937), xi.

74. J. G. Pillow, "Cavalry in Recent and Future Wars" (lecture, Marine Corps Schools, 14 October 1927), Folder 12/1, Box 1, Lecture Collection, Marine Corps University Research Archives, Quantico, VA.

75. Charles P. Summerall, "Cavalry in Modern Combat," *CJ* 39 (October 1930): 491.

76. George S. Patton to "Dear Gene," 8 October 1940, Folder 48, Box 2, Eugene A. Regenier Papers, Manuscripts and Archives Collection, Stirling Library, Yale University, New Haven, CT.

77. George S. Patton, "What the World War Did for Cavalry," *CJ* 31 (April 1922): 172.

78. George S. Patton, "Success in War," *CJ* 40 (January 1931): 26–30.

79. Brigadier General Elmer Zilch [Joseph M. Scammell], "Some Comments on the Caribbean War," *IJ* 41 (January–February 1934): 9–14. Joseph M. Scammell to Basil Liddell Hart, 4 March 1934, LH 1/622/3, Liddell Hart Papers; Joseph M. Scammell, "Side Lights on Orange Doctrine" [1922?], Box 1, RG 17, Naval Historical Collection, Newport, RI.

80. Bond and Carey, *Wars of the American Nation,* 206. Bloxham Ward, "An Educational Military Policy," *IJ* 16 (July 1919): 21–25.

81. Lewis Steward Chappelear, "Pacifism, Its Effects upon Christianity and the Future of the United States" [1926?], Box 30, Summerall Papers.

John W. Lang, "Militarist or Pacifist," *CJ* 40 (March–April 1931): 32–36; Sherman Miles, "The Problem of the Pacifist," *North American Review* (March 1923): 319–20.

82. Dennis P. Quinlan, *Military Protection* (n.p., 1922), 40. William G. Haan to AGO, sub: War Plan—White, 24 May 1920, AGO 381 (5-24-20), Box 52; G-2 Annex, Emergency Plan—White, 9th Corps Area, 1923, Box 45, both in E 37B, RG 407; W. W. Hick, "Estimate of the Radical or Revolutionary Situation in the United States" (lecture, AWC, 16 December 1920), AWCCA.

83. H. G. Bishop, "What of the Future?" *FAJ* 12 (September–October 1922): 368. David A. Shugart, "On the Way: The U.S. Field Artillery in the Interwar Period" (Ph.D. diss., Texas A&M University, 2002).

84. C. M. Bundel, "What Is Wrong with Our Principles of War," *IJ* 33 (October 1928): 330.

85. Draft of 1936 Revision: Industrial Mobilization Plan, 7 May 1936, Box 131, RG 80. Hugh A. Drum to C/S, sub: Missions of the Regular Army, 15 February 1924, WPD 1549, RG 165.

86. Hjalmar Erickson, "War, Its Nature, Doctrines, and Methods," *CAJ* 57 (October 1922): 306.

87. Ibid., 310–11. Emphasis in original.

88. Nelson M. Walker, "The Technical Education of the Regular Officer," SRP #71, 1930, CARL.

89. Walter S. Grant, "The Army Commander: The Machine Which the Army Commander Operates" (lecture, AWC, 9 February 1925), AWCCA.

90. Charles P. Summerall, "Morale and Leadership" (lecture, AWC, 16 October 1930), AWCCA. E. F. McGlachlin, "The Art of Command, Part 3" (lecture, AWC, 17 December 1921), AWCCA.

91. R. S. Bratton, "A Study to Determine the Basic Principles Involved in the Troop Leading of an Infantry Division," SRP #17, 1931, CARL.

92. Committee No. 1, "Organization of Nations for the Support of Wars and for National Defense," Doct. 406-1, 1933–1934 AWC, AWCCA.

93. Thomas R. Kershner, "The Relationship between the Soldier and the Statesman," SRP #59, 1932, CARL. John M. Erwin, "Democracy and the General," *Army Ordnance* 15 (November–December 1934): 157–58;

George Van Horn Moseley, "Industry and National Defense (III)," *CJ* 40 (March–April 1931): 21–23.

94. L. B. Magruder, "Our Military Policy," *CAJ* 64 (May 1926): 503.

95. Briant H. Wells, Memorandum for C/S, sub: A Pacific Policy for the United States, 31 October 1921, AGO 381 (11-2-23), Security Classified Files, Box 50, RG 407. A. G. Rudd, "The Public and the Army," *IJ* 24 (January 1924): 25–32; David C. Shanks, "The Army and the People," *IG* 16 (February 1920): 623–29.

96. Quoted from a speech written by Eisenhower, Frederick H. Payne, Address to AWC, 6 January 1931, in Daniel D. Holt and James W. Leyerzapf, eds., *Eisenhower: The Prewar Diaries and Selected Papers, 1905–1941* (Baltimore: Johns Hopkins University Press, 1998), 147–56. Kerry E. Irish, "Apt Pupil: Eisenhower and the 1930 Industrial Mobilization Plan," *JMH* 70 (January 2006): 31–62.

97. Quoted from a speech written by Eisenhower, Frederick H. Payne, "To the Graduating Class [USMA]," 10 June 1931, in Holt, *Eisenhower,* 174.

98. Dwight D. Eisenhower to Manuel Quezon, 8 August 1940, cited in Holt, *Eisenhower,* 483. Underlined in original.

99. C. C. Williams, "Ordnance Service in the Theater of Operations" (lecture, AWC, 1 March 1928), MHI.

100. Bishop, "What of the Future?" 365–74.

101. Bonner F. Fellers, "The Psychology of the Japanese Soldier," 39, SRP #34, 1935, CARL. Bradford G. Chynoweth, "Infantry Equipment," *IJ* 20 (March 1922): 277–83; Rene E. D. Hoyle, "Mechanization," *FAJ* 8 (May–June 1928): 238–48.

102. John H. Burns, "The Dead Hand," *IJ* 44 (April 1937): 103.

103. S. D. Rockenbach, "Tanks in the World War" (lecture at Marine Corps Schools, 23 March 1922), Folder 5/1, Box 1, Lecture Collection, Marine Corps University Research Archives. *FSR 1923,* 13.

104. Johnson Hagood, "The United States in the Next War," *JUSA* 53 (July 1920): 3.

105. R. E. Callan to CG, 3rd Crops Area, 2 October 1925, AGO 381 (10-2-25), Box 15, E 37B, RG 407.

106. Stanley D. Embick, "Military Aspects of the Situation That Would

Result from the Retention by the United States of a Military (Including Naval) Commitment in the Philippine Islands" [2 December 1935], Box 3, E 207, RG 107. Hugh A. Drum, ACS, G-3, to C/S, sub: transmittal memorandum . . . relative to War Plan Orange, 18 July 1925, F 1991, WPD, RG 165.

107. WK [Walter Krueger], Memo: Our Policy in the Philippines, 28 October 1935, F-573, Box 17, E 284, RG 165. Ronald Schaffer, "General Stanley D. Embick: Military Dissenter," *MA* 37 (October 1973): 89–95.

108. Wilson B. Burtt, "The Fighting Unit," *IJ* 29 (September 1926): 239.

109. Ely, "Battlefield Psychology."

110. Walter R. Wheeler, "Some Thoughts on Military Leadership," p. 72, Box 16, Williston B. Palmer Papers, USMA. Francis Bonham, "A Study of Combat Morale," SRP #14, 1931, CARL.

111. Anon., "Infantry in Battle," *IJ* 25 (August 1924): 125. Joseph M. Scammell, "Fear in Battle," *JUSA* 55 (July 1921): 30–38; Wise, "Soldier's Life," 929–38.

112. James Jay Carafano, *GI Ingenuity: Improvisation, Technology, and Winning World War II* (Westport, CT: Praeger, 2006); Michael D. Doubler, *Closing with the Enemy: How GIs Fought the War in Europe, 1944–1945* (Lawrence: University Press of Kansas, 1994).

113. Charles E. T. Lull, "War of Tomorrow," *Army Ordnance* 15 (September–October 1934): 81.

114. St. Clair Streett, "What Principles Should Govern the Strategical Employment of the Air Force, with Particular Consideration to the Most Suitable Objectives?" SRP #112, 1933, CARL.

115. J. N. Douglas, "A Study of Applied Psychology and Its Practical Application to the Army," 1, SRP #31, 1932, CARL. Conrad H. Lanza, "Aspects of Modern War," *FAJ* 28 (September 1938): 341–63.

6. Atomic War

1. Maxwell D. Taylor, *The Uncertain Trumpet* (New York: Harper and Brothers, 1959), 6. Maxwell D. Taylor, "On Limited War," *AID* 13 (June 1958): 4–5.

2. Andrew Krepinevich, Jr., *The Army and Vietnam* (Baltimore: Johns Hopkins University Press, 1986).

3. Remarks of Gen. J. Lawton Collins, Background Material for the War Department Presentation to the Committee on the Armed Services, 11 February 1947, N-15083-C, CARL.

4. Eugene P. Forrester Oral History, 1985, SOOHP, 64.

5. OCAGF Staff Study: Organization and Assignment of Special Task Force from Parakeet Units, 29 August 1947, File 370.5/7-2, Box 11, E54, RG 337; OCAGF Staff Study: Task Force from General Reserve Units . . . for Overseas Duty in Greece, 28 August 1947, File 370.5/1, Box 11, E54, RG 337.

6. "Beyond the Stars," p. 129, James M. Gavin Papers, MHI.

7. AFF Staff Study: To determine the degree and system of protection . . ., 20 December 1947, Binder 2A, File 381, Box 12, E 54, RG 337.

8. Presentation Given to President by Major General Lauris Norstad, 29 October 1946, Strategy and the Army Files, Folder 10, Box 2, RG 319.

9. *War Department Equipment Board Report,* 29 May 1946, copy in MHI.

10. J. Lawton Collins, "Role of the Army in Future Global Warfare" (lecture, Armed Forces Staff College, 5 February 1948), Box 43, J. Lawton Collins Papers, DDEL.

11. William R. Desobry Oral History, 1977, SOOHP, 66. US Army Forces Information, *The Army Almanac: A Book of Facts Concerning the Army of the United States* (Washington, DC: GPO, 1950), 625.

12. Joint Planning Staff 789, Concept for Operations for "Pincher," 2 March 1946, F 3; JCS 1641/5, sub: Estimate Based on Assumption of Occurrence of Major Hostilities, 11 April 1946, F 4; JWPC 432/7, sub: Tentative Over-All Strategic Concept and Estimate of Initial Operations, "Pincher," 18 June 1946, Folder 6, all in Strategy and the Army Files, Box 1, RG 319.

13. Jacob L. Devers, "The Future of Armor," *ACJ* 57 (July–August 1948): 5. U.S. Forces, European Theater, *The General Board,* 1945, CMH; Report of Army Advisory Panel on Joint Amphibious Operations, 15 January 1949, F 2, Box 20, Lucien K. Truscott, Jr., Papers, George C. Marshall Library, Lexington, VA, [hereafter Truscott Board].

14. Testimony of Albert C. Wedemeyer, Minutes of Army Equipment Policy Panel, 18 July 1949, F 334, Box 21, E 54, RG 337.

15. John L. Homer, "Guided Missiles and Future Warfare," *CAJ* 90 (November–December 1947): 24–26; Floyd A. Lambert, "Air Defense of the United States," *AAJ* 92 (May–June 1949): 31–32; David B. Parker, "Death Takes a Sleeping City," *CAJ* 90 (March–April 1947): 12–14.

16. Charles L. Bolté, "Military Concepts Influencing the European War" (lecture, Air War College, 4 November 1947), K239.716247-11, AFHRA.

17. Walter Krueger Testimony, Truscott Board.

18. S. L. A. Marshall, *Men against Fire: The Problem of Battle Command in Future War* (New York: William Morrow, 1947), 208.

19. Albert C. Wedemeyer, "Concept for Employment of Military Forces in Future War" (lecture, Air War College, 18 April 1952), K239.716252-73, AFHRA.

20. Omar N. Bradley, "Our Military Requirements," *IJ* 64 (April 1949): 46.

21. Manton Eddy, "Relationship of Land Power to Air Power" (lecture, Air War College, 1 March 1949), K239.716249-28, AFHRA; George A. Lincoln, "Military Strategy in Cold War" (lecture, 14 October 1949, Air War College), K239.716249-58, AFHRA.

22. Paul M. Robinett, "Ground Force Mobility," *Armor* 52 (March–April 1953): 10. Jacob L. Devers to CGs, sub: Future of Armor, 19 November 1947, N1-15937, CARL; George F. Hoffman and Donn A. Starry, eds., *Camp Colt to Desert Storm: The History of U.S. Armored Forces* (Lexington: University Press of Kentucky, 1999), 217–62, 298–323.

23. Melvin Zais, "Developments in Ground Warfare from 1939 to 1948 and Future Potentialities," 31 May 1949, SRP, N-2253.147, CARL.

24. James M. Gavin, *Airborne Warfare* (Washington, DC: Infantry Journal Press, 1947), 175. Lewis H. Brereton, "Role of Airborne Forces in Future Warfare" (lecture, Naval War College, 3 February 1947), N-15262, CARL; James M. Gavin, "The Future of Airborne Operations," *MR* 27 (December 1947): 3–8; James M. Gavin, "The Future of Armor," *IJ* 62 (January 1948): 7–11.

25. Report of the Army Equipment Board, 8 March 1950, Box 17,

E 66A, RG 337. G-2/GS, Comparison of Current and Future Capabilities of U.S. and Soviet Tanks, 22 April 1949, F 461.01, Box 22, E 54, RG 337.

26. Matthew B. Ridgway, *The Korean War* (Garden City, NY: Doubleday, 1967), vi.

27. Mark Clark to Wade H. Haislip, 8 August 1950, F 381, Box 22, E 54, RG 337.

28. *Semiannual Report of the Secretary of the Army, January 1 to June 30 1950* (Washington, DC: GPO, 1950), 67.

29. George B. Pickett, "Tanks in Korea, 1950–1951," *Armor* 60 (November–December 1951): 12–16.

30. Earle E. Weaver, "Strategic Mobility," *AID* 12 (January 1957): 6.

31. Roy K. Flint, "Task Force Smith and the 24th Division: Delay and Withdrawal, 5–19 July, 1950," in *America's First Battles, 1776–1965*, ed. Charles E. Heller and William A. Stofft (Lawrence: University Press of Kansas, 1986), 266–99; Dennis J. Reimer, *Soldiers Are Our Credentials: The Collected Works and Selected Papers of the Thirty-Third Chief of Staff, United States Army*, ed. James Jay Carafano (Washington, DC: Center of Military History, 2000), 7–8, 234.

32. Matthew B. Ridgway to J. Lawton Collins, 8 January 1951, Matthew B. Ridgway File, Box 17, Collins Papers.

33. [R. P. Shugg] to C/S, sub: Will Our Present Doctrine and Organization Produce an Army Which Can Stop the Russians in 1952? 20 June 1951, 461/31, Box 90, E 55B, RG 337.

34. Ed., "For Continental Warfare . . . an Armored Corps," *Armor* 52 (January–February 1953): 21.

35. George Decker, "Army Survey of Defense of Western Europe," 19 April 1950, File 381, Box 22, E 54, RG 337.

36. Collins, "Role of the Army."

37. J. Lawton Collins, "National Strategic Objectives" (lecture, Air War College, 20 April 1950), Box 43, Collins Papers.

38. J. Lawton Collins (untitled lecture to Air War College, 28 April 1953), Box 43, Collins Papers.

39. Dwight D. Eisenhower, *Mandate for Change, 1953–1956* (Garden City, NY: Doubleday, 1963), 446.

40. Dwight D. Eisenhower to "Monty," 2 May 1956, copy in Eisen-

hower (1956) File 2, Box 1, Eisenhower Correspondence Series, 1941–78, Alfred M. Gruenther Papers, DDEL.

41. Interview with Matthew B. Ridgway by Maurice Matloff, 14, 19 April 1984, Matthew B. Ridgway Papers, MHI. Andrew J. Bacevich, "The Paradox of Professionalism: Eisenhower, Ridgway, and the Challenge to Civilian Control, 1953–1955," *JMH* 61 (April 1997), 303–34.

42. Matthew B. Ridgway as told to Harold H. Martin, *Soldier: The Memoirs of Matthew B. Ridgway* (New York: Harper and Brothers, 1956), 274.

43. Ibid., 280.

44. Matthew B. Ridgway, "Current Army Tasks" (lecture, Air War College, 6 December 1954), K239.716254-90, AFHRA.

45. Remarks at Secretary's Conference, 16 July 1955, Item 6, Box 5, Maxwell D. Taylor Papers, National Defense University Library, Fort McNair, DC.

46. Taylor, *Uncertain Trumpet*, 146. Maxwell D. Taylor, "A National Military Program" (lecture, Council on Foreign Relations, 14 May 1956), Box 4, Taylor Papers.

47. Charlton Ogburn, "The United States Army," *Holiday* 28 (September 1960): 102.

48. DOA Pamphlet 355-5: *The Soldier and Army,* April 1956, Item 55 (15), Box 5, Taylor Papers.

49. *Field Service Regulations, Operations, ST 100-5-1* (June 1960), copy in CGSC Files, Box 39, RG 498. David T. Fautua, "The 'Long Pull' Army: NSC 68, the Korean War, and the Creation of the Cold War U.S. Army," *JMH* 61 (January 1997): 93–120.

50. Wallace M. Hanes, "Guerrilla Warfare," 14 March 1955, AWCSP.

51. William D. McKinley, "Army Concepts of Future War" (lecture, Air War College, 18 May 1954), K239.716254-46, AFHRA.

52. Lyman L. Lemnitzer, "The Army's Role in General War and Conflict Short of General War" (lecture, Air War College, 21 May 1959), K239.716259-11, AFHRA.

53. OCAFF, "Tactical Employment of the Atomic Bomb," 7 October 1951, 000.9/35, Box 4, E 55B, RG 337. John M. Midgley, Jr., *Deadly Illusions: Army Policy for the Nuclear Battlefield* (Boulder, CO: Westview Press, 1986).

54. Combat Development Objectives Guide—Atomic Operations, 1954, Box 33, E 55F, RG 337.

55. Frank J. Sackton, "The Changing Nature of War," *MR* 34 (November 1954): 58.

56. AWC, Advanced Study Group, "Project Binnacle: Concepts and Doctrine for Future Warfare, Conventional or Nuclear, 1960–1970," 1956, MHI.

57. CGSC, Syllabus: The Army and National Security, (1000/8), 1957–1958, CARL.

58. John P. Rose, *The Evolution of U.S. Army Nuclear Doctrine, 1945–1980* (Boulder: Westview Press, 1980), 57.

59. Sackton, "Changing Nature of War," 58.

60. William C. Westmoreland, "Our Twentieth Century Army" (lecture, Airborne Conference, 7 May 1957), Box 1, William C. Westmoreland Papers, USMA.

61. Gavin, *Airborne Warfare,* 170.

62. Benjamin F. Taylor, "The Destiny of the Army," 15 March 1954, AWCSP. Andrew J. Bacevich, *The Pentomic Era: The U.S. Army between Korea and Vietnam* (Washington: National Defense University Press, 1986); Don Alan Carter, "From G.I. to Atomic Soldier: The Development of U.S. Tactical Doctrine, 1945–1956" (Ph.D. diss., Ohio State University, 1987).

63. John F. Rhoades, "Are We Training Leaders?" *Armor* 67 (January–February 1958): 44.

64. Ridgway, "Current Army Tasks."

65. Paul W. Caraway, "Army Views on the Attack" (lecture, Air War College, 8 February 1955), K239.716256-50, AFHRA.

66. Robert B. Rigg, *War—1974* (Harrisburg, PA: Military Service Publishing Co., 1958).

67. *The Role of the Infantry* (Fort Benning, GA: Infantry School, 1955), 22.

68. Ogburn, "The United States Army," 102. Herbert B. Powell, "The Infantryman in the Atomic Age," *AID* 13 (April 1958): 34.

69. Department of the Army, *Progress 57* (Washington, DC: GPO, 1957), Box 13, Theodore J. Conway Papers, MHI.

70. Karl T. Gould, "Individual Requirement Study No. 12," 2 April 1952, K239.716252-26, AFHRA.

71. "The Other Side of the Coin" [1957], draft, Box 5, Arthur S. Collins Papers, MHI.

72. T. J. H. Trapnell, "The Army Views on the Use of Force in Limited War" (lecture, Air War College, 12 April 1957), K239.716257-37, AFHRA.

73. Sidney B. Berry, Jr., Oral History, 1983, SOOHP, 411. CGSC, *Draft Annual Report*, 15 February 1958, CGSC Curriculum Files, CARL; Lionel McGarr, "Special Report of the Commandant," 1 January 1959, CGSC, Box 34, RG 337; "The Regulars," pp. 575–78, Donald A. Siebert Papers, MHI.

74. OCAFF Reports of Observers: Exercise Flash Burn, 10 May 1954, 354-Folder 2, Box 28, E 55F, RG 337.

75. Observer Reports: Exercise Indian Summer, in John W. Callaway to John A. Heintges, 15 October 1954, F 2, Box 28, E 55F, RG 337.

76. Paul D. Harkins to CG, CONARC, sub: Observation of Sage Brush, 30 December 1955, Binder 8, AGO 354 (Sage Brush) 1955, Box 125/154, HQ CONARC Central Administrative Files, RG 338. One minor point of confusion was that the exercise was referred to as both Sagebrush and Sage Brush.

77. John E. Dahlquist, Remarks at Joint Critique for Exercise Sagebrush, 17 November 1955, John E. Dahlquist Papers, MHI; HQ, Exercise Sagebrush, Final Report, 1955, HRC 353.2 Maneuvers—Sage Brush File, CMH.

78. Maxwell D. Taylor, "Role and Capability of the Army World-Wide" (lecture, Quantico Conference on Defense Leaders, 16 July 1955), Maxwell D. Taylor File, Box 13, Bio Files, RG 407.

79. *Public Information Policy and Guidance,* 15 February 1955, USAREUR Manual 360-10, E 33043, EUCOM, RG 338.

80. Combat Developments Office, Infantry Fighting Vehicle for the PENTANA Combat Group (U), 29 May 1958, MHI.

81. William E. DePuy, *Selected Papers of General William E. DePuy: First Commander, U.S. Army, Training and Doctrine Command,* compiled by

Richard M. Swain, ed. Donald L. Gilmore and Carolyn D. Conway (Fort Leavenworth, KS: Combat Studies Institute, 1994), 266.

82. Forsythe Oral History, 333.

83. Department of the Army, *Progress 57.*

84. Desobry Oral History, 14.

85. Berry Oral History, 410–11.

86. James M. Gavin Oral History, 1975, SOOHP, 45.

87. Melvin Zais Oral History, 1977, SOOHP, 335–41.

88. Paul C. Jussel, "Intimidating the World: The United States Atomic Army, 1956–1960" (Ph.D. diss., Ohio State University, 2004), 208.

89. T. L. Sherburne, "Reorganizing the 101st Airborne," *AID* 12 (June 1957): 13–23.

90. HQ, 25ID, After Action Report—Reorganization 1957, F 250/15, Box 5, E 34431, RG 338.

91. HQ, 25ID to CG, USARPAC, sub: Organization of 25th Infantry Division, 5 June 1957, Box 5, E 34431, RG 338.

92. Maxwell D. Taylor, Statement at Army Commanders' Conference, 5 April 1956, Box 9, Taylor Papers.

93. Maxwell D. Taylor, "Security through Deterrence" (lecture, Army War College, 20 August 1956), Box 4, Taylor Papers.

94. Taylor, *Uncertain Trumpet*, 6.

95. Ibid.

96. Ibid., 62.

97. CGSC, "Study of Army Attitude toward Arming Partisans," 1950, File 334, Box 21, E 54, RG 337. Fred L. Walker, Jr., "Your Next War," *IJ* 61 (August 1947): 42.

98. AFF Inspection Team, Infantry: Report of Army Field Forces Inspection of European Command, October 1951, 333.144, Box 41, E 55B, RG 337.

99. John E. Dahlquist (untitled lecture, CGSC, 17 December 1954), Dahlquist Papers.

100. Gordon Charles Gill, "Unconventional Warfare," 25 March 1952, AWCSP.

101. Orlando C. Troxel, Jr., "Special Warfare—A New Appraisal," *AID* 12 (December 1957): 2–11. Douglas S. Blaufarb, *The Counterinsurgency Era: U.S. Doctrine and Performance, 1950 to the Present* (New York: Free Press, 1977).

102. Glenn F. Rogers, "Unconventional Methods of Warfare," 24 March 1952, AWCSP.

103. Paschall, "Low-Intensity Conflict," 41; Edson D. Raff, "Fighting behind Enemy Lines," *AID* 11 (April 1956): 13.

104. Taylor, "Transcript of Statement at Army Commander's Conference." Lionel C. McGarr, "The Commandant's /60 Curriculum Guidance and Decisions on /60 Curriculum," 3 November 1958, CGSC, Box 3, RG 337; Armored School Research Report, "Security of the Trains of Armored Units against Guerrilla Type Activity," 7 March 1952, Box 35, E 35004, RG 338.

105. John W. Romlein, "Unconventional Methods of Warfare," 24 March 1952, AWCSP.

106. Robert G. MacDonnell, "Unconventional Methods of Warfare," 1 March 1952, AWCSP.

107. Bruce Palmer, Jr., "The Modern Role of Unconventional Warfare," 1 March 1952, AWCSP.

108. Peter Schmick, "Partisan Warfare," 22 February 1951, AWCSP.

109. John V. Roddy, "Anti-Guerrilla Warfare," 15 March 1955, AWCSP.

110. William F. Lewis, "National Policy for Limited War," 14 March 1955, AWCSP, emphasis in original.

111. Neil Sheehan, *A Bright Shining Lie: John Paul Vann and America in Vietnam* (New York: Random House, 1988).

112. Krepinevich, *Army and Vietnam,* 56–90.

113. Taylor, "Security through Deterrence." Army Operations Research Office, Defense of the North American Continent, 30 November 1954, 350.001-Folder 2, Box 22, E 55F, RG 337.

114. S. R. Mickelsen, "Army Antiair—The Nation's Shield," *AID* 12 (November 1957): 9.

115. George A. Cahill, "ARADCOM's Hawk and Hercules," *Recruiting Journal* (September 1957): 8–9.

116. Ibid.

117. Mickelsen, "Sentry of the Skies," 9. "A Proven Sales Package with a Brand-New Wrapper," *Recruiting Journal* (May 1962): 11–13.

118. Mickelsen, "Army Antiair—The Nation's Shield," 10.

119. Bruce Siemon, "U.S. Army Air Defense Europe, 1948–1970," 1971, Historical Files, 7th Army CY 2, copy in CMH.

120. Collins, "National Strategic Objectives."

121. Maxwell D. Taylor, "The Army's Role in the Future," *AID* 13 (January 1958): 4.

122. Siemon, "U.S. Army Air Defense Europe, 1948–1970."

123. Lincoln, "Military Strategy in Cold War."

124. Thomas J. O'Connor, "Unconventional Warfare Today," 24 March 1952, AWCSP. Walter R. Goodrich, Albert O. Connor, G. A. Williams, "A National Strategy for the United States, 1956–1970," [1955], AWC Z-G62, MHI; George W. Wear, "The Meaning of Winning," 3 May 1965, AWCSP.

125. Lucius D. Clay, "Concept for Employment of Military Forces in Future War" (lecture, Air War College, 10 April 1952), K239.716252-106, AFHRA.

126. "America in the World Today" (speech, High Twelve International Convention, 18 June 1952), Box 5, Paul M. Robinett Papers, MDLC.

127. H. I. Hodes to James A. Van Fleet, 19 May 1952, F-28, Box 69, Van Fleet Papers.

128. Virginia Weisel Johnson, *Lady in Arms* (Boston: Houghton Mifflin, 1967), 79. Romlein, "Unconventional Methods of Warfare."

129. Floyd Parks, "Information Aspects of Planning" (lecture, AWC, 25 April 1953), Box 13, Floyd L. Parks Papers, DDEL.

130. Annual Historical Report, 1 July 1954–30 June 1955, Historical Division, USAREUR, Historical Manuscript Files 8-3.1 CL, at CMH. Lori Bogle, *The Pentagon's Battle for the American Mind: The Early Cold War* (College Station: Texas A&M University Press, 2004).

131. Heinz P. Rand, "Mental Conditioning of the Soldier for Nuclear

War," in CGSC, *Selected Readings in Leadership in Higher Commands*, 15 August 1960, Box 39, RG 498.

132. John H. Cushman, "What Is the Army's Story?" *CFJ* 5 (October 1954): 49.

133. John T. Corley, "Lean and Hungry Soldiers," *CFJ* 1 (July 1951): 16–18; Maurice D. Stratta, "Soldier Morale in a Non-Atomic Limited War," 15 March 1955, AWCSP.

134. William G. Van Allen, "Revitalization of Senior Army Leadership," 14 March 1955, AWCSP.

135. Earle E. Weaver, "Strategic Mobility," 5.

136. W. G. Wyman, "Adaptability: Index to Survivability," *AID* 12 (June 1957): 4.

137. Matthew B. Ridgway to Gerald G. Gibbs, in Gerald B. Gibbs, "United States Policy towards Future Wars of National Liberation," 1970, AWCSP, italics are capitalized in original.

7. From Reformation to Reaction

1. James E. Chapmen, "Vietnam: Strategic Incompetence, Its Causes and Implications," 18 October 1973, AWCSP. Many of the ideas in this chapter were first presented at the 2006 Chief of the Australian Army's History Conference. My thanks to General Peter F. Leahy, Jeffrey Grey, Peter Dennis, and the conference participants for their comments and suggestions.

2. Department of the Army, *FM 100–1: The Army* (August 1981), 9. Department of the Army, *A Study of the Strategic Lessons Learned in Vietnam*, 8 vols. (McLean, VA: BDM Corporation, 1979); AWC curriculum pamphlets, 1974–1978, MHI; CGSC, *75–76 Catalog* and *76–77 Catalog*, both in CARL; Conrad C. Crane, *Avoiding Vietnam: The U.S. Army's Response to Defeat in Southeast Asia* (Carlisle, PA: Strategic Studies Institute, 2002); Michael J. Brady, "The Army and the Strategic Military Legacy of Vietnam" (MMAS, 1990).

3. Zeb B. Bradford, "US Tactics in Vietnam," *MR* 52 (February 1972): 64.

4. Ibid., 72.

5. Ibid., 75.

6. Harry G. Summers, Jr., *On Strategy: The Vietnam War in Context* (Washington, DC: GPO, 1981).

7. Tom Clancy with Fred Franks, Jr., *Into the Storm: A Study in Command* (New York: G. P. Putnam's, 1997), 84. Peter Maslowski, "Army Values and American Values," *MR* 70 (April 1990): 10–23.

8. Geoffrey G. Prosch and Mitchell M. Zais, "American Will and the Vietnam War," *MR* 70 (March 1990): 80. David T. Twining, "Vietnam and the Six Criteria for the Use of Military Force," *Parameters* 14 (Winter 1985): 10–18.

9. Colin Powell with Joseph E. Persico, *My American Journey,* rev. ed. (New York: Ballantine, 2003), 144–45.

10. AWC, "Study on Military Professionalism," 13–14, 30 June 1970, copy in MHI. Llyle H. Barker et al., "Professional Military Development of the Military Executive," 27 May 1975, AWCSP; Richard Lock-Pullan, "'An Inward Looking Time': The United States Army, 1973–1976," *JMH* 67 (April 2003): 483–511.

11. *E. C. Meyer, General, United States Army Chief of Staff, June 1979–June 1983* (Washington, DC: Department of the Army, 1983), 294.

12. Ibid., 69.

13. Powell, *My American Journey,* 292.

14. Donald M. Snow and Dennis M. Drew, *From Lexington to Desert Storm: War and Politics in the American Experience* (Armonk, NY: M. E. Sharpe, 1994), 325–26.

15. Wesley K. Clark, *Waging Modern War: Bosnia, Kosovo, and the Future of Combat,* rev. ed. (New York: Public Affairs, 2002), 450.

16. Chapmen, "Vietnam: Strategic Incompetence, Its Causes and Implications." Thomas E. Lett, Jr., "Military Power in a Limited War," 21 September 1975, AWCSP.

17. Oral History, 232, 1996, Box 1, Joseph T. Palastra Papers, MHI. Kevin Corcoran, "Maneuver Company Commanders and Their Battalion Commanders in Vietnam: No Shared Value," 31 March 1989, AWCSP.

18. Dennis S. Langley, "Management and Mismanagement in War: Issues from the Vietnam War," 19 April 1982, AWCSP.

19. Louis J. Zeleznikar, "The Military Executive: The Trend of the 80s," 2 March 1973, AWCSP.

20. CGSC, *1976–1979 Catalogs,* CARL.

21. "Frederick Taylor and Scientific Management," www.netmba.com/mgmt/scientific, accessed 16 October 2006.

22. Robert M. Cassidy, "Back to the Street without Joy: Counterinsurgency Lessons from Vietnam and Other Small Wars," *Parameters* 34 (Summer 2004): 74.

23. William E. DePuy to Fred C. Weyand (C/S), 18 February 1976, in William E. DePuy, *Selected Papers of General William E. DePuy: First Commander, U.S. Army, Training and Doctrine Command,* compiled by Richard M. Swain, ed. Donald L. Gilmore and Carolyn D. Conway (Fort Leavenworth, KS: Combat Studies Institute, 1994), 180. Paul H. Herbert, *Deciding What Has to Be Done: General William E. DePuy and the 1976 Edition of FM 100–5 Operations* (Fort Leavenworth, KS: Combat Studies Institute, 1988); John Romjue, *From Active Defense to AirLand Battle: The Development of Army Doctrine, 1973–1982* (Fort Monroe, VA: TRADOC, 1984).

24. Donn A. Starry Oral History, 19 March 1993, SOOHP, 2.

25. Richard W. Wilmot et al., "An Examination of the Utility of the First Use of Tactical Nuclear Weapons in the Defense of Western Europe," 6 June 1975, AWCSP. Syllabus: Forward Deployed Operations (European Setting) (M3161); Syllabus: Fundamentals of Combined Arms Warfare (M3121), both in 1976–1977 Course, CGSC, CARL.

26. HQ, Department of the Army, *FM 100–5: Operations* (1 July 1976), 1. Hereafter cited as *FM 100–5* (1976).

27. Ibid, 2–3.

28. Jeffrey W. Long, "The Evolution of U.S. Army Doctrine: From Active Defense to AirLand Battle and Beyond" (MMAS, 1991), 35.

29. *FM 100–5* (1976), 1–2.

30. Ibid, 43–44.

31. Philemon A. Erickson, Jr., "The '73 War: Implications for U.S. Army Forces in NATO" (MMAS, 1978), 150.

32. James G. Burton, *The Pentagon Wars: Reformers Challenge the Old Guard* (Annapolis, MD: Naval Institute Press, 1993); W. Blair Haworth,

The Bradley and How It Got That Way: Technology, Institutions, and the Problem of Mechanized Infantry in the United States Army (Westport, CT: Greenwood Press, 1999); *The Pentagon Wars,* DVD (1998, HBO Home Video).

33. Mark R. Hamilton, "Maneuver Warfare Revisited: A Plea for Balance," April 1984, AWCSP. Grant T. Hammond, *The Mind of War: John Boyd and American Security* (Washington, DC: Smithsonian Press, 2001); Richard D. Hooker, Jr., ed., *Maneuver Warfare: An Anthology* (Novato, CA: Presidio Press, 1993); Robert Leonard, *The Art of Maneuver: Maneuver-Warfare Theory and AirLand Battle* (Novato, CA: Presidio Press, 1991); Huba Wass de Czege, "Toward a New American Approach to Warfare," *The Art of War Quarterly* 2 (September 1983): 31–62.

34. *E. C. Meyer,* 295.

35. Ibid., 155.

36. Ibid., 52–54.

37. Department of the Army, *FM 100–1: The Army* (August 1981), 7.

38. Louis C. Menetrey Oral History, 1996, SOOHP, 113–14.

39. *E. C. Meyer,* 97.

40. Ibid., 222.

41. Starry Oral History, 24. William R. Richardson Oral History, 2000, SOOHP; Donn A. Starry, "A Tactical Evolution—FM 100–5," *MR* 58 (August 1978): 2–11.

42. Sidney B. Berry, Jr., Oral History, 1983, SOOHP, 1077.

43. HQ, Department of the Army, *FM 100–5: Operations (1982),* 1. William G. Hanne, "AirLand Battle: Doctrine, Not Dogma," *MR* 63 (June 1983): 11–25; Long, "Evolution of U.S. Army," 30–77; Donn A. Starry, "To Change an Army," *MR* 63 (March 1983): 20–27; Huba Wass de Czege and L. D. Holder, "The New FM 100–5," *MR* 62 (July 1982): 53–70.

44. *FM 100–5: Operations (1982),* 2–4.

45. Ibid., 2–2.

46. Roger Spiller, "In the Shadow of the Dragon: Doctrine and the US Army after Vietnam," *R.U.S.I. Journal* 142 (December 1997): 52.

47. Richard M. Swain, "Removing Square Pegs from Round Holes: Low-Intensity Conflict in Army Doctrine," *MR* 67 (December 1987): 2.

48. Course Syllabus: Forward Deployed Operations, European Setting (M3161), 1976–1977; Course 3—Tactics: Defensive Tactics (M313/83),

1982–1983; Course Syllabus: Contingency Force Operations (M3141), 1976–77; *The Leavenworth Assessment of the Warsaw Pact Threat in Central Europe (Revised)* (Fort Leavenworth, KS: U.S. Army Combined Arms Combat Development Activity, 1977), all in CARL; Edward D. Baisden et. al., "Validation of the USAWC Student War Gaming Model," 18 May 1983, AWCSP.

49. *E. C. Meyer,* 292.

50. The "Big Blue Bedroom" is the main lecture room at CGSC. "Buzzword Bingo" was played with bingo cards containing the latest army slogans and catchphrases, which were then marked off as lecturers regurgitated them. A variation was "Springbutt Bingo," played with cards having the names of students who repeatedly asked questions (termed "springbutts" because they spring from their chairs to ask their questions).

51. Richardson Oral History, 4. John L. Gifford, "Teaching and Learning the Operational Art of War: An Appraisal of the School of Advanced Military Studies," 2000, SAMSM.

52. Christopher L. Baggott, "The School of Advanced Military Studies in the 21st Century," 21 May 1998, SAMSM. Robert H. Scales, Jr., *Certain Victory: The US Army in the Gulf War* (Washington, DC: Office of the Chief of Staff, 1993), 27–28, 109–10.

53. Donald B. Vought, "Preparing for the Wrong War?" *MR* 57 (May 1977): 20.

54. HQ, Department of the Army, *FM 100–5: Operations* (1986), 4–5. Walter E. Kretchik, "Peering through the Mist: Doctrine as a Guide for U.S. Army Operations, 1775–2000" (Ph.D. diss., University of Kansas, 2001), 181–97, 205–11.

55. Brady, "Army and Strategic Military Legacy," 146; Proposed Essay Requirement Memo, in Postinstructional Conference for P-851, Low-Intensity Conflict, P-851/86 Box 1, 1985–1986 Course; CGSC, 1978–1988 course catalogs, all in CARL. CGSC did offer electives in unconventional warfare and included some highly qualified faculty, such as Vought, Peter Leahy, John Waghelstein, and Lawrence Yates.

56. Cited in Michael J. Mazarr, *Light Force and the Future of U.S. Military Strategy* (New York: Brassey's, 1990), 163–64.

57. John A. Wickham, Jr., Oral History, 1991, SOOHP, 74.

58. William B. Caldwell IV, "Not Light Enough to Get There, Not Heavy Enough to Win: The Case of US Light Infantry," 4 December 1987, SAMSM; Charles C. Campbell, "Light Infantry and the Heavy Force: A Marriage of Convenience or Necessity?" 2 December 1985, SAMSM; Richard St. John, "Antitank Tactics for the Light Infantry: Can History Help?" 7 April 1986, AWCSP.

59. Alan R. Cocks, "Objective: NTC. Some Ideas for Leaders on How to Get There from Here," 28 February 1986, AWCSP.

60. Daniel P. Bolger, *The Battle for Hunger Hill: The 1st Battalion, 327th Infantry Regiment at the Joint Readiness Training Center* (Novato, CA: Presidio Press, 1997), 9–15, 21–39. Daniel P. Bolger, *Dragons at War: 2/34 Infantry in the Mojave* (Novato, CA: Presidio Press, 1991); Anne W. Chapman, *The Origins and Development of the National Training Center, 1976–1984* (Fort Monroe, VA: TRADOC, 1992); Glynn C. Mallory, "Combat Training Centers: Training the Force to Fight," *MR* 57 (October 1987): 2–7; James R. McDonough, *The Defense of Hill 781: An Allegory of Modern Mechanized Combat* (Novato, CA: Presidio Press, 1988).

61. Steven N. Collins, "*Just Cause* Up Close: A Light Infantryman's View of LIC," *Parameters* 22 (Summer 1992): 57.

62. Thomas E. Ricks, *Fiasco: The American Military Adventure in Iraq* (New York: Penguin Books, 2006), 132–33; Antulio J. Echevarria II, *Toward an American Way of War* (Carlisle, PA: Strategic Studies Institute, 2003).

63. Reforger was an acronym for Return of Forces to Germany, and usually capitalized. HQ USAREUR and 7th Army, *After Action Report: Reforger 79,* MHI.

64. *Reforger V After Action Report,* 15 January 1974, MHI

65. L. D. Holder, "Training for the Operational Level," *Parameters* 15 (Spring 1986): 7.

66. *Reforger 76: After Action Report: Exercise Lares Team,* 11 October 1976, MHI; Frederick J. Kroesen Oral History, 1987, SOOHP, 331–32; HQ USAREUR and 7th Army, *After Action Report for Reforger 76* and *After Action Report: Reforger 79.*

67. *FTX Carbon Edge Reforger 1977: Final After Action Report,* 11. John M. Midgley, Jr., *Deadly Illusions: Army Policy for the Nuclear Battlefield* (Boulder, CO: Westview Press, 1986), 129–85.

68. David A. Bouton, "The US Military and Future War: Ready or Not?" 19 May 1987, AWCSP.

69. John N. Abrams, "Warfighter and Pilot," 8 April 1986, AWCSP.

70. Robert L. Maginnis, "The Warrior Spirit," *MR* 67 (April 1987): 69–70.

71. Bruce A. Malson, "Tarnished Armor: Erosion of Military Ethics," 23 March 1988, AWCSP; Anneliese M. Steele, "Are the Relationships between Junior and Senior Officers in the U.S. Army Officer Corps Dysfunctional?" 30 April 2001, SAMSM; Dudley L. Tademy, James A. Musselman, Donald L. Woodhouse, "Lieutenant Colonel and Colonel Command Declinations during FY 79," June 1980, AWCSP.

72. Daniel P. Bolger, "Two Armies," *Parameters* 19 (September 1989): 27.

73. Kretchik, "Peering through the Mist," 205–6.

74. James M. Simmons, "Operation Urgent Fury: Operational Art or a Strategy of Overwhelming Combat Power," 6 May 1994, SAMSM, 41.

75. "Introduction," *Operation Just Cause: The Incursion into Panama* (Washington, DC: Center of Military History, 2004), 3.

76. Frederic J. Brown, "The Uncertain Path," *MR* 70 (June 1990): 2–13; Stephen Silvasy, Jr., "AirLand Battle Future: The Tactical Battlefield," *MR* 71 (February 1991): 2–12.

77. Quoted in Steven W. Senkovich, "From Port Salines to Panama City: The Evolution of Command and Control in Contingency Operations," 7 June 1990, SAMSM, 45.

78. Scales, *Certain Victory,* iii.

79. Douglas A. Macgregor, "Future Battle: The Merging Levels of War," *Parameters* 22 (Winter 1992–1993): 33.

80. William E. DePuy to Colin Powell, 26 September 1991, in DePuy, *Selected Papers,* 466.

81. Leonard, *Art of Maneuver,* 261, see also 262–99.

82. Daniel P. Bolger, "The Ghosts of Omdurman," *Parameters* 21 (Autumn 1991): 28–39. Joseph J. Collins, "Desert Storm and the Lessons of Learning," *Parameters* 22 (Autumn 1992): 83–95.

83. Timothy M. Karcher, "Understanding the 'Victory Disease': From the Little Bighorn, to Mogadishu, to the Future," 22 May 2003, SAMSM.

84. Richard M. Swain, *"Lucky War": Third Army in Desert Storm* (Fort Leavenworth, KS: CGSC, 1997), 71.

85. Clancy with Franks, *Into the Storm,* 442.

86. David McCormick, *The Downsized Warrior: America's Army in Transition* (New York: New York University Press, 1998); Dennis J. Reimer, *Soldiers Are Our Credentials: The Collected Works and Selected Papers of the Thirty-Third Chief of Staff, United States Army,* ed. James Jay Carafano (Washington, DC: Center of Military History, 2000), 32–33.

87. Tim W. Quillin, "Force Protection in Support and Stability Operations (SASO)," 31 December 1999, SAMSM. Robert Baumann, Lawrence Yates, and Versalle F. Washington, *My Clan against the World: US and Coalition Forces in Somalia, 1992–1994* (Fort Leavenworth, KS: Combat Studies Institute, 2004).

88. Mark F. Duffield, "Into the Beehive: The Somali Habr Gidr Clan as an Adaptive Enemy," 17 December 1999, SAMSM.

89. Roger N. Sangvic, "Battle for Mogadishu: Anatomy of a Failure," 16 December 1998, SAMSM.

90. Carl E. Vuono, *A Trained and Ready Army: Collected Works of the Thirty-First Chief of Staff, United States Army* (Washington, DC: Department of the Army, 1994), 135.

91. Ibid., 294.

92. Carl E. Vuono, "The Strategic Value of Conventional Forces," *Parameters* 20 (September 1990): 7.

93. Richardson Oral History, 26.

94. Reimer, *Soldiers Are Our Credentials,* 15–16.

95. Quoted in James L. Yarrison, *The Modern Louisiana Maneuvers* (Washington, DC: Center of Military History, 1999), 129.

96. William R. Moyer, "The 1994 Louisiana Maneuvers: Is Back to the Future What Our Army Needs?" 23 May 1992, SAMSM.

97. Thierry Gongora and Harald von Riefhoff, eds., *Toward a Revolution in Military Affairs: Defense and Security at the Dawn of the Twenty-First Century* (Westport, CT: Greenwood Press, 2000); David Jablonsky, *The Owl of Minerva Flies at Twilight: Doctrinal Change and Continuity and the Revolution in Military Affairs* (Carlisle Barracks: Strategic Studies Institute, 1994); Thomas A. Keaney and Elliot A. Cohen, *Revolution in War-*

fare? Air Power in the Persian Gulf (Annapolis, MD: Naval Institute Press, 1995).

98. Reimer, *Soldiers Are Our Credentials,* 81–89.

99. Department of the Army, *FM 1: The Army* (14 June 2001), i.

100. "Army Posture Statement, Fiscal Year 2001," http://www.Army.mil/aps/01, accessed 15 November 2006.

101. Vuono, *A Trained and Ready Army,* 310.

102. Kretchik, "Peering through the Mist," 219–71; John L. Romjue, *American Army Doctrine for the Post-Cold War* (Fort Monroe, VA: TRADOC, 1996).

103. CGSC, *Catalog, Academic Year 1992–1993,* CARL.

104. CGSC, *Advanced Application Course Guide for AY 1996–97,* CARL. CGSC, Lesson 2: European Operational Situation, Corps and Division Combat Operations (C320), 1994–95, CARL.

105. CGSC, Summary of C320 [Corps and Division Combat Operations Course], 10 February 1994, CARL.

106. Robin L. Swan, "Vision Statement," 1998, cited in Gifford, "Teaching and Learning." Baggott, "School."

107. AWC, Syllabus: Advanced Warfighting Studies Program, 1993, MHI. AWC, Department of National Security and Strategy, Core Curriculum, Course 2, "War, National Policy & Strategy," Academic Year, 2000, in author's possession.

108. Paul S. Warren, "New Kind of War: Adaptive Threat Doctrine and Information Operations," 1 February 2001, SAMSM. Michael P. Noonan and Mark R. Lewis. "Conquering the Elements: Thoughts on Joint Force (Re)Organization," *Parameters* 33 (Autumn 2003): 31–45.

109. Justice S. Stewart, "Sumo in a Ninja Fight: A Critical Study of Army Force Structure in the 21st Century Environment," 27 May 1997, SAMSM.

110. Gary E. Luck, Jr., "Conceptual Leadership Skills for the Twenty-first Century: A Means of Dealing with Complexity, Ambiguity, Uncertainty, and Speed," 16 December 1998, SAMSM.

111. Robert H. Scales, Jr., *Firepower in Limited War,* rev. ed. (Novato, CA: Presidio Press, 1995); Robert H. Scales, Jr., *Future Warfare* (Carlisle, PA: Army War College, 2000).

112. Clark, *Waging Modern War,* xxiv. Shawn Prickett, "Developing Operational Leaders for the 21st Century," 2003, SRP, NWC Classified Library, Newport, RI.

113. Douglas A. Macgregor, *Breaking the Phalanx: A New Design for Landpower in the 21st Century* (Westport, CT: Praeger, 1997). Douglas A. Macgregor, *Transformation under Fire: Revolutionizing How America Fights* (Westport, CT: Praeger, 2003).

114. Ralph Peters, "The New Strategic Trinity," *Parameters* 28 (Winter 1998–1999): 78–79. Ralph Peters, *Red Army* (New York: Random House, 1992); Ralph Peters, *The War in 2020* (New York: Pocket Books, 1991); Ralph Peters, "The Plague of Ideas," *Parameters* 30 (Winter 2000–2001): 4–20; Ralph Peters, "The Human Terrain of Urban Operations," *Parameters* 30 (Spring 2000): 4–12.

115. Ralph Peters, "The Author Replies," *Parameters* 29 (Spring 1999): 167.

116. Douglas V. Johnson, "Doctrine That Works," www.strategicstudiesinstitute.Army.mil/pdffiles/pub724.pdf, accessed 22 August 2006.

Acknowledgments

This project began during my tenure as the Harold K. Johnson Visiting Professor of Military History at the U.S. Army War College. It would not have been possible without the insight and encouragement of Dean William T. Johnsen, the faculty, and the students—particularly those in Seminar 19. A special thanks is due to Mike and Anne Perry and to Paul and Debbie Jussel, who provided a home away from home. A fellowship from the John S. Guggenheim Memorial Foundation allowed me to complete my research. A fellowship at the Woodrow Wilson International Center provided a stimulating environment to write the first draft. Claudius M. Easley, Jr., provided funding through a faculty fellowship. Texas A&M University, and especially department head Walter Buenger and Dean Charles Johnson, provided outstanding support. I also have the pleasure of working with great colleagues such as R. J. Q. Adams, Terry Anderson, Daniel Bornstein, Joseph G. Dawson, and Adam Seipp.

Over the three decades I've built up a formidable debt to archivists. This book would not have been possible without the help of Dr. Timothy Nenninger and the military records specialists at the National Archives and Marty Andresen, Robert Dalessandro,

Louise Arnold Friend, David Keough, Richard Sommers, and the rest of the staff at the U.S. Army Military History Institute. The archivists at the Hoover Institution, the U.S. Army Center of Military History, the U.S. Navy Historical Center, the U.S. Naval War College Naval Historical Collection, Liddell Hart Centre for Military Archives at King's College, the U.S. Air Force Historical Research Agency, the Library of Congress, the Dwight D. Eisenhower Presidential Library, the Combined Arms Research Library, the National Defense University Library, the U.S. Marine Corps University Research Archives, and the U.S. Marine Corps Historical Center have all been most helpful.

I have greatly benefited from the advice of soldiers and scholars, many of whose contributions are not properly acknowledged due to rigorous pruning at the end. Edward M. Coffman, Pete Maslowski, and David Vaught read the complete manuscript. Andrew J. Bacevich, James Jay Carafano, Joseph Cerami, Antulio Echevarria II, Jeffrey A. Engel, Jeffrey W. French, Henry Gole, Paul H. Herbert, Paul C. Jussel, Tim Nenninger, Bill Odom, Samuel Watson, and Robert Wooster all read and commented on individual chapters. Dozens of people share credit for intellectual inspiration, including Lance Betros, John S. Brown, Sandy Cochran, Eliot Cohen, Robert Doughty, Tom Dye, David Fitzpatrick, Kurt Hackemer, Peter Herrly, Douglas V. Johnson, Richard Kohn, David Kyvig, Robert Litwak, Tom Mahnken, Lloyd J. Matthews, Brad Meyer, Allan R. Millett, Richard R. Muller, John A. Nagl, Carol Reardon, Tom Ricks, Gordon Rudd, Douglas Smith, and Kevin J. Weddle. I'd like to thank Mark Parillo and Kansas State University, Lieutenant General Peter Leahy, Chief of the Australian Army, and Peter Dennis and Jeffrey Grey of the Australian Defense Forces University for permission to use material from published papers.

A special thanks goes to my editor, Joyce Seltzer, and to Harvard University Press. My father, James R. Linn, did yeoman service proofing my drafts, and my mother, Kay, and my in-laws, Robert and Shirley Kamins, provided inspiration and support. Most of all, this book owes its existence to my wife, Dinny. She trekked to the archives, took copious notes, read numerous drafts, and served as a compassionate listener and insightful reader.

INDEX